JOHN F. ROONEY, JR.
Oklahoma State University

A GEOGRAPHY OF AMERICAN SPORT

From Cabin Creek to Anaheim

ADDISON-WESLEY PUBLISHING COMPANY
Reading, Massachusetts
Menlo Park, California • London • Don Mills, Ontario

(1974)

This book is in the
ADDISON-WESLEY SERIES IN
THE SOCIAL SIGNIFICANCE OF SPORT

Consulting Editor
JOHN W. LOY

ISBN 0-201-06491-X
ABCDEFGHIJ-MA-7987654

To Doreen, who knew the true meaning of sport.

Foreword

The ubiquitous presence of sport cross-nationally and cross-culturally strongly attests to the fact that modern man is deeply engrossed in sport as an actual or vicarious, voluntary or conscripted participant. Moreover, the constant inclusion of sport in various institutional sectors such as economics, education, politics, and religion shows that sport permeates and affects many aspects of man's daily life. This pervasive presence of sport demands explanation.

The goal of the Social Significance of Sport Series is to provide an initial understanding of the interrelationships between sport, culture, and society. This objective will be achieved through the publication of several books which examine the social phenomenon of sport from different theoretical and methodological perspectives. The core of the series consists of a set of books dealing with the major areas and substantive topics of sport studies. Major areas to be covered include the history, philosophy, and sociology of sport. Substantive topics to be treated include women and sport, sport and social stratification, and the mass media and sport.

Toward a Philosophy of Sport (1972) by Harold VanderZwaag was the first text to appear in the series. In this initial volume Professor VanderZwaag raises a number of critical questions which are to be answered from different theoretical viewpoints in the course of the series. These questions include: *Who* is involved in sport? *When* are they involved? *Where* are they involved? *How* are they involved? *Why* are they involved? *What* are the personal and social consequences of their involvement? John Betts addresses these questions from a historical perspective in the second text of the series, *America's Sport-*

ing Heritage: 1850–1950. The present and third volume in the series, *The Geography of Sport* by John Rooney largely focuses on the single question, "*Where* are people involved in sport?"

At first glance the question, "*Where* are people involved in sport?" appears to be rather simple and thus readily answerable. However, the present book clearly reveals that the question is a complex one requiring a great deal of geographical research for an adequate answer. Professor Rooney notes that although geographers have largely ignored or only superficially studied the spatial and environmental aspects of sport, a valid justification can be made for the development of a subfield of sport geography. He suggests that the major conceptual subdivisions of a geography of sport might well include the following:

1. the spatial variation in sports, that is the place-to-place differences in the games which people play and with which they identify;

2. the spatial organization of sport at different competitive levels;

3. the origins and diffusion of sports and sportsmen;

4. the social and symbolic impact of the spatial organization of sport;

5. the effect of sport on the landscape;

6. the relationship between the spatial organization of sport and national character.

The content of *The Geography of Sport* well illustrates the nature of the outlined subdivisions of sport geography and gives direction for the future development of each area. Rooney's work should provide geographers with a fresh perspective and offer stimulation for the growth of a new and exciting subfield within their discipline. Moreover, his book is long overdue for physical educators interested in the social dimensions of sport. Although physical educators have long alluded to the importance of studying the origins and diffusion of sports (see Philip Smithells' enticing notion of the "sport ethnogram" in his *Principles of Evaluation in Physical Education* with Peter C. Cameron. New York: Harper & Row, 1962), and while a few exploratory examinations of the relation between sport and geography have been made (see Ernst Jokl's *Medical Sociology and Cultural Anthropology of Sport and Physical Education.* Springfield, Ill.: Charles C. Thomas, 1964), no individual has attempted a full-scale geographical analysis of a country's national sports. Professor Rooney's book is thus an important addition to the Social Significance of Sport Series for it is the first of its kind and affords a unique analysis of the spatial organization of sport in America.

John W. Loy
Departments of Physical Education and Sociology
University of Massachusetts, Amherst

Preface

This book represents an initial examination of the geographical aspects of American sport. Its focus is on "the national" games, their origin and diffusion, their spatial organization, and their regional associations. It also deals with the geographically based rivalries which have been spawned by the development of sports regions and the desire by so many places to be recognized as sports centers. An effort is made to develop explanations for sport consciousness and for the great geographical variation so characteristic of our major games.

My research has grown out of a persisting love for sport, coupled with a great curiosity about the character of place. It has been my belief for some time that the total feeling which a place transmits is integrally tied to the sports which it embraces. Cricket and soccer are somehow symbolic of England, hurling, of Ireland, and football, of present day America. This book then endeavors to provide a better understanding of the American scene through the media of sport and geography.

My involvement in the study of sport came initially as a result of many friendly arguments concerning the origins of the country's best football players. My first goal was to identify the geographical variations in the production of players, to examine regional differences in the importance of the game, and, if possible, to settle the arguments once and for all. It was in this spirit that I published my findings. At that time I was almost totally unaware of probings by sociologists, psychologists, philosophers, and historians into the role and meaning of sport. Thanks to considerable interdisciplinary cooperation since then, this book is placed in the context of that original work and should help all of us who are interested in sport to better understand its social function.

I would like to express my sincere gratitude to several people who inspired me to attempt this project. For numerous reasons (none of them good) academicians have largely eliminated sport from their accepted list of research topics. Any misgivings which I may have had were quickly eliminated by the strong encouragement I received from John Fraser Hart, Peirce Lewis, Campbell Pennington, and the late Vince Lombardi. Those who helped with the original data collection, analysis, and display include Marvin Swartz, Dan Irwin, Tso Hwa Lee, James H. Stine, Gayle Maxwell, Mark Gregory, and Rodney Fry. Among my graduate students, Douglas McDonald, Mark Miller, Mike Bernard, Ron Pearson, Robert Ingle, Roger Jenkinson, Russ Lura, Phil Adrian, Don Rominger and Paul Bolstad deserve special thanks. I want to thank Donald Meinig for his penetrating comments and suggestions. Generous grants from Southern Illinois University, The Oklahoma State University Research Foundation, and the University of Exeter, England were vital to the completion of this work. I would also like to thank Elizabeth Flippin, Janice Harris, and Diana Frank for their patience and fine work in typing the manuscript.

Stillwater, Oklahoma   J. F. R., Jr.
December, 1973

Contents

1   INTRODUCTION   1

Sport and Place   1
Sport and Geography   3

2   SCOPE AND PURPOSE   14

The Growth of College and Professional Sport   19

3   THE ORIGIN AND DIFFUSION OF SPORT IN
    THE UNITED STATES   21

The Historical Antecedents of American
Spectator Sport   21
Baseball   23
Collegiate Football   36
Professional Football   47
Basketball   48
Collegiate Wrestling   58
Golf   58

4   THE SPATIAL ORGANIZATION OF SPORT IN
    THE UNITED STATES   64

Interscholastic Athletics   66
State-to-State Variations in Participation   70
Why the Variation?   77
Intercollegiate Athletics   78
The Conference Pattern of Organization   89
The Junior Colleges   95

	Professional Sport	97
	Another Form of Spatial Organization	99
5	IDENTIFYING SPORTS REGIONS	102
6	FOOTBALL: WHERE THEY COME FROM	112
	Regional Productivity Based on City-County Units	122
	State Performance	132
	Why Football Fever	134
	Deficit Areas	142
7	BASKETBALL: WHERE THEY COME FROM	147
	Toward a State-Based Regionalization	153
	The Major Source Regions	154
	Toward Explanation	160
	Other Important Areas	169
	The Deficit Areas	171
8	BASEBALL: WHERE THEY COME FROM	175
	The Origin of Players	176
	Regional and State Production	176
	City and County Output	182
	Changes in Productivity	183
	Toward Explanation	184
9	THE RECRUITING GAME: FOOTBALL	187
	Football Recruiting	189
	Interregional Migration	190
	The Conferences	207
	The Little People	213
10	THE RECRUITING GAME: BASKETBALL	220
	The IllInKy Surplus	220
	The Pennsylvanio-Ohio Surplus	228
	Recruiting from the Northeast	231
	Recruiting from California	231
	General Patterns	235
	The Overemphasizers	236
	Differences between the Majors and Minors	237
11	WOMEN'S SPORT	242
	Geographic Variations	242

Intercollegiate Sport 248
Sports Centers 251
Professional Prospects 252

12 OTHER AMERICAN SPORTS 254

Track and Field 254
Wrestling 257
Golf 259
Soccer 264
Tennis 267
Swimming 269
Gymnastics 272
The Snow and Ice Sports 274
The Regional Sports 277

13 SOME CONCLUDING STATEMENTS 283

The Sport Region 283
The Price of Producing Athletes 285
The Challenge 288

BIBLIOGRAPHY 290

INDEX 303

Biographical Sketch

John F. Rooney, Jr. is Professor and Head of the Department of Geography at Oklahoma State University. Before receiving his Ph.D. degree in geography from Clark University in 1966, he taught at the University of Wyoming. He then went on to teach at U.C.L.A. and at Southern Illinois University and during 1968–1969 was Visiting Lecturer at the University of Exeter in England. Dr. Rooney's abiding interest in the character of place, coupled with a persisting love of sport, have shaped this study of the American scene through the media of sport and geography.

1 / Introduction

SPORT AND PLACE

Wrigley Field, located on Chicago's near north side amid decaying apartment houses, taverns, the "L," and an endless supply of minute parking lots, is a relic of another era. There is no night baseball at Wrigley Field, but it has real grass and ivy-covered walls. On a sunny July afternoon 30,000 of the faithful typically jam the ballpark, agreeing with ageless Ernie Banks's, "It's a beautiful day to play baseball." After the National Anthem, Pat Peiper, and the starting lineup, it's "Play ball." Shouts of "Beer here, red hots, and peanuts" can be heard over the din. Whether the Cubs win or lose, the people at Wrigley Field and those watching and listening to broadcasts have been whisked back to a time when American sport was dominated by baseball, a game played on a spacious green expanse in the bright light of day.

Babysitters are lined up a year in advance; parties are scheduled around the matches; takedowns, escapes, and riding time are a part of the day-to-day conversations of housewives and dentists, plumbers, and professors. At almost every Oklahoma State University wrestling meet, 8500 people crowd into stuffy old Gallagher Hall to watch a team that has lost only 23 dual matches in 44 years. Collegiate wrestling got its start in Stillwater, Oklahoma, and still ranks with football as a primary sporting attraction there. Wrestling mania has spread to Ames, Corvalis, Seattle, East Lansing, and Carbondale, but devotion to wrestling and its ability to control social events, conversation time, and media coverage remains unequaled except in Stillwater, Oklahoma.

Fig. 1.1 Wrigley Field, the homeground of the Chicago Cubs National League Baseball Club, is one of the few old stadia left in the United States. Located in a crowded residential and commercial area, it has limited parking and poor access to the city's residents. (Courtesy of the Chicago Cubs.)

What is the major event in a small Illionois or Indiana community on a wintry Saturday night? In most, is a high school basketball game. Hoops and backboards adorn garages and barns. Signs promoting the "Warriors," "Eagles," or "Red Devils" are displayed in downtown store windows. The gymnasium usually stands out as the most impressive structure around. Everyone seems to know the names and backgrounds of the players, the scoring averages, the rebounders, the playmaker, and the promising 6'5" freshman. The coach is one of the most important men in town, and opinions concerning his abilities generally run strong. A casual observer can hear basketball talk everywhere—post office, grocery, tavern. For here basketball is life's biggest diversion, and for many from November to mid-March, it is life itself. (For a description of the importance of basketball in this area of the country see *Hoosier Hysteria* by Herb Schwomeyer.)

Stores are closed, the downtown area is nearly deserted on a clear, warm Friday evening. Half the town is cheering the McKinney High gridders to another victory. Nearly 7000 people are jammed into the modern stadium where over 100 players and sixteen coaches

ring the field. Like many other games being played throughout
the state of Texas this game is very important. Community prestige,
a possible trip to the state playoffs, and scholarship offers for the
best individual performers are all on the line. On Saturday morning
the town will dissect the game. Players will be praised or chastised,
and the turning points established. By afternoon all attention will
be focused on college football: the University of Texas, SMU, A &
M, Tech, Rice, or Baylor. Sunday means the Dallas Cowboys or the
Houston Oilers, and then the wait for the next Friday night. Football and Texas are synonomous.

In Nebraska all the action is in Lincoln, the home of the Cornhuskers, where on six autumn Saturdays the town and the stadium
are colored a bright red. The women wear red suits and sweaters,
the men red blazers and hats, and even babies and pets are appro-
priately attired. Nebraskans believe that football has put their
state on the map and that Bob Devaney was divinely inspired; they
are hoping that his youthful successor, Tom Osborne, is also. It is
the one thing that unites the dry and windswept western part of the
state around North Platte and Scottsbluff, with the lush corn country
around Omaha and Lincoln. It is the one thing that a Nebraskan can
talk to an Alabaman or a Californian about and feel superior over
the Trojans or Crimson Tide. A typical football day finds 76,000 of
the faithful descending upon Lincoln. Traffic jams around the
stadium are monumental as people wind their way through the
heterogeneous midwestern architecture. After the game the flow to
Omaha, or west on Interstate 80, is as thick as it ever gets in this
sparsely populated land. But there are many watering holes where
people gather for brief celebrations along the way. Most Nebraskans
would like to do it more than six times a year. In a word, the pre-
dominance of particular sports varies from place to place. Some
areas are totally committed to a single sport—basketball in Harlem
and Indiana, football in Green Bay and Texas, hockey in Boston
and Ontario. Other regions, for example California, embrae many
sporting activities. These geographical variations in sport preferences
and game involvement require explanation. There is a need for a
geography of sport.

SPORT AND GEOGRAPHY

Geography as a discipline is concerned with the character of place,
with the spatial arrangement and organization of the myriad phenomena on the earth's surface. Geography is primarily an exercise in

locational analysis and human spatial behavior and seeks to understand why various things are where they are. Recently practitioners
of the discipline have begun to focus on where people and things
will be in the future vis-a-vis where they should be. Thus geography
is becoming a prescriptive science. Geographic research has focused
on virtually every segment of man's spatial behavior, from manufacturing and agriculture to settlement patterns, transportation, and
communication networks. It has also concentrated on the tangible
results on man's spatial behavior: the distributions and effects of
his value systems, languages, religions, architecture, music, and
politics. Although geographers as a research group have largely
ignored the spatial and environmental aspects of sports there is
strong justification for a subfield of sports geography, perhaps as
a segment of a total geography of leisure.[1] Geographic analysis
can produce a better understanding of the significance of sport to
society and the manner in which the role of sport has changed.
The geography of sport is conceptually very great because the com-
binations of games and places are immense and ever changing. Sport
can be examined from either a systematic or regional geographic
viewpoint. The following section describes and illustrates what
appear to be the major conceptual subdivisions of the field.

THE SPATIAL VARIATION IN GAMES

The geography of sport is concerned with the place-to-place variations
in the games which people play and with which they identify. It is
also concerned with the degree of emphasis that characterizes these
games in different areas. To illustrate the spatial variation of a sport
let us consider rugby. Basic to the geographic study of rugby would
be an examination of where the game is currently being played, and
how it came to be played in those areas. Rugby is a major sport
throughout the British Isles, France, South Africa, Australia, New
Zealand, and Fiji and is also developing strength as a secondary
sport in Canada, Germany, Italy, and in some sections of the United
States. The variations in the degree of attachment to rugby within
the regions where it is played can be measured by identifying the
source areas of the first-class players and teams, press coverage of
the games, the number of teams and players per capita, attendance
at contests, and the amount of time that people spend discussing the
sport. From this kind of information, primary rugby zones can be
isolated and analyzed in greater detail.

Another consideration in the study of rugby would involve
geographical variations in the style of play. The diffusion of

different types of rugby strategy which affect general playing styles would fall under the same game–place type of analysis. These geographical patterns can be studies for all games, for there is a geography of every game, one which is subject to constant change and evolution.

THE SPATIAL ORGANIZATION OF SPORT

Sports geography also deals with the spatial organization of competition. American football provides a good illustration of the components of spatial organization. The geographic study of American football would involve consideration of the spatial organization associated with all levels of competition from the professional level through the midget or "pee wee" schoolboy leagues. The spatial arrangement of university and collegiate conferences and the various classes of professional teams are a necessary ingredient of any thorough geographic analysis. The role of distance and regional social differences as a scheduling variable must be assessed, as well as the impact of changes in franchise location or conference memberships. Conference locations might be compared with culture regions such as the Deep South, New England, and California. The effect of the spatial organization on fan movements and attendance and upon intercommunity and intercollegiate cooperation might also be included. In addition, the provision or marketing of sports entertainment services at various scales and to varying populations would fall into this general category.

The geographical organization of the sports hierarchy begins at the high school and junior league level. In many states the organizational hierarchy has been given official recognition by the establishment of numerous competitive classes based on school enrollment. The "Texas Interscholastic League" exemplifies the degree to which the formal organization of high school athletics can progress. Texas has six classes of competition to which a high school can be assigned, depending upon its enrollment.[2] Each class is divided into districts which combine six to eight schools located in relatively close proximity to one another. These alignments are frequently evaluated with boundary and class changes commonly recommended. Similar arrangements exist in many other states.

The spatial organization of sport has a profound effect on the intensity of competition and fan interest. Long-term rivalries exist throughout the sporting world and have generally stemmed from geographical proximity. Examples include Liverpool–Manchester (soccer), Los Angeles–San Francisco (basketball, football, baseball), and Chicago–Green Bay (football). The list is endless and includes all levels of the sporting activity hierarchy.

ORIGIN AND DIFFUSION OF GAMES AND PLAYERS

Geographers have long concerned themselves with the origin and diffusion of various activities.[3] However, little is know about the origin and spread of games. What causes a game to diffuse? Why have so many remained confined to one nation or area or within small groups of nations? Again, rugby is an excellent case in point. The amateur category of the game has diffused throughout much of the old British Commonwealth and Western Europe and has spread to North America. In fact, the brand of football played in the United States is a derivitive of rugby. Today both football and rugby are played in the United States and Canada. On the other hand, professional rugby is mired in profound spatial stability within three countries of the English Midlands, although one related type, Australian Rules Football, is that nation's biggest sporting attraction.

Why was cricket so unsuccessful in America? Why did baseball become the American national game and later gain similar status in Japan? And why has basketball spread so vigorously from its birthplace in Massachusetts?

Voight's work on the concerted attempts to spread American baseball to other areas is an outstanding contribution to the meager understanding of that sport's diffusion process.[4]

The migratory behavior of athletes and other athletic personnel is also of fundamental interest to the sports geographer. Migration is generally in response to monetary, educational, or fame-related inducements of one sort or another. Recruitment patterns can be mapped for any sporting activity but are generally more meaningful when the distance between the potential players and the location of the sporting franchise or institution means little, and when many players and possible destinations are involved. American collegiate football provides an excellent example, with an abundance of playing opportunities and a huge pool of potential recruits.[5]

At the professional level of sport, the geographer is concerned with the location and locational changes of franchises. Professional baseball was geographically stable for the first fifty years of this century, despite significant changes in the location of the American population. The sixteen major teams were clustered in the northeast with eleven of them concentrated in five cities, New York, Boston, Philadelphia, Chicago, and St. Louis. This resulted in a public exposure that was far from national. The stimulus for change and the subsequent migration was triggered by the movement of the Boston Braves to Milwaukee. Six of the original sixteen teams have now moved, and two of those have moved twice. In addition, eight new teams have been added giving baseball a much more nationally representative locational pattern.

Many exciting geographical questions are raised by the locational changes in Major League Baseball. What has happened to the geography of communications and broadcasting where baseball is concerned? How have minor league locations been affected? What geographical impacts have occurred in collegiate baseball? How have fan loyalties and identifications with urban centers been altered?

THE SPORT REGION

Sport has a profound spatial impact which radiates out from the point of actual competition. Though a contest involving the Chicago Cubs may be played at a location on Chicago's north side, the results have meaning to many people who are far removed from that point. The geographical area in which a significant portion of these residents are interested in a given sporting activity and identify with a given team can be termed a fan region. For example, a line which divides the St. Louis Cardinals fan area from that of the Chicago Cubs could be drawn, at a point where fifty percent of the area baseball fans follow each team. Seventy-five or ninety percent lines could be plotted closer to each of the cities.

Fan loyalties are among the strongest human attachments. Weiss describes the importance of this fan devotion in relation to other forms of human activity. He states:

> Agriculture, manufacturing, and business play a much larger role in our economy than is possible to sport, though of course sport is not without economic importance. The economically important enterprises, however, do not arouse the full attention of most men. Rarely do they enter into man's daily disputes or lay claim to the basic loyalties in the way or to the degree that sport does. It is sport that catches the interest and elicits the devotion of both the young and old, the wise and foolish, the educated and the uneducated.[6]

Fan regions, like any other nodal or functional geographic region, are dynamic and very responsive to change. In the case of sport a winning or losing year stimulates expansion or contraction of the fan region. The introduction of a competitive force also exerts a significant impact. Major League baseball again provides an excellent illustration.

When the Boston Braves moved to Milwaukee in 1953, they received instantaneous support from throughout Wisconsin, a state that contained many residents with loyalties to the Chicago Cubs. As the Braves improved, their fan region grew, and during the championship years, it included much of Minnesota, the Dakotas, and even parts of northern Illinois. The 1957–1958 period saw the Braves establish Major League home attendance records which included many pilgrimages by fans who traveled hundreds of miles to Milwaukee.

In 1962 a competitive force (in technical geographic terms, an intervening opportunity) was introduced. The Minnesota Twins were located in Bloomington, Minnesota in the midst of the Milwaukee fan region. The Minnesota team lured many of the fans away from Milwaukee, and as they became an immediate American League pennant threat, they cut severely into the attendance at Milwaukee. As the young Twins team rose, the aging Braves sank in the standings and at the box office. The Minnesota fan region expanded, while the Milwaukee one contracted. Finally, in 1966 the Milwaukee franchise was moved again, this time to Atlanta. As a result, a new fan region was established in Georgia with spatial ramifications throughout the Southeast.

Another kind of sport region is an area where a given sport or set of sports is played or dominates. Thus there are football regions, basketball regions, lacrosse regions, rugby–soccer regions, and so on. It is reasonably easy to identify and bound the regions where an individual sport or combination of sports is played. However, it is extremely difficult to identify and bound many of the areas which are dominated by a sport or group of sports. It is this question of regional sport dominance that much of this book is devoted to answering.

THE EFFECT OF SPORT ON THE LANDSCAPE

Sport has a considerable effect on the visible cultural landscape. Open space and facilities constructed for the purpose of sport are common elements in communities throughout the world. The effect of sport on the landscape is perhaps most dramatized by the recent stadium construction within the cores of American cities. St. Louis, Atlanta, Oakland, and Pittsburgh are good examples. The resurgence of downtown St. Louis has been stimulated by the construction of

Fig. 1.2 Busch Stadium in St. Louis has been a significant force in the rejuvenation of the downtown area. Note the open space reserved for parking and the parking garages.

Fig. 1.3 The new Atlanta stadium has been integrated with the vertically expanding downtown area. Expressway connections with all sections of the city are excellent.

Fig. 1.4 The new Riverfront Stadium in Cincinatti is utilized for both baseball and football. The stadium is a part of a redevelopment project adjacent to the Ohio River.

Fig. 1.5 (upper right) Chavez Ravine in Los Angeles, home of the Dodgers, is typical of the modern stadium. It has a profound influence on surrounding land use and traffic patterns in this section of the city.

Fig. 1.6 (lower right) Yankee Stadium like Wrigley Field is one of the oldest edifices of American professional sport. Here much of the surrounding open space has been preserved for recreational activity in contrast to the Los Angeles situation.

Busch Stadium, the home of the St. Louis professional teams. Ramshackle tenements and marginal business establishments have been replaced by the stadium, a parking structure, stores, and restaurants. The success of the nearby Gateway Arch and Spanish Pavilion have also been influenced by the stadium location, not to mention the impact of three million fans who flock to the downtown area each year. The Houston Astrodome has had substantial influence upon surrounding land and is now the center of a vast entertainment complex in that city. Oakland and Atlanta have experienced great economic and social benefits from major league sports. Considerable building activity has occurred in both places in response to stadium and coliseum construction. Furthermore, there are many possibilities for future developments both within and around our central cities.

In the small communities the sports complex, whether it be a gymnasium or outdoor facility, is often the largest gathering place. Its location affects the location of other types of open space: parks, ballfields, and playgrounds, as well as influencing street and traffic patterns, property values, and residential perception. The same can be said for school sports facilities in large urban areas.

SPORTS AND NATIONAL CHARACTER

Every country, or for that matter, every area has a sports geography which is representative of a segment of its overall socio-cultural geography. Different regions have identified with different games, and the degree of this identification varies dramatically at the micro scale. In most nations one to three games are dominant. We associate bull fighting with Mexico, baseball, football, and basketball with the United States, skiing with Switzerland, and sumo wrestling with Japan. Soccer reigns supreme in Britain, but rugby and cricket are also very important. Soccer is number one in Brazil and throughout much of Latin American, and ice hockey is the national game of Canada.

Some nations are more sporting minded than others and participate and spectate to a much greater extent. Concern is at least in part a function of the amount of gambling associated with sporting activities. The British and Australian football pools, American football cards, and the "track," all work to stimulate interest in sport.[7] It would also seem that the games which a nation embraces reflect to some extent the value system of its people. Sport as a communication form is related to the major social institutions of an area. These include home, school, church, political, and economic systems.

NOTES

1. By comparison, other social scientists have been reasonably active. Research by an interdisciplinary group known as sports sociologists has been the most abundant, focusing primarily on the social ties and structures which have been shaped by sport. Studies dealing with the role of sport as a unifying force, in the face of national, religious, social, political, and economic barriers, have been numerous. Literature concerned with racial, sex, and ethnic discrimination throughout the sporting world also abounds. The most important works from a geographic standpoint have centered on sport as a cultural element, the significance of high school sport in the United States, race and sport, and social attitudes toward sport. Historians, philosophers, psychologists, anthropoligists, and economists have also devoted serious attention to sport research. However, the vast majority of sports-related literature is preoccupied with personalities, teams, and statistical information. Sports encyclopedias generally include a brief history of the game involved, but the bulk of the contents deal with record keeping: the scores of past contests and discussions of the "greatest" games, players, and coaches. Much of this work lacks a geographical perspective or treats space as a neutral variable.

2. *Texas Inter-Scholastic League Bulletin,* 1970.

3. Two diffusion studies which apply to sport are Campbell W. Pennington, "La Carrera de bola entre los tarahumaras de Mexico. Un Problema de difusion," *America Indigena* 30 (1970) 15–40 and J. W. Loy, "Social Psychological Characteristics of Innovators," *American Sociological Review* 34 (1969) 73–82.

4. David T. Voight, "American Baseball and the Mission of America," paper presented at the third International Symposium on the Sociology of Sport, University of Waterloo, Ontario, Canada, August 26, 1971. Also see David T. Voight, *American Baseball* (Norman, Oklahoma: University of Oklahoma Press, 1968).

5. John F. Rooney, Jr., "Up From the Mines and Out From the Prairies: Some Geographical Implications of Football in the United States," *The Geographical Review* LIX (October, 1969) 471–472 and "A Geographical Analysis of Football Player Production in Oklahoma and Texas," *Proceedings, Oklahoma Academy of Science* 50 (1970) 114–120. Also see J. F. Rooney, Jr., "A Geography of Basketball," paper presented at the Rocky Mountain Social Science Meeting, Fort Collins, Colorado, May, 1971.

6. Paul Weiss, *Sport, A Philosophic Inquiry* (Carbondale, Ill.: Southern Illinois University Press, 1969), p. 9.

7. For a discussion of the role of betting on interest levels associated with professional football see Larry Merchant, *The National Football Lottery,* New York, Holt Rinehart & Winston, 1973.

2 / Scope and Purpose

This book is concerned with the geography of sport in the United States, a nation in which the sporting scene consists of a conglomeration of games and activities. Although Americans identify with a great variety of sports, there are three (football, basketball, and baseball) that have great national appeal. They are the national games and play a role similar to that played by soccer, rugby, and cricket in Great Britain and most of the nations formerly affiliated with the rapidly vanishing British Commonwealth.

Other important American sports include golf, track and field, horse and automobile racing, boxing, wrestling, swimming, bowling, tennis, and hockey. Winter activities such as curling, skiing, skating, and sledding are more spatially confined, and in some cases more popular than the "national" games within their regions of concentration. Rodeo, polo, lacrosse, handball, badminton, racketball, and squash are popular with many people, but they receive only spotty attention from the news media. Hunting, fishing, hiking, and climbing, individual activities based on the idea of competition between man and his natural environment, are also popular.

Conceptually, sport must be viewed as just one aspect of leisure behavior. Its role in the total leisure spectrum varies considerably from place to place. The importance of sport at any place is in part a function of the range of available leisure opportunities present there. The popularity of a certain sport or sports in any region is a result of a combination of historical, social, economic, demographic, and environmental conditions.

14

The subfields of the geography of sport outlined in the preceding chapter form the basis for the analysis that follows. Included is an investigation of the geographical organization of sport. The present geographical organization is a function of the origin and diffusion of our major national games, a topic which also receives considerable attention here.

As with other social phenomena, there is great regional variation throughout the United States in the sports which people play, watch, or otherwise identify with. It is the primary purpose of this book to examine, identify, and interpret the regional differences which characterize the sports geography of the United States.

These regional differences can be investigated in several possible ways. The importance of sport to any place or region can be assessed by measuring the amount of participation, the interest level of the local population which is visible in terms of monetary support, game attendance, press coverage, and the nature of the playing facilities. Another measure of a place's involvement with sport is the ability to generate high-quality players. It is this latter variable which is perhaps easiest to monitor, especially for the major sports. For example, most athletic teams record basic geographical information about their players and coaches; virtually all maintain lists of the home towns and the high schools for their varsity athletes. Hence by obtaining roster information from a representative national sampling of college, university, and professional teams, it is possible to measure the geographical variations in the production of various types of athletes and to identify different kinds of sports regions. The data-processing task for this type of analysis is a huge one, but compared to the inherent difficulties in the acquisition of financial-support information or in the undertaking of a content analysis of press coverage, it is the only feasible course to follow.

The identification of sports regions within the nation is, as a result, primarily based on the spatial variability of raw athletic talent. Two major talent questions are answered. Where are the players who staff the burgeoning rosters of American sports coming from, and what is the geographical nature of the recruiting that gets them there? To put it simply—where are they coming from, and where are they going?

The geographical treatment of American sport included here is by no means exhaustive, since it is chiefly confined to football, basketball, and baseball. However, some coverage of hockey, golf, collegiate wrestling, gymnastics, track, swimming, winter sports, and regional ports is also included. The data on player origins are supplemented, where possible, by statistics on participation in high school athletics, appropriations for athletic programs, size of coaching staffs, attendance, and facilities.

The origin of college-bound athletes in the United States has been debated for a long time. It has been common knowledge among recruiters and sports enthusiasts that some areas excel in the production of large quantities of first-class players, while others produce few or none at all. The locations of these "hotbeds" of sporting activity have been the subject of considerable controversy, with opinions highly tainted by one's regional background.

The Blue Grass country of Kentucky has come to be associated with thoroughbred horses, and the South with stock-car racing; we have been told that Indiana and Illinois are the basketball leaders and that Pennsylvania and Texas are the nation's football talent factories. Even if these and other claims about sporting superiority are authentic, there is still little known concerning the relative producing capacities of these areas in comparison to the rest of the country. The problem with all these notions is that there has been no measure against which to judge an area's output of athletes. There have been no data on normal production, so about all that could be said about places like Pittsburgh or Amarillo was that they were very good sources of football players. We knew that Pennsylvania and Texas were football states but were probably not aware of how localized the source regions of players were within these states.

Most ideas about sports have been clouded or influenced by geographical place–pride biases. Illinoisans are partial to Illinois basketball, Hoosiers to the Indiana game, and New Yorkers to theirs. Prejudice of this nature is understandable within a people–place framework, but it has led to a host of falsehoods regarding regional differences in athletic ability and emphasis.

This work cannot answer the question of which region's basketball, football, or baseball is best, but it does provide the data for making realistic quantitative comparisons between places. It establishes norms against which the output of any region can be judged. It also demonstrates that many of our cities and towns are not characterized by well-balanced high school athletic programs, that some areas are out-performing others by more than twenty to one, and that many large American cities are failing to give schoolboys the opportunity to develop their athletic potential. On the other hand, we

The installation of Astroturf at Oklahoma State University. There is a great deal of controversy about injury rates on artificial turf, yet conversion from grass continues at an unparalleled pace.

find that some places are giving so many young men a chance to play a variety of organized sports that few of them become proficient enough at any one game to make a college team. Programs of that nature reflect a different and perhaps more defensible concept of the purpose of interscholastic sport.

A secondary objective of this volume is to consider the geographic, economic, social, and political influences which sport has exerted on the American scene. One indication of the importance of sports is contained in the Department of Commerce data covering personal consumption expenditures for recreation. Their estimate places annual spending in the vicinity of $30 billion.[1]

It is in this environment, which combines more leisure with greater on-the-job pressures, that organized sports can fulfill multiple sets
of needs. Ours is rapidly becoming an amenity-oriented society. Decisions regarding the location of such things as factories, offices,
shopping plazas, housing developments, and expressway routes are
being influenced substantially by the availability of entertainment
facilities and aesthetically pleasing surroundings. Sports are a vital entertainment medium, as ambitious Chambers of Commerce in cities
like Atlanta, Denver, Houston, and Oakland have discovered.

Thus the expansion of amateur and professional sports can be
viewed as simply an attempt to satisfy our ballooning wants. Even our
investments reflect a preoccupation with the package of sports-related
industries. Those who follow the stock market are aware that recre-
ation-oriented companies are now in the same league with such glam-
our fields as computers, oceanography, electronics, and data communications. Once the national economy returns to its expansionary
trend, we will probably witness another speculative boom in the recreation industry.

The growth in spectator-oriented competition has spurred the
demand for all kinds of sporting equipment. Sales of traditional gear
for football, basketball, and baseball have risen steadily. Expansion
of the National Hockey League has given a monumental boost to the
retailing of hockey items. For example, the success of the St. Louis
Blues has created an unbelieveable demand for hockey sticks, pucks,
skates, and related ensemble, in relatively warm eastern Missouri. One
St. Louis chain reported sales of 3600 hockey sticks for one January
weekend[2] despite the fact that the ice is so unreliable that most of the
competition must take place on asphalt playgrounds. But this has
not stopped the St. Louis kids. They are playing with an iceless puck.

The rush to participate has also created a growth market for
many types of expensive equipment. America's attraction to the water has been manifested in spending for boats, motors, diving gear,
skis, and so on. Bicycle riding has experienced an unprecedented re-
vitalization, and participation in winter sports has increased dramatically. During the past decade the number of skiers has been com-
pounding at a rate of 15 percent annually. Sales of snowmobiles
have increased from a few thousand in 1963 to last year's registration
total of 1,216,000 machines.[3] The makers of pleasure aircraft are
among the fastest growing corporations in the United States. The
point is apparent: the recent spurt in all kinds of recreational activity has far outstripped the increase in population.

THE GROWTH OF COLLEGE AND PROFESSIONAL SPORT

The American enthusiasm and seemingly insatiable demand for more exposure to sport have resulted in an unprecedented expansion of professional franchises. The television and press coverage of their activities has grown even faster. Consider the following statistics. The number of professional football teams has increased from twelve to twenty-six in just eight years. Baseball has expanded from sixteen to twenty-four units, and basketball, long the stepchild of the professional athletic world, has more than tripled from eight to twenty-seven quintets. The number of professional golfers has mushroomed to the accompaniment of a trememdous increase in financial support, and hockey has literally exploded. Other sports like automobile racing, horse racing, tennis, track and field, and even roller derby have participated in the upward spiral. Only boxing has suffered in recent years, and it too is showing signs of a resurgence.

Colleges and universities have also been involved in the growth, and in many ways have made the professional expansion possible. Pressures in the early fifties to de-emphasize athletics have largely abated, and have only been revived during the last few years. High-calibre play is now characteristic of every section of the country. The football dominance of the Northeast, and later the Midwest, has given way to a truly national fight for mythical collegiate dominance. Even teams from the sparsely populated Rocky Mountain region are proving to be formidable opponents in intersectional contests. The South has spawned numerous football powers since the days of tiny Centre College's rise to prominence. More recently the football fortunes of the region's black schools like Grambling, Alcorn, A & M, Jackson State, and Florida A & M have also improved. At the same time the list of first-class teams in Texas and the Pacific Coast states continues to grow as former unknowns like Houston, U. T. E. P., North Texas State, San Diego, Fresno, Long Beach, and San Jose State take their place in the national spotlight.

New names are constantly flashing upon the basketball scene with superb teams cropping up all over. How many avid followers of the college game would have expected first-class play from such schools as Southern Illinois, U. T. E. P., Weber State, St. Peter's, Kentucky Wesleyan, Tennessee, Jacksonville, or Southwest Louisiana, to mention just a few of the new arrivals? And there has been no decline in the level of competition elsewhere to offset this improvement. Better basketball is virtually ubiquitous throughout the country.

With the collapse of a large segment of professional baseball's minor league system, college baseball has rushed in to fill the void. Numerous schools have extended their schedules from the traditional 15 to 20 games even to as many as 60 or 70. The movement which started in California and the Southwest has now been adopted by numerous institutions. And the number of athletic scholarships allocated to the sport has also leaped dramatically.

The so-called minor collegiate sports have benefited too. Opportunities for intercollegiate competition in track and field, cross country, golf, gymnastics, wrestling, tennis, swimming, lacrosse, ice hockey, fencing, and crew are greater than ever before. European sports—soccer, and rugby—are now included by many schools and are beginning to generate considerable enthusiasm. With the persisting emphasis on physical fitness and participation, intramural programs have also begun to receive sorely needed attention.

NOTES

1.   Department of Commerce, Office of Business Economics, *Survey of Current Business*, Washington, D.C., 1969.

2.   G. Ronberg, "An Icy Love-In with the Red-Hot Blues," *Sports Illustrated*, April 7, 1961, pp. 52–54.

3.   Data provided by the International Snowmobile Industry Association, 5100 Edina Industrial Blvd., Minneapolis, Minn.

3 / The Origin and Diffusion of Sport in the United States

THE HISTORICAL ANTECEDENTS OF AMERICAN SPECTATOR SPORT

Organized sport in the United States dates from the 1820's. The most popular sports of that era were horse racing, sailing regattas, and professionsl running. Their rise was accompanied by the rise of urbanization, which produced a market for spectator sport. Industrialization resulted in higher living standards and more leisure time to spend on sporting activity.

The popularity of American spectator sport was hastened by the technological revolution of the nineteenth century. It also benefited greatly from the movement away from Puritan orthodoxy, a similar sporting thrust in England, steady immigration from Europe, the persisting frontier traditions of ruggedness and strength, and the contributions of enthusiastic promoters.

Betts claims that the Industrial Revolution was the key factor in the rapid expansion which took place between 1850-1900.[1] He states,

> Organization, journalistic exploitation, commercialization, inter-community competition, and sundry other developments increased rapidly after 1850 as the agrarian nature of sport gave way gradually to the influences of urbanization and industrialization.[2]

The prominence that sport had attained by 1900 was only possible because of great progress in transportation, communications, lighting, photography, and manufacturing. Railroad expansion tied cities together and allowed for the development of interstate baseball competition. The "Sport of Kings" flourished after rail connections permitted the rapid shipment of horses and racing fans. Most of the early prize fights took place along the rivers served by steamboats.[3] In addition, excursion trains for sporting events were common by 1869.[4]

The development of the railroads coincided with the diffusion of the telegraph. Wire coverage produced a speedy growth in the volume of sporting news. And the Western Union offices themselves attracted huge crowds during the big events.[5] Box scores, betting odds, fight news, and regatta results were transmitted across the country, and by 1870 numerous city papers were publishing daily reports.[6]

Newspapers expanded their coverage of sport to meet the ballooning public interest in the 1880's and 1890's. The telegraph made the sports pages timely, and the development of specialist sports writers like Leonard Washburne, Charles Seymour, and Harry Weldon made them humorous and interesting. Printing and photographic innovations were also vital.

Technical improvements in the quality of athletic goods aided the boom in sporting activity. Baseball and fishing equipment, bicycles, pool tables, and other items were standardized during the 1850's.[7]

Edison's incandescent light bulb (1879) spawned a new era of both participation and spectating. By 1882 electric lights had been installed in Madison Square Garden.[8] Soon after, the majority of YMCA's, gymnasiums, athletic clubs, and armories had lights too. The greatest benefactor was basketball, which quickly caught on as a major spectator attraction. Electric lighting made sport a nighttime phenomena in cities and hamlets throughout the country.

Spectator sports in these days provided the same kinds of diversion that they do today. They were an escape for a large group of people, who were not yet used to the severe confines of urban existence. Crowds of 50,000, including all segments of society, were not uncommon for racing and regattas. Professional running was moved from city streets to race tracks, where admission fees could be charged. Although illegal, prize fighting was also extremely important during the first half of the nineteenth century.

The 1860's and 1870's witnessed the development and spread of baseball as a participatory and spectator sport. Croquet, lawn tennis, archery, bicycling, and roller skating were also very popular during this period.

BASEBALL

Although the origin of baseball is clouded in controversy, it is likely that the game evolved from the English sport of "rounders," which was a semiorganized bat-and-ball game played primarily by children. Voight writes: "If not by the 1820's, certainly by the 1840's, baseball evolved to a point where a twentieth-century observer, watching a team like the aristocratic New York Knickerbockers, would have recognized the game."[9]

A committee of Knickerbockers headed by Alexander Cartwright established the basic rules and laid out a standard diamond in 1845.[10] Cartwright migrated from New York to California during 1849 and demonstrated his version of baseball at many points along the way.[11] By 1858 there were at least twenty-five clubs playing the game on an organized and gentlemenly basis.[12] Excluding the Knickerbockers, these clubs met and organized the "National Association of Baseball Players" in 1859.[13] By the following year there were some sixty teams spatially concentrated in the East.[14] St. Louis and Chicago were western members, but there was no representation from the South. This early period was epitomized by great emphasis on sportsmanship and stressed the gentlemen's element of the game. Most of the participants were men of position and at least moderate wealth.

The game spread vigorously after the Civil War, with towns in the East and Midwest fielding teams. The object began to move from "sport for sport's sake" to winning for the "glory of the town,"[15] thus strengthening the people–place relationship, which is so common in present day sport. Admission fees were charged during the 1860's, setting the stage for full-fledged professional competition. This decade also witnessed a rules-standardization movement which included the establishment of the nine-inning game, called balls, and iron plates for the pitcher's box and home plate.

The 1860's were characterized by semiprofessional teams such as the Excelsiors, Eckfords, and the Atlantics from Brooklyn, the New York Mutuals, the Washington Nationals, the Philadelphia Athletics, the Rockford, Illinois City Club, and teams from Morrisania and Troy, New York, as well as from Chicago, Pittsburgh, Cincinnati, Fort Wayne, and Columbus. The 1869 Cincinnati Red

TABLE 3–1
THE GEOGRAPHIC ORGANIZATION OF BASEBALL: 1870–1900

National Association

Baltimore	1872–1874	Middletown	1872
Boston	1871–1875	New Haven	1875
Brooklyn (2)	1872–1875	New York	1871–75
Chicago	1871 1874–75	Philadelphia (3)	1871–75
Cleveland	1871–1872	Rockford	1871
Elizabeth	1873	St. Louis	1875
Fort Wayne	1871	Troy	1871–72
Hartford	1874–75	Washington (2)	1871–75
Keokuk	1875		

National League

Baltimore	1892–99	Milwaukee	1878
Boston	1876–	New York	1876–
Brooklyn	1890–	Pittsburgh	1887–
Buffalo	1879–85	Philadelphia	1876–
Chicago	1876–	Worcester	1880–92
Cincinnati	1876–80 1890–	Providence	1878–85
Cleveland	1879–84 1889–99	St. Louis	1876–77 1885–86
Detroit	1881–88		1892–
Hartford	1876–77	Syracuse	1879
Indianapolis	1878 1887–89	Troy	1879–82
Kansas City	1886	Washington	1886–89 1892–99
Louisville	1876–77 1892–99		

Union Association

Baltimore	1884	Philadelphia	1884
Boston	1884	Pittsburgh	1884
Chicago	1884	St. Louis	1884
Cincinnati	1884	St. Paul	1884
Kansas City	1884	Washington	1884
Milwaukee	1884		

Stockings were the first all-salaried ball club. Under the management of Harry Wright, who was nationally acclaimed as "the father of the professional game,"[16] the team toured the East and recorded an incredible record of 57 wins and one tie. The first franchise relocation in professional baseball involved the movement of the Cincinnati team to Boston in 1871. A professional baseball league was officially established in 1871 and included Wright's Boston team and members from New York, Chicago, New Haven, Brooklyn, Philadelphia (3), and Fort Wayne. The first decade was dominated by Boston and Philadelphia and featured many short-lived and terribly outclassed franchises in the West, such as Keokuk and St. Louis.

The National League began operation in 1876 with eight clubs.[17] The league had representatives from Boston, Chicago, St. Louis, Louisville, Hartford, Cincinnati, Philadelphia, and New York. The geography of the league was very unstable during these early years. Milwaukee, Indianapolis, and Providence soon replaced St. Louis, Hartford, and Louisville. In 1879 Milwaukee and Indianapolis dropped out and Troy, Buffalo, Syracuse, and Cleveland were admitted, once more creating a circuit, with an almost total eastern contingent (Table 3-1).

During the 1880's era which was dominated by Pop Anson, the National League relocated in the nation's largest cities. Detroit, New York, Washington, Kansas City, and Philadelphia were granted permission to participate because of growing competition from the American and Union Associations and failure of the small city franchises in Buffalo and Providence. Baltimore and Brooklyn were also added forming a twelve-club "big city" league in the 1890's.

By 1902 a dual National and American League structure had been firmly established. The spatial organization of competition that was set up at that time remained essentially unchanged until 1953, when the Boston Braves moved to Milwaukee. Despite the westward movement of the population, major league baseball remained confined to the Northeast. The South and West had no representation whatsoever.

The first half of the twentieth century was characterized by the spread of minor league baseball to every nook and cranny of the nation. It was extremely rare for a community of 25,000 or more to be without a professional baseball club. Some form of professional baseball was an entertainment medium within easy access of nearly every American. In 1949, prior to the expansion and relocation of the major league teams, there were 59 leagues and over 500 minor league teams. By 1951 the number of leagues had decreased to 49 and the number of clubs to 360.[18]

The diffusion of baseball can be pinpointed through an examination of the geographical origins of the best players over an extended period of time. In general, the best players are the ones who made it to the Major Leagues. It is possible to plot the birthplaces of all major league baseball players by using data contained in the *Encyclopedia of Baseball*.[19] This source contains a short biography of everyone who played in the "majors" for one game, or over a twenty year career. By taking the midpoint of each player's major league tenure, it is possible to assign him to a ten year period. Thus the time sequence of player origins like that shown in Fig. 3-1 can be generated for the period 1876–1958.

During the first period, 1871–1880, when the National League was organized, most of the players came from the Northeast. Pennsylvania, New York, and Massachusetts led in producing players. Maryland had the highest per capita index of 4.68, but even New York was generating players at a rate of three times the national norm. Minnesota, Iowa, Missouri, and Louisiana provided the only players from west of the Mississippi, and Missouri was the only state west of Pennsylvania to exceed the national average on a per capita basis.

The next decade witnessed a substantial westward movement. California's player output jumped to 21, a per capita rate of 1.36. Washington, Wyoming, and Nebraska also sent forth a few players. In the Northeast the dominance of Pennsylvania and Massachusetts was maintained, as New York began to fall. The pattern changed very little during the 1890's with high per capita production almost entirely confined to the Northeast. Kentucky began to emerge as a baseball state, a prelude to the great southern love affair with the game. The period also saw Ohio move into second place behind Pennsylvania.

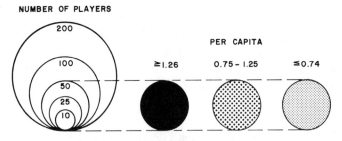

Fig. 3.1 Key to maps on the following pages. A per capita index of 1.00 equals national average production for the ten-year period in question. Dark circles indicate high per capita output.

THE DIFFUSION OF MAJOR LEAGUE BASEBALL AS MEASURED BY PLAYER ORIGIN

1871 - 1880

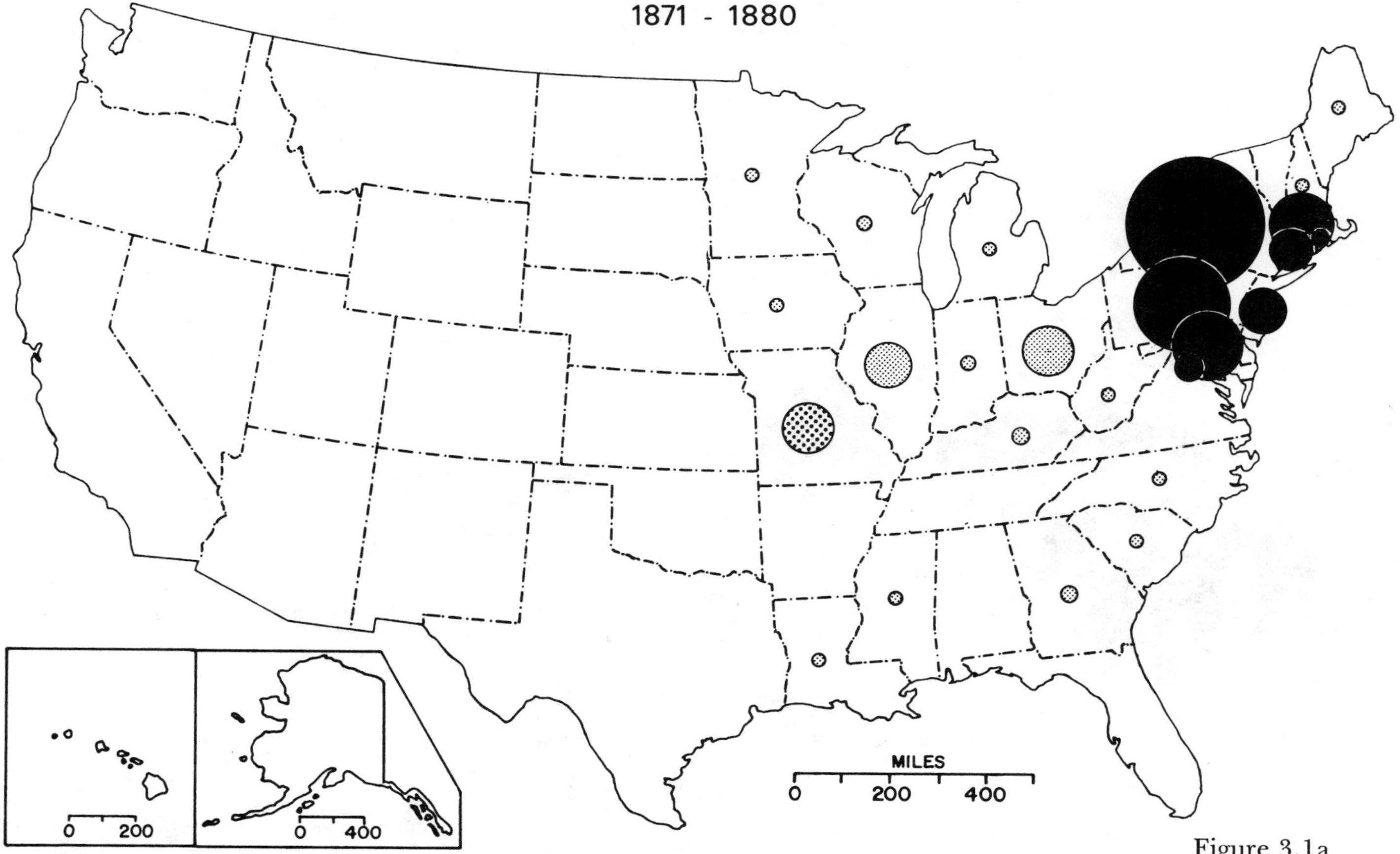

MILES

0   200   400

0   400

0   200

Figure 3.1a

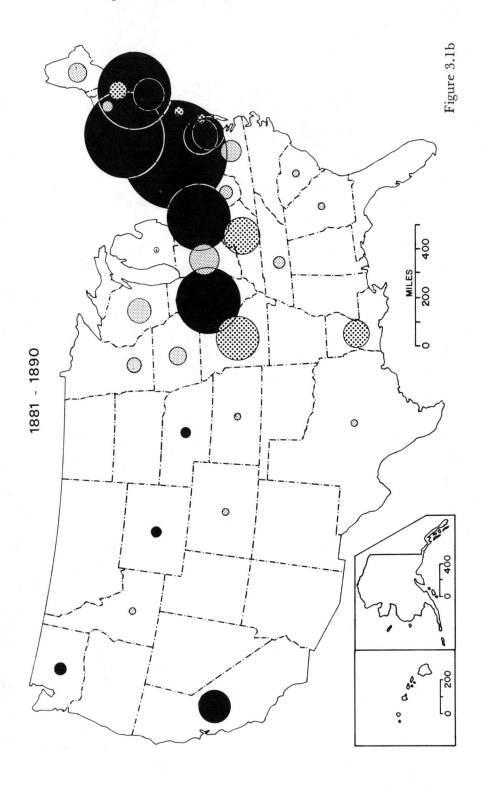

1881 - 1890

Figure 3.1b

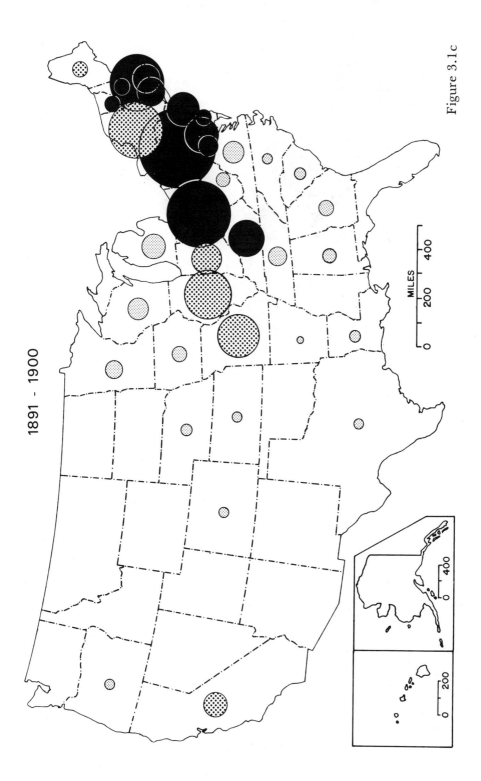

Figure 3.1c

1891 - 1900

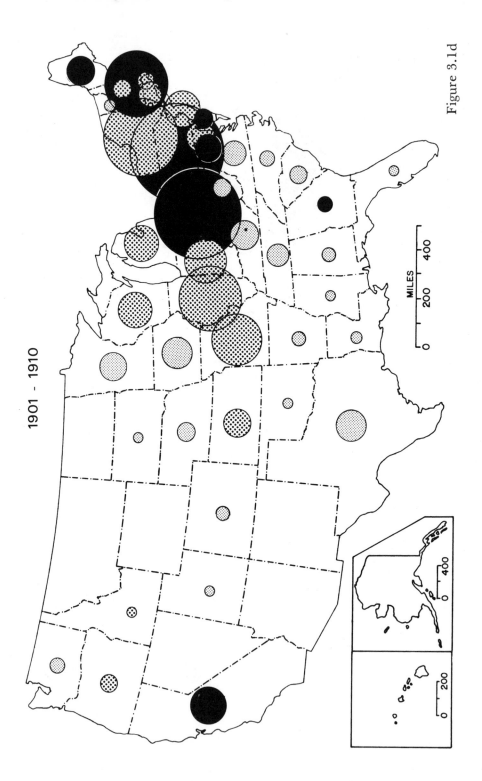

Figure 3.1d

1901 – 1910

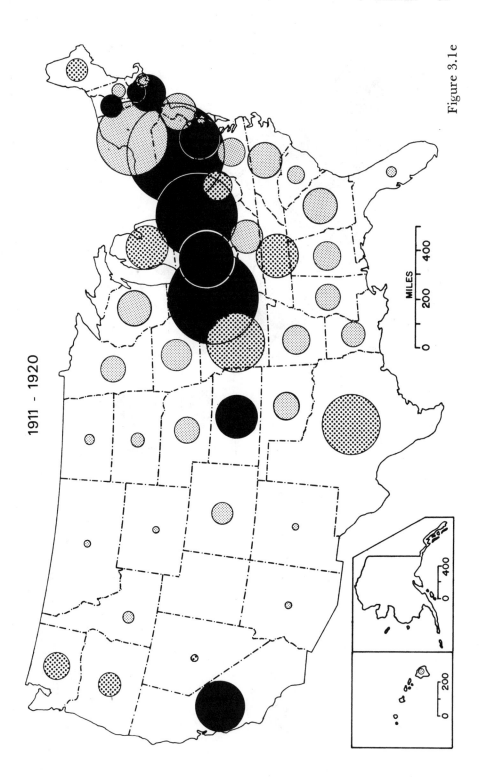

Figure 3.1e

1911 - 1920

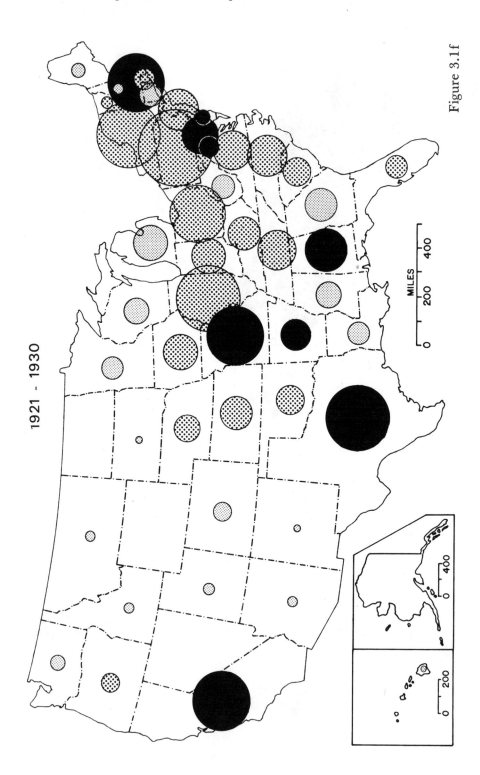

Figure 3.1f

1921 - 1930

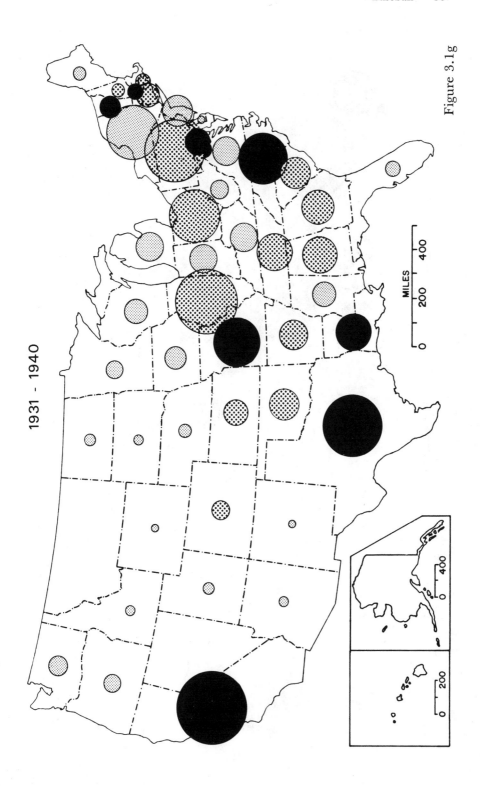

1931 - 1940

Figure 3.1g

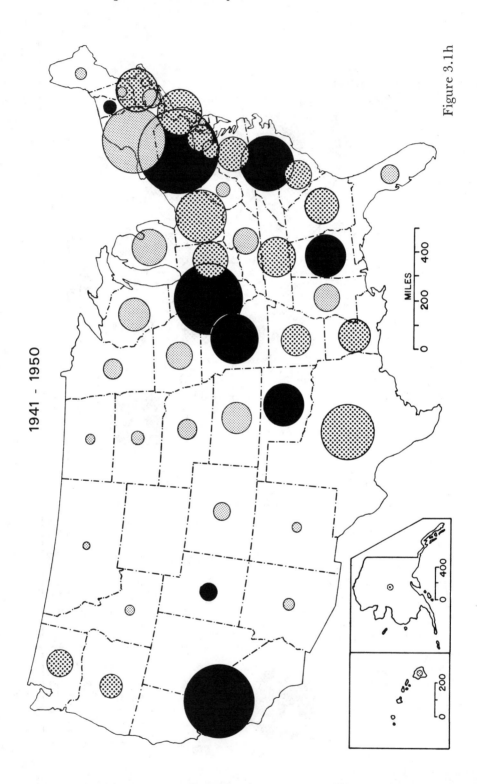

1941 - 1950

MILES

Figure 3.1h

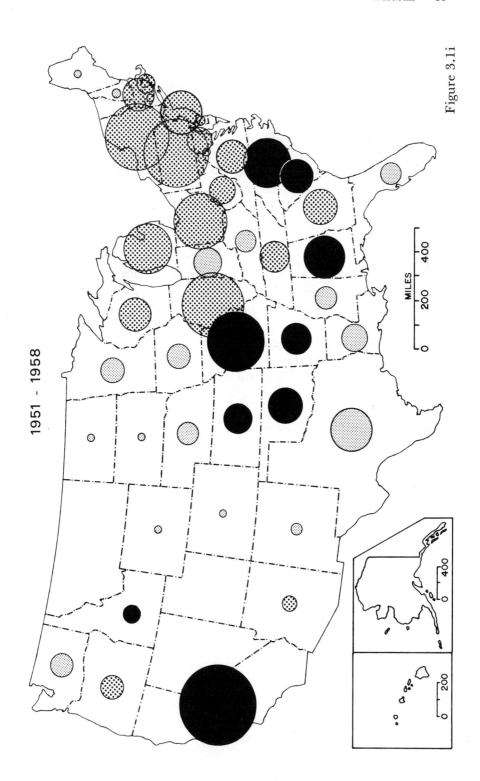

Figure 3.1i

1951 - 1958

By the turn of the century, baseball players were coming from all sections of the United States. However, Ohio and Pennsylvania were still the leading states. The second decade was characterized by the emergence of Illinois, and Texas. Aside from Washington, D.C., the South remained far below average.

The 1920's witnessed the continued growth of California and Texas baseball. Missouri, Alabama, and North Carolina also developed a great number of players during this period. The Pennsylvania-Ohio dominance had finally begun to crumble.

California became the leading producer of major leaguers during the 1930's, followed closely by Illinois, Pennsylvania, and Texas. Only Masschusetts and Vermont maintained their characteristically high production rates in the Northeast. This was the period that saw most of the southern states move above the national per capita average for the first time. There was little change during the 1940's and by the 1950's the production of baseball players had finally become a national phenomenon.

The geographical structure of major league baseball is now more representative of the national population distribution than at any-time before. Major league baseball is finally becoming a truly national game, at least from a geographical standpoint. This nationalization, in combination with the advent of televised contests, has been accompanied by drastic losses and consolidations at the minor league level. There are now just 21 leagues and less than 150 teams (Fig. 3-2). The tremendous loss has been partially offset by advances at the collegiate level. However, the relatively few universities who are taking their baseball seriously, in no way counteract the decline of the major leagues. At the same time, semiprofessional and amateur baseball have experienced a precipitous decline. Increased wealth has brought with it a much greater range of leisure time choices, and baseball has lost many participants and fans to endeavors like boating, golf, tennis, cycling, and flying. But regardless of where it stands relative to football, the bat-and-ball game is still the major American summer sport, and to many, it still ranks at the top.

COLLEGIATE FOOTBALL

Intercollegiate football competition has been going on for over one hundred years, since the first contest took place between Princeton and Rutgers, at New Brunswick, New Jersey on November 6, 1869. Games of ball involving the use of the foot date back many centuries.

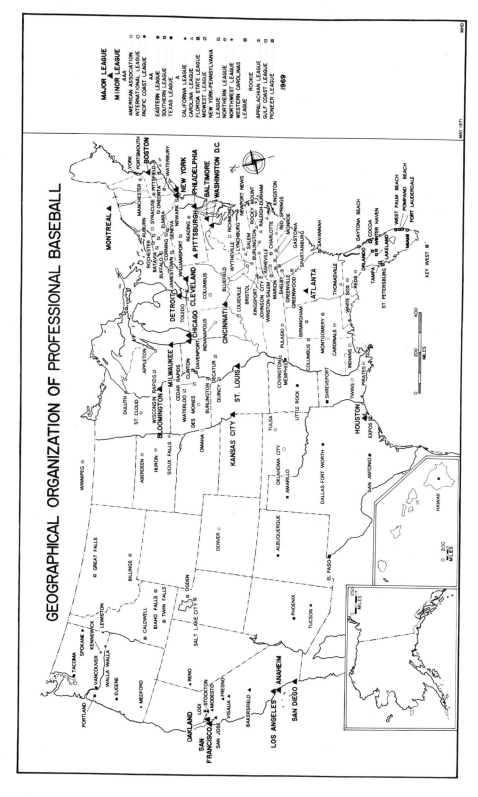

GEOGRAPHICAL ORGANIZATION OF PROFESSIONAL BASEBALL

Figure 3.2

In England the first written reference to football was in 1175. The early game was disorganized and extremely rough. The following quote from the *Anatomy of Abuses* presents an excellent description:

> . . . football playing . . . may rather be called a friendly kind of fight than a play or recreation, a bloody and murthering practice than a felowly sport a pastime. For dooth not everyone lye in waight for his adversarie seeking to overthrow him and to picke him on his nose, though it be uppon hard stone? In ditch or dale, in valley or hill, or what place so ever it be, hee careth not so he have him down . . . and by this meanes sometimes their neckes are broken, sometimes their backes, sometimes their legs, sometimes their arms, sometimes one part is thurst out of joint, sometimes their eyes start out and sometimes hurt in one place, sometimes in another . . . And no mervaile, for they have the sleights to meet one betwixt two, to dash him against the hart with their elbowes, to hit him under the short ribs with their griped fists, and with their knees to catch him upon the hip and pick him on his neck with a hundred other such murthering devices: and hereof groweth envie, malice, rancour, choler, hatred, displeasure, enmitie and what not els; and sometimes fighting, brawling, contention, quarrel picking, murther, homicide and great effusion of blood as experience daily teacheth.[20]

Football was played in essentially this manner until the nineteenth century. It was during this period that the sport began to truly resemble what is now referred to as football (the rugby version), a contest which involves running with the ball.

It is not possible to say exactly when football was first played in the English public schools. It was being played at Eton, Charterhouse, Harrow, Rugby, Shrewsbury, Westminister, and Winchester by the end of the eighteenth century.[21] At this time there were no written rules. However, the game was played on a weekly basis during established spring and autumn seasons. English public school football was an extremely violent game as illustrated by the following description:

> When running . . . the enemy tripped, shinned, charged with the shoulder, got you down and sat upon you . . . in fact might do anything short of murder to get the ball from you.[22]

Early football did not involve any carrying of the ball. The carrying game evolved sometime during the 1820's and, according to legend, first took place at Rugby School.[23] Rugby was formalized during the 1840's with the establishment of uniform written rules. It was at this time that the distinction between "rugger" and "soccer" occurred. Both forms continued to diffuse throughout the American school systems.

In America, as in England, the game progressed from legalized brawling to a semiorganized attempt to move the ball toward, and eventually over, the opponent's goal. There continued to be two versions, one relying solely on kicking and the other allowing running and handling of the ball. A number of high schools, particularly in the Boston area, sponsored teams and established what might now be called an interscholastic conference or league. This eventually led to the commencement of intercollegiate competition at New Brunswick.[24]

The first game had little in common with modern football. It was played with 25 men on a side and resembled present-day soccer. No ball handling was permitted. By 1872, Columbia, Harvard, and Yale had joined Princeton and Rutgers in intercollegiate competition. Harvard favored a carrying game, similar to Rugby Union, and their persistence led to the first rules convention of 1873. Three years later, Rugby Union rules were officially adopted, and the carrying game was in to stay.[25] Between 1876 and 1883, two developments placed football on a path which was to change it drastically from rugby. Possession of the ball (the line of scrimmage) was legalized, and a team was given three downs to move five yards forward, or if it chose, to move ten yards backward. The era of mass or power football had begun.

The period 1883-1906 was dominated by strategy designed to produce power and momentum. It was the roughest, most dangerous period the game has ever known. Notable plays included the "flying wedge" and the "V" trick. Both relied upon the forward movement of an interlocked group surrounding the ball carrier. The objective was to flatten any person between it and the opponent's goal. These, and the more sophisticated "guards and tackles back" plays which were smaller and faster versions of the wedge, resulted in unacceptable injury and mortality levels. During 1905 the *Chicago Tribune* reported 18 deaths and 159 serious injuries. Many people demanded that the game be banned, and some colleges followed their suggestion.

Finally in 1905, President Theodore Roosevelt invited delegates from Harvard, Princeton, and Yale to the White House to discuss the deteriorating football situation. That White House conference was followed by a meeting of representatives from 62 colleges and the establishment of the American Intercollegiate Football Rules Committee. Drastic rule changes followed, most of which were geared to opening the game up and thereby reducing the risk to life and limb.

The most basic change, and the second major step away from rugby, was the introduction of the forward pass. In the beginning, there were many restrictions on the use of the pass (the receiver had to be five yards downfield, and incomplete passes resulted in 15-yard penalties). Another rule change involved the decision to require a 10-yard advance for a first down. This forced the game to open up, with the old power plays losing in favor of end runs and slants. The accent shifted from power to a combination of power and speed. In 1910 interlocked interference was outlawed, and there was an immediate shift in advantage from the offense to the defense. In order to compensate, restrictions on the forward pass were lifted the next year, and the number of downs was increased from three to four. Rule changes since then have been minor, and the football of today is very similar to that of 1912. In summary, the emphasis moved from kicking, to mass momentum, to power, and finally to a combination of power, speed, and deception.

THE GAME SPREADS

The cradle of football was the Northeast, but the game spread quickly to the Midwest, where the University of Michigan was the pioneer. A band of Wolverines traveled East in the early 1880's to engage Harvard and Yale in the Nation's first intersectional battles. The decade witnessed the establishment of the Western Conference, now known as the Big Ten, and the adoption of football by Notre Dame. During the late 1880's and early 1890's, several schools in Kentucky, Virginia, and North Carolina began to participate. The decade also saw California and Stanford schedule games on the West Coast. The success of the new entrants was hastened by the importation of coaches from the established institutions (Fig. 3–3). Camp, Yost, and Dobie moved to the West Coast. Heisman, Warner, and McGugin went South, while Stagg, Cavanaugh, and Williams migrated from the East to the Midwest.[26]

COACHING MIGRATIONS 1879 – 1911

COLLEGE HEAD FOOTBALL COACHES

EASTERN ORIGINS

MIDWESTERN ORIGINS

DESTINATION

FLOW LINES

MILES
0 100 200 300

Figure 3.3

THE LOCATION OF COLLEGIATE FOOTBALL STRENGTH - 1889 - 1930

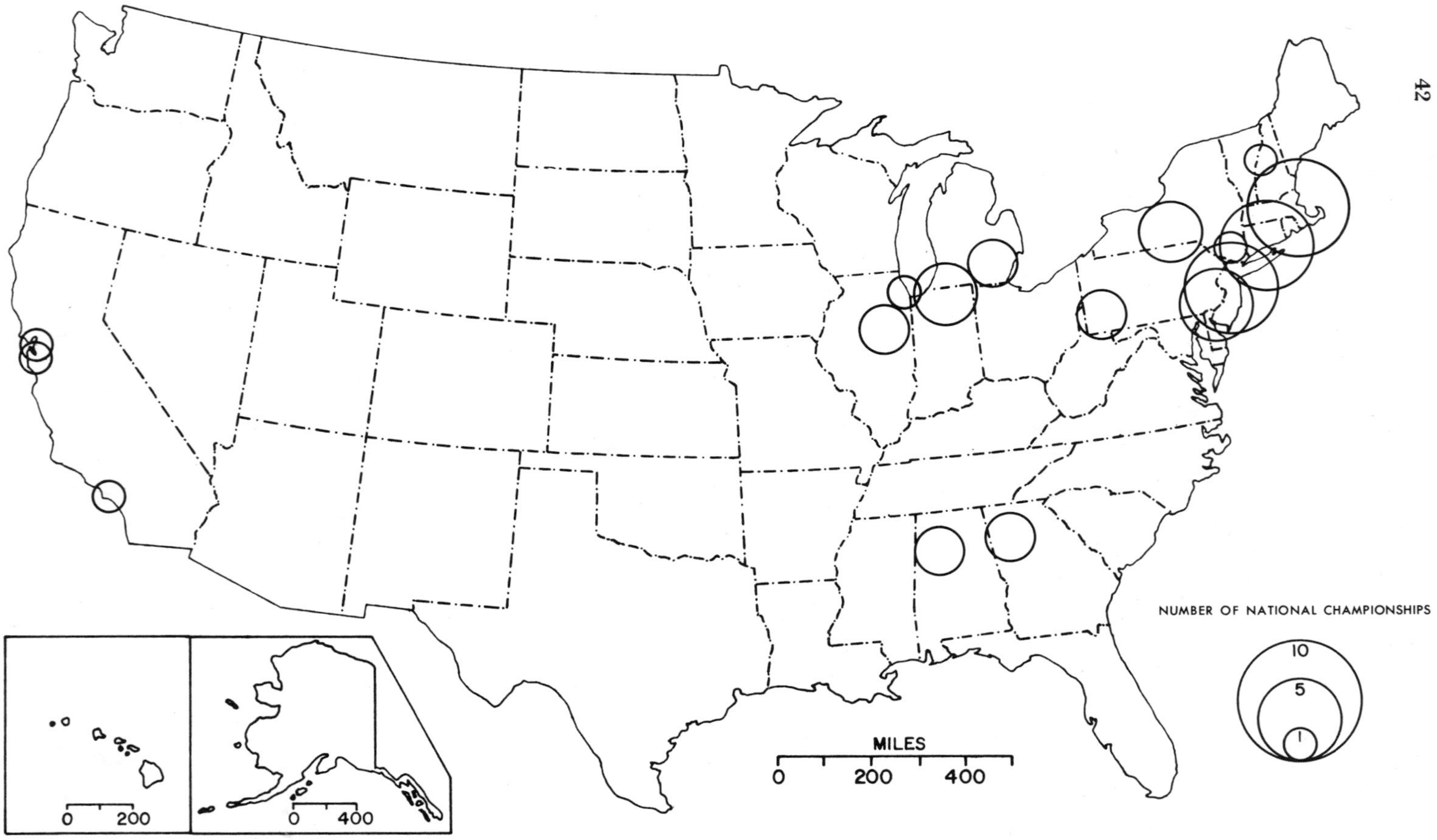

NUMBER OF NATIONAL CHAMPIONSHIPS

MILES

Figure 3.4

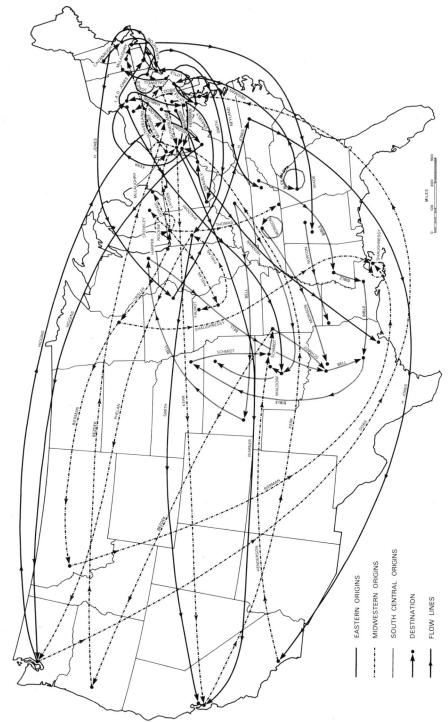

COACHING MIGRATIONS 1912 – 1930

COLLEGE HEAD FOOTBALL COACHES

Figure 3.5

EASTERN ORIGINS

MIDWESTERN ORIGINS

SOUTH CENTRAL ORIGINS

DESTINATION

FLOW LINES

MILES
0   100   200   300

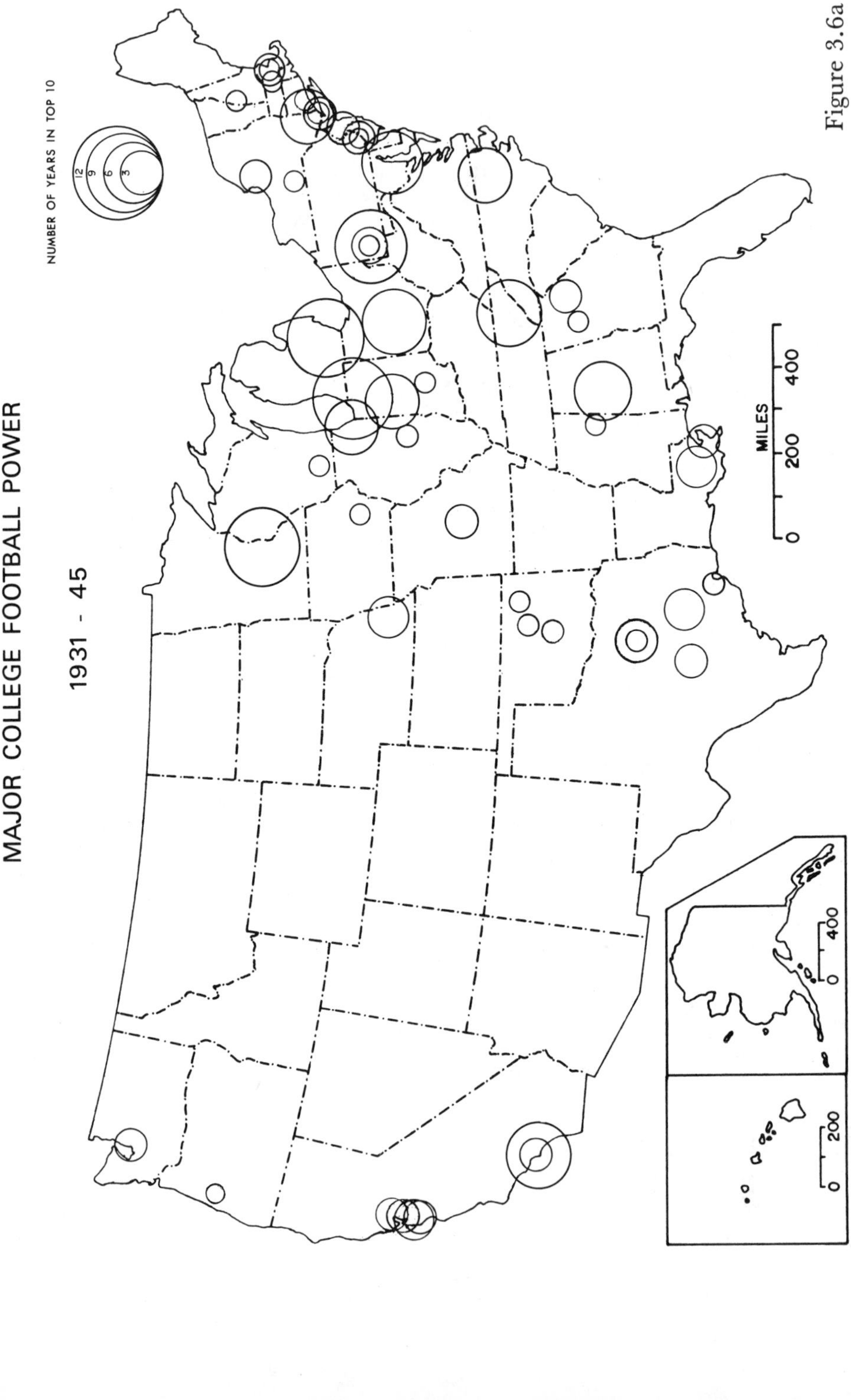

MAJOR COLLEGE FOOTBALL POWER

1931 - 45

NUMBER OF YEARS IN TOP 10

MILES

0   200   400

0   200

0   400

DETERMINED BY TOP 10 AND NUMBER 1 RANKINGS

Figure 3.6a

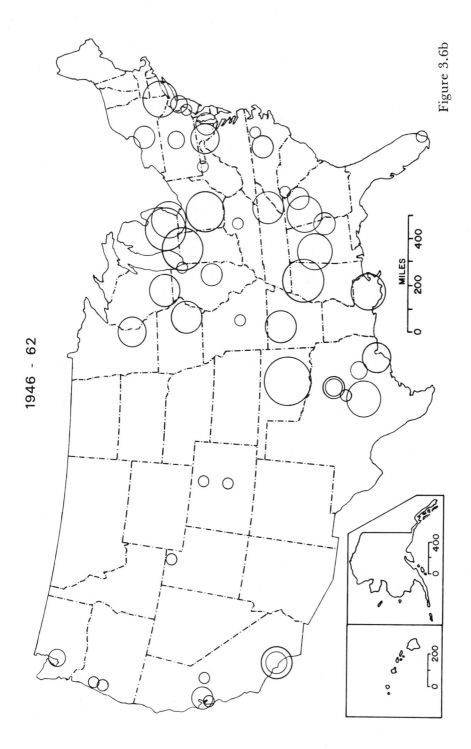

Figure 3.6b

1946 - 62

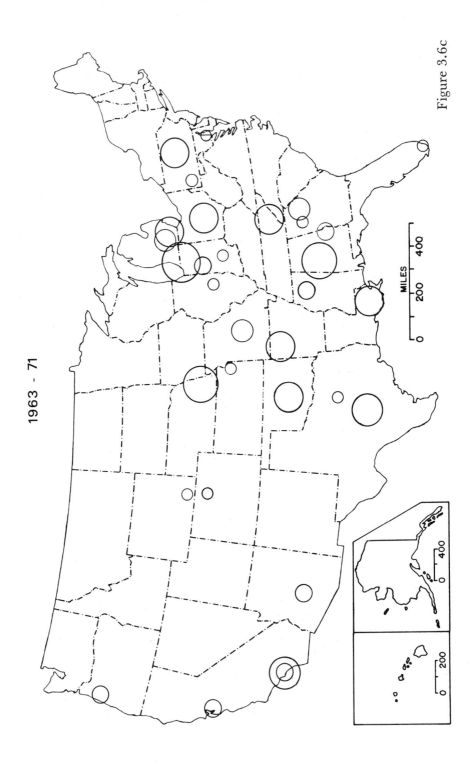

1963 - 71

MILES

400

200

0

400

0

200

0

Figure 3.6c

The Ivy League dominated the game prior to World War I, although there were a few exceptions, such as Michigan, Purdue, and Chicago (Figure 3-4). During the period immediately following the war, good coaching and raw material began to diffuse at a faster rate to the "provinces." Small schools like Notre Dame, Centre, and Texas A & M came to the forefront. With the help of more eastern coaching transplants like Warner, Jones and Andy Smith, the game began to thrive again on the Pacific Coast (Fig. 3-5).

The postwar era saw Alabama, Georgia Tech, and Tennessee replace Sewannee, Vanderbilt, and Virginia as the southern stalwarts. Nebraska was the chief force in the plains. Football was also attractive to the people of the Southwest, a region which developed an early reputation for its passing game. This was an era when coaches like Rockne, Bierman, Zuppke, Waldorf, Neyland, and Crisler caught the fancy of the American public and functioned as major forces in the diffusion of the game (Fig. 3-6).

The meteoric expansion of an exciting brand of football with such coaches as Rockne, Halas, and Warner was accompanied by a tremendous boom in stadium construction. Most facilities were built with borrowed funds and paid for with gate receipts. Since attendance was influenced greatly by the quality of play, the stadium debt provided a powerful motive to field successful teams. Attempts by many schools to do so created severe competition for the available talent and marked the beginning of the intense player recruiting which is so common today. Many violations of the amateur code occurred in these days, spurring the establishment of national financial standards for athletic scholarships. This allowed all schools (at least theoretically) to compete for athletes on equal grounds.

PROFESSIONAL FOOTBALL

According to popular opinion, the first game between professional teams was played in 1895 at Latrobe, Pennsylvania, although some players had performed for pay as much as three years before.[27] The strong relationships between early professional football and steel was in part due to financial support from the steel companies. The miners and mill hands were logical supporters of the hard-nosed Sunday entertainment, perhaps because it was something even more difficult than their typical daily activity in the mines and mills.[28]

Until 1920, when the National Football League was founded, most of the professional activity took place in Pennsylvania, New York, and Ohio. Standouts of the period—Canton, Massillon, and Columbus, Ohio, Franklin, Pennsylvania, and Watertown, New York—no longer field major professional teams. However, minor league professional football continues to thrive throughout this cradle area.

There were eleven original National Football League franchises. Five were in Ohio including Massillon, Canton, Akron, Cleveland, and Dayton. Rock Island, Chicago and Decatur, were the Illinois members. Muncie and Hammond, Indiana and Rochester, New York rounded out the league. George Halas of the Decatur Staleys was the leading figure during these early days.[29] He moved his team to Chicago in 1921, changing their name from the Staleys to the Bears. Four years later professional football began to gain attention when Halas signed Red Grange from the University of Illinois campus. The Bears dominated the game during the ensuing years, earning the nickname "Monsters of the Midway." Halas and his colleague, Clark Shaughnessy continued their innovative role. They perfected the "T formation," dramatically unveiling it in the 1940 championship game with a 73–0 victory over the Washington Redskins.

By this time the National Football League had moved its franchises to the larger cities setting the pattern for the present geographical organization. Today professional football is confined to the largest urban centers, with the exception of Green Bay, Wisconsin. Twenty-six teams comprise the National and American conferences, with each franchise worth at least $20 million to its owners and many times that to the city or area in which it is located (Fig. 4.2). The scramble for expansion teams has been frenzied with most of the new ones going to rapid-growth areas like Atlanta, San Diego, Minneapolis—St. Paul, Miami, and Dallas.

BASKETBALL

Basketball is now second in importance to football as a university sporting activity, and at many schools, it is the bellwether of the athletic program. Schools like Marquette, St. Bonaventure, Manhattan, Seattle, San Francisco, and now Jacksonville, have made their mark on the college athletic scene with little or no help from football. In fact, there are more schools competing in top-flight basketball than in any other sport. New and spacious field houses provide

a visible manifestation of the game's popularity in places which
formerly regarded it as just something to fill the long winter void.
Outstanding play has now spread to nearly all sections of the country
as the old-line powers have rapidly discovered. The "soft touches"
to which they had become accustomed are no longer so numerous.

The sport of basketball dates back to 1891. Historians of the
game are in agreement that James Naismith started it in Springfield,
Massachusetts. Since the early days, basketball has undergone numerous
rule changes, and there is little resemblance between the first contest
at the International Young Men's Christian Association Training
School and the fast-paced game of today.[30]

The rule changes and refinements began almost immediately.
Backboards were installed in 1893, a step which kept spectators
from participating in the action. Five-man teams became manda-
tory in 1897. The continuous dribble was instituted the next year,
and for over thirty years, basketball, the center jump variety, changed
little. In 1937, the center jump was eliminated, shortly after the
ten- and three-second rules had been added. Those changes coincided
with the emergence of the game as a major spectator attraction and
the beginning of Madison Square Garden doubleheaders, the AAU,
NCAA, and NIT post-season tournaments, and the development of
serious Olympic competition. Scores doubled, games were longer,
and crowds were larger and louder from grade school through the
professional ranks.

Rule changes since 1937 have been minor and were generally in
response to the extraordinary talents of a handful of players. The
game's domination by big men, or "goons" as they were so often
called, prompted the widening of the free-throw lane, the goal-
tending rule, and more recently, the hotly contested collegiate
"dunking" ban. The defensive wizardry of Bill Russell and the
offensive ability of Wilt Chamberlain, Kareem Jabar (Lew Alcindor),
and Elgin Baylor were largely responsible for the recent rule al-
terations.

Today basketball is the leading spectator game in the United
States. Its greatest following is at the grass roots level, in the hamlets and small towns of Mid-America and in the close-knit neighbor-
hoods and ghettos of the nation's largest cities.[31] Total attendance
at basketball games now approaches 150 million annually, which is
more than attendance at football, baseball, ice hockey, and tennis
combined! There are some indications that the sport may be losing
its grip in rural America, but any decline there may well be offset by
growth in the urban centers.

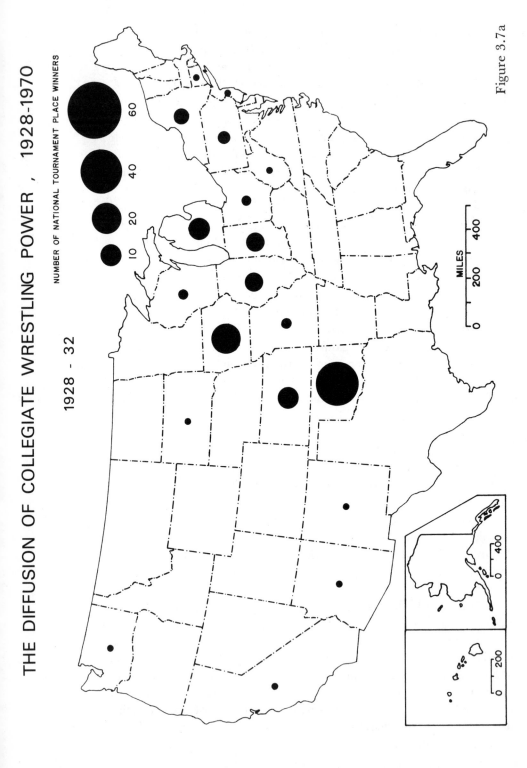

THE DIFFUSION OF COLLEGIATE WRESTLING POWER , 1928-1970

NUMBER OF NATIONAL TOURNAMENT PLACE WINNERS

1928 - 32

Figure 3.7a

1933 - 37

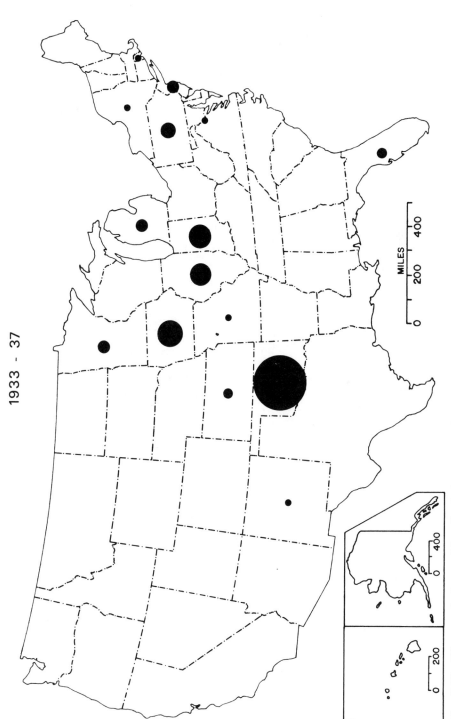

Fig. 3.7b The symbols used in all of the parts of Fig. 3.7 indicate the origin of the wrestlers by state of high school graduation.

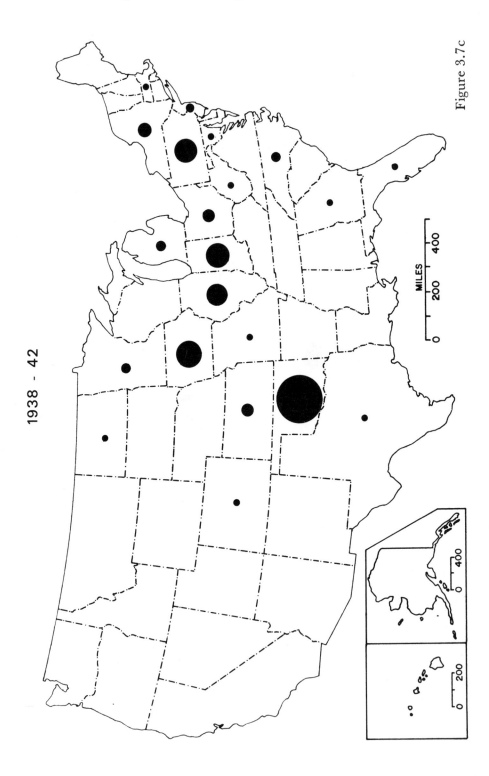

1938 - 42

Figure 3.7c

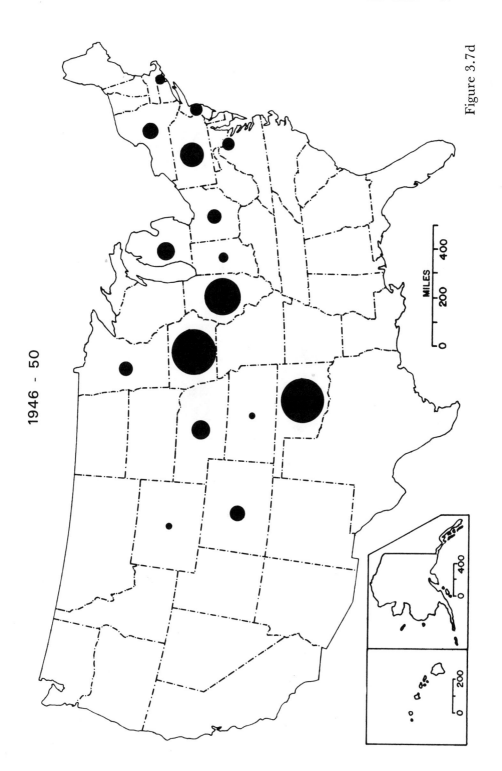

Figure 3.7d

1946 - 50

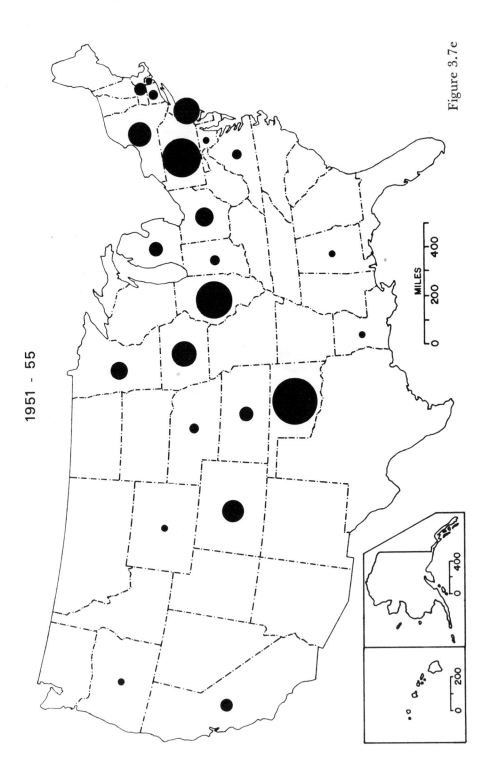

Figure 3.7e

1951 - 55

Figure 3.7 f

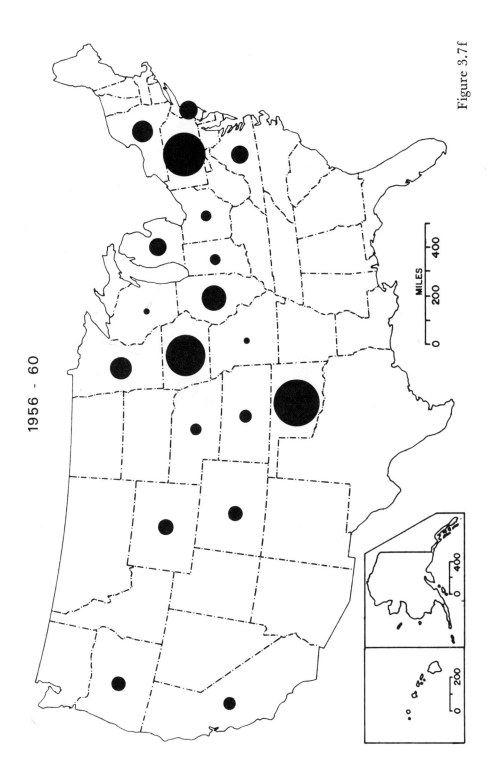

1956 - 60

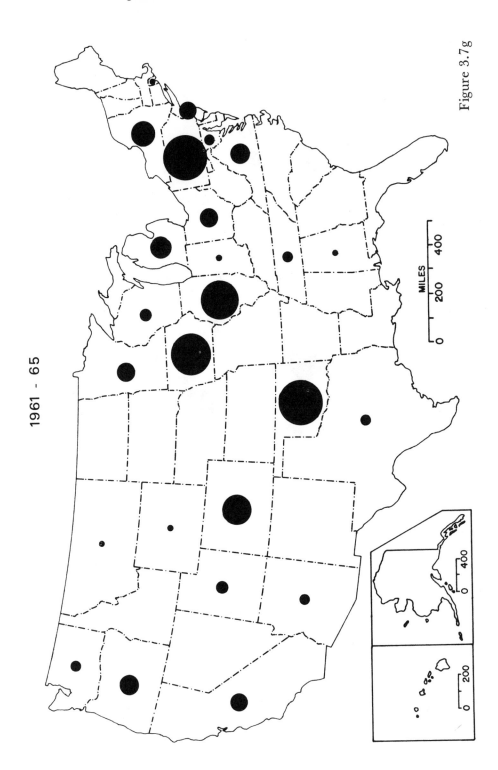

Figure 3.7g

1961 - 65

Figure 3.7h

1966 - 70

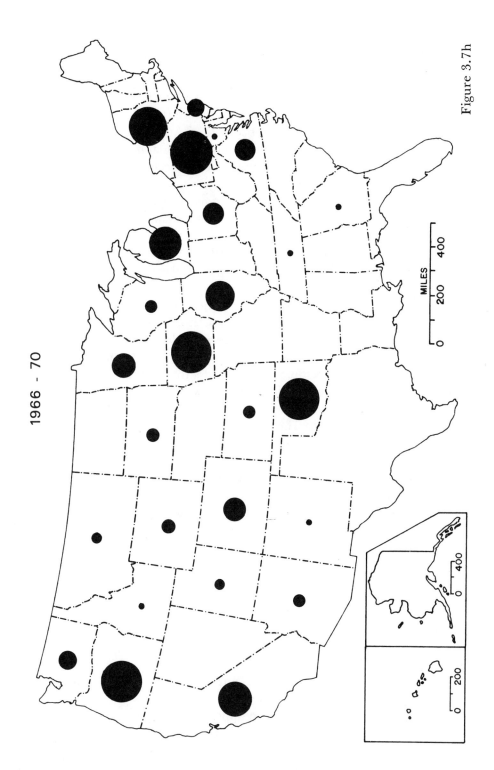

COLLEGIATE WRESTLING

Collegiate wrestling provides an excellent case study in the diffusion of a sport from a single dominant center. Under the direction of Edward C. Gallager, Oklahoma A & M College (now Oklahoma State University) developed into an unbeatable wrestling power. From 1916 to 1940 "Gallager's grapplers" won 138 dual matches with just five losses and four ties. The reign included a record of 68 consecutive victories.

The diffusion process from Oklahoma outward to the rest of the United States from 1928 to 1970 can be examined. Data on national tournament (NCAA) place winners have been assembled for every five-year period beginning with 1928.[32] They include the hometown and the college attended by each place winner. The information on hometowns was calculated on a state per capita basis for each of the time periods under consideration.

Oklahoma dominates over all competitors during the first two time periods, although Iowa makes a reasonable showing (Fig. 3–7). During the next period, New York, New Jersey, and Pennsylvania emerged as distinct wrestling centers, and a total of 21 states were represented. The following five years show little change. By period five Pennsylvania had become a major force, and westward diffusion was becoming apparent. The ensuing periods demonstrated an increased westward movement, especially to Wyoming and adjacent Rocky Mountain states. By the final period, the West, focusing on Oregon and California has become established as a wrestling node. The sport has now diffused to all areas with the exception of the South, and upper New England. The whys and hows of the diffusion process pose an exciting research problem.

GOLF

Golf historians are uncertain when the sport was adopted in the United States. It is generally accepted that the first *permanent* course was constructed at Yonkers, New York in 1888, but there is evidence of play at least 100 years before that.[33] In any event, once the game started it experienced a phenomenal and immediate expansion. There were over 1000 courses by 1900—most of them were concentrated in the Northeast.[34]

Golf, like tennis, began as an upper-class sport. And even today the initial investment and the cost of play make it almost inaccessible

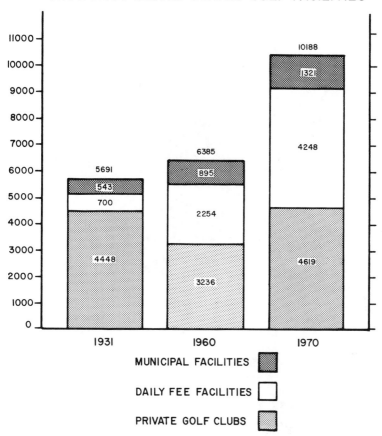

GROWTH IN UNITED STATES GOLF FACILITIES

SOURCE: NATIONAL GOLF FOUNDATION INFORMATION SHEET ST I

Fig. 3.8 This graph depicts the growth in all types of golf
courses during the Arnold Palmer era. (Courtesy of Mark M.
Miller.)

to the poor. The sport has grown tremendously during the last 15
years, as measured by media coverage, number of participants, number and quality of facilities, and the recognition accorded to the best
players. Based on National Golf Foundation estimates, there are
now over 10 million American players, utilizing over 10 thousand
courses. The great ones, Arnold Palmer, Jack Nicklaus, Gary Player,
and Lee Trevino, have attained celebrity status. Palmer, Nicklaus,
and Trevino have each been voted "sportsman of the year," and
Palmer was named athlete of the 1960-1970 decade. The professionals are now competing for tournament purses that have increased

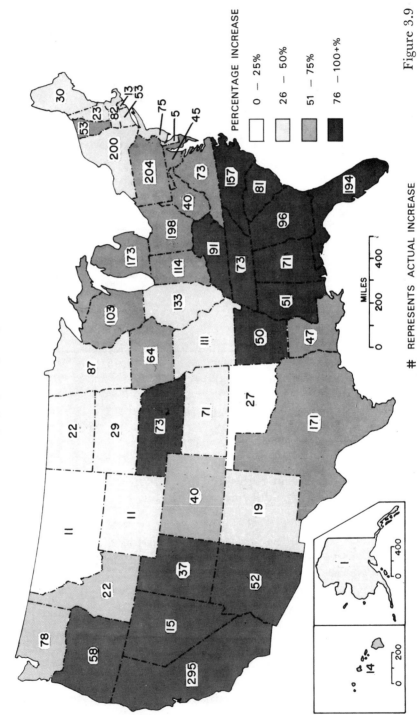

INCREASE IN GOLF FACILTIES
1960-1970

PERCENTAGE INCREASE

0 – 25%
26 – 50%
51 – 75%
76 – 100+%

MILES

0   200   400

REPRESENTS ACTUAL INCREASE

Figure 3.9

twentyfold since the days of Hogan, Sarazen, Hagen, Nelson, and Snead. Nicklaus pocketed over $300,000 as the leading money winner in 1972 as compared to Paul Runyan's $6800 earnings as the 1934 leader.[35] Most of the present events pay out more prize money than the entire tour did before World War II.

A large portion of the increased popularity is attributable to the success and magnetic personality of Arnold Palmer. He dominated the game to a greater extent than Jones, Hagen, and Hogan before him; much the way that Nicklaus does now. The combination of his daring play and personality caught the fancy of the public like no one else. Palmer helped the Professional Golf Tour to compete with baseball, football, and basketball for attention and prestige. And as a result, amateur golf, men's and women's, juniors and seniors, high school and collegiate, also benefited.

One way to measure the golf explosion in the United States is through the facilities themselves. During the 1931–1960 period there was an increase of less than 700 courses (Fig. 3-8). Then came Arnold Palmer. There was a *75 percent* jump in the number of American courses between 1960–1970 (Fig. 3-9).[36] Northern New England was the first golf resort area in the United States. A significant number of the courses and hotels there were built to attract tourists from the major eastern cities. Resort courses developed in the Catskills and Adirondacks and at many seaside locations throughout the East. In recent years, most of the resort courses have been built in the Southeast, particularly in the Carolinas, Florida, and in the Southwest. The "Dixie Golf Circle" and the Grand Strand area around Myrtle Beach, South Carolina are prominent among the new developments, as are the PGA Course, and those built in and around the Florida Disneyland.

Southwestern golf expansion has centered on Phoenix, Tucson, Las Vegas, and Reno, and the desert area east of Los Angeles. A good part of the course construction has been in association with real estate speculation. The leisure revolution has spawned the golf-housing or fairway lot life style, and today it is estimated that there are over one million residents in golf-housing developments.[37]

NOTES

1. John Richards Betts, "The Technological Revolution and the Rise of Sports, 1850-1900," *The Mississippi Valley Historical Review* 40 (September, 1953) 231.

2. *Ibid.*, p. 231.

3. *Ibid.*, p. 234.

4. Alexander Johnson, *Ten-and Out! The Complete Story of the Prize Ring in America* (New York: 1947), 42–43.

5. *Daily Picayune* (New Orleans), July 6, 1870. See also *New York Times*, October 21, 1858; *Harper's Weekly* XXVII (October 13, 1883) 654.

6. Betts, *op. cit., p. 239.*

7. See *Spirit of the Times* XX (May 4, 1850) 130; *Courier* (Natchez), November 26, 1850; *Daily State Journal* (Madison), March 26, 1855.

8. *New York Herald*, October 23, 1882.

9. David Quentin Voight, *American Baseball* (Norman, Okla: University of Oklahoma Press, 1966), pp. 7–8.

10. *Ibid.*, p. 8.

11. Harold Peterson, "Baseball's Johnny Appleseed," *Sports Illustrated*, April 14, 1969, pp. 57–76.

12. Voight, *op. cit.*, p. 8.

13. *Ibid.* p. 8.

14. *Spalding's Official Baseball Guide*, 1900, pp. 51–70.

15. Marshall B. Davidson, *Life in America*, Vol. II, (Boston: Houghton Mifflin Co., 1951), p. 61.

16. John Kiernan, "Henry Wright," *Dictionary of American Biography* (ed. by Dumas Malone) Vol. XX, New York, Scribner, p. 554.

17. Spalding, *op. cit.*, p. 68.

18. *Study of Monopoly Power* (Excerpt from the 1953 Senate Subcommittee on Professional Baseball), Washington, 1953, p. 992.

19. Hy Turkin, and S. C. Thompson, *The Official Encyclopedia of Baseball* (New York: A. S. Barnes and Company, 1956), p. 59–382.

20. Philip Stubbes, *Anatomy of Abuses*, 1583.

21. E. G. Dunning, "Football in Its Early Stages," *History Today*, Vol. 13 (December, 1963), pp. 841.

22. *Ibid.*, p. 843.

23. There is a great deal of controversy surrounding the claim that William Webb-Ellis first ran with the football during a contest at Rugby during 1823.

24. For an account of this first game, see John W. Herbert, "How it All Started" circulated by the Associated Press, November 23, 1933.

25. Walter Camp, who is generally referred to as the father of the game, was instrumental in formulating the early rule changes and selling them to other members of the rules committee.

26.   The coaching migration maps are based on information assembled by Don Rominger, in his unpublished paper, "Diffusion of Big Time Football Power and Some Resulting Migratory Patterns of Successful Coaches," Stillwater, Oklahoma, 1972.

27.   Hamilton Maule, *The Game* (New York, Random House 1964), p. 5.

28.   *Ibid.* p. 5.

29.   Allison Danzig, *Oh How They Played the Game* (New York: MacMillan, 1971), pp. 303–314.

30.   William G. Mokray, *Ronald Encyclopedia of Basketball* (New York: Ronald Press, 1963), pp. 1–16.

31.   For a colorful account of what basketball can mean to an area see: John R. Tunis, *The American Way in Sport* (New York: Duell, Sloan and Pearce, 1958), pp. 79–98.

32.   Don Chalmers, Joe Cox and Richard Kunze, *A Geographic Study of NCAA Wrestling Tournament Placewinners*, Unpublished seminar paper, Stillwater, Oklahoma, April 19, 1971.

33.   There seems to be some controversy over the location of the first permanent golf course in the United States. Sources have credited both the Foxburg Country Club, Foxburg, Pennsylvania and St. Andrews Golf Club, Yonkers, New York, with being the first permanent courses. The majority of sources indicate that the St. Andrews Club was the original course, and it is accepted as the original for the purposes of this book.

34.   Nevin H. Gibson, *The Encyclopedia of Golf* (New York: A. S. Barnes 1964), p. 181.

35.   Professional Golf Association, *The P.G.A. Tour Book* (New York: Professional Golf Association, 1971), p. 60.

36.   Mark M. Miller, *A Spatial Analysis of Golf Facility Development in the United States, 1931–1970*, Unpublished Master's Thesis, Oklahoma State University, May, 1972.

37.   Bill Hartley and Ellen Hartley, "125 Places to Live Along a Golf Course," *Golf Digest*, 18 (November, 1967) p. 45.

4 / The Spatial Organization of Sport in the United States

The present geographical organization of American sport has been shaped primarily over the past 100 years. In simplest terms, we can consider the spatial organization of sport as consisting of three levels. The function of levels one and two is the promotion of mass participation, while that of the third level is to market sport as an entertainment medium for the spectator, and, of course, to generate profits for the franchise owners.

The participatory activities are geared to serve small-group markets. They are found almost everywhere that there are enough people to make up a team. Among the most common organizations for participatory sport are the "little leagues" for preteens, the interscholastic sports spectrum, and the adult-oriented organizations, which are usually administered by city, industrial, or religious groups. Some of the mass-participation sports are universally available (football, basketball, baseball, softball, and bowling), while others such as hockey, lacrosse, and cricket are regionally concentrated.

The spectator-oriented activities include "big time" college athletics, particularly football and basketball, and the major professional sports. They are much more geographically concentrated than the participant-based activities. Since they are highly dependent on gate receipts for survival, they have generally gravitated to locations where a profit is likely, even during poor seasons. Hence they are very market-oriented. The highest caliber professional teams (Major League baseball, The National Football League, The National and American Basketball Associations and The National and World Hockey Leagues)

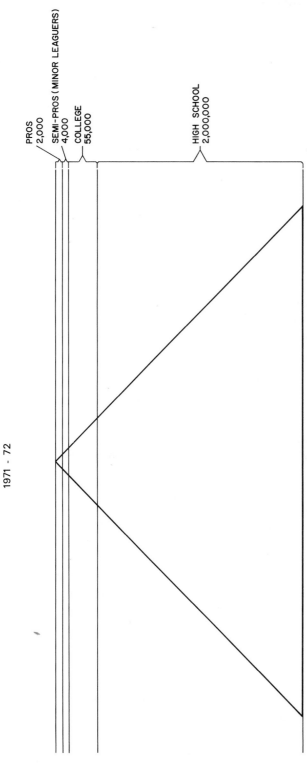

FOOTBALL, BASKETBALL AND BASEBALL PARTICIPATION BY LEVEL OF COMPETITION

1971 - 72

PROS
2,000

SEMI-PROS (MINOR LEAGUERS)
4,000

COLLEGE
55,000

HIGH SCHOOL
2,000,000

Fig. 4.1 Most Americans participating in organized sport are of high school age or younger. Yet the ethics which shape and govern sport are largely the product of professional and collegiate competition.

are almost entirely confined to the largest metropolitan areas. Minor league franchises are located in smaller markets or in less accessible areas.

College and university sport fits somewhat nebulously between the professional and youth-oriented activities. In some sports like college football and basketball, the highest caliber university competition serves a role that ranges somewhere between the Minor and the Major professional leagues. The location of the "big-time" collegiate programs has emerged in such a way as to provide first-class spectator attractions in college towns located in predominantly rural areas, which are deemed as poor risks for professional franchises. College sport, especially football, has become the most place-oriented of the spectator activities. Thus Nebraskans, Oklahomans, and Texans (whether alumni or not) demonstrate a fanatic degree of loyalty to their university teams—teams in most cases which are located in relatively small potential market areas compared to their professional kin. However, there are instances, i.e., the University of Michigan, UCLA, USC, and Georgia Tech, where collegiate and professional sport successfully coexist in the same market areas.

The spatial organization of sport can be depicted as a pyramid, with professional sport located at the tip and the mass-participation activities forming the base. It is from this base that the talent which stocks the professional teams is developed, gradually moving upward to the pinnacle, but only after a harsh selection process removes most of the original aspirants (Fig. 4–1).

The readily available data permit the examination of the major American games at three levels of competition. By looking at the spatial organization of interscholastic, intercollegiate, and professional sport, several generalizations concerning varying degrees of regional emphasis, opportunity to participate, and spatial organization are possible. The interscholastic setup forms the base on which higher echelon competition depends, and therefore merits initial consideration.

INTERSCHOLASTIC ATHLETICS

The geographic organization of interscholastic athletics is quite similar throughout the United States. Virtually every small high school is a member of a league or conference. Large communities are likewise grouped together for the purpose of competing against one another. The big city high schools usually play each other with leagues commonly divided into public and parochial contingents. Suburban leagues are also typical, and in many cases do not interact with their adjacent inner-city organizations.

The state of Illinois provides a fairly standard example of the geographic organization of high school athletics. Nearly 100 leagues and conferences accomodate the state's 800-plus high schools. The conferences usually have between six and ten members. Most of them are made up of small schools with enrollments of 100 to 500 students. The greatest distance between communities in these conferences seldom exceeds 30 miles. In central Illinois the large towns like Champaign, Danville, Decatur, and Urbana belong to the same league. This is also true in the southern part of the state where Carbondale, Centralia, Benton, West Frankfort, and Marion compete for the conference title. In these conferences the greatest distances between members approaches 100 miles. Chicago schools are apportioned between public and private leagues. The city's suburban ring is divided into small regional groupings such as the West Suburban, Southwest Suburban, Northwest League and so on.

Until 1969 all the Illinois high schools competed for a single title in baseball, basketball, tennis and other sports. The state was divided into 64 regions. Each of the regions crowned a champion. The regional tournament winners then advanced to one of sixteen sectional tournaments, of which fifteen were located outside the city of Chicago. Sectional winners played one more game with a team from their part of the state. Then the eight remaining teams went to the state tournament in Champaign. Since 1969 the Illinois schools have been divided into two groups based upon their enrollment. But the geographical organization of state title competition remains essentially unchanged.

For tournament purposes most states have assigned schools to one of four to six classes, depending upon its enrollment. This results in four to six state champions in each sport. The system also calls for regular evaluation of each school's status and constant changes of class assignments and regional divisions.

PARTICIPATION IN SPORT AS AN INDICATOR OF GEOGRAPHIC ORGANIZATION

Reliable data on sports participation are hard to come by. And virtually all the information available is at the national level. There are estimates on the number of people who play golf, football,

TABLE 4–1

1971 SPORT PARTICIPATION SURVEY

Compiled by
National Federation of State High School Associations

	Boys		Girls	
	Number of Schools	Number of Participants	Number of Schools	Number of Participants
Badminton	769	9,797		
Baseball	12,896	400,906		
Basketball	19,647	645,670	4,856	132,299
Bowling	785	11,931	21	370
Cross Country	8,263	166,281	77	1,719
Curling	417	4,174		
Decathlon	75	233		
Fencing	27	324		
Field Hockey	153	2,286	159	4,260
Football—11 Man	14,004	878,187		
8 Man	541	15,727		
6 Man	109	7,125		
9 Man	126	3,130		
12 Man	494	28,522		
Golf	8,645	120,078	116	1,118
Gymnastics	1,861	40,530	1,006	17,225
Ice Hockey	573	22,656		
Lacrosse	171	3,520	15	450
Riflery	107	2,085		
Rugby	69	1,460		
Skiing	478	9,787	142	2,659
Soccer	2,290	78,510	28	700
Softball	208	3,982	373	9,813
Swimming	3,078	91,309	853	17,229
Tennis	6,312	91,179	2,648	26,010
Track & Field (Indoor)	1,697	49,761	2,992	62,211
(Outdoor)	16,383	642,639		
Volleyball	3,826	63,544	1,550	17,952
Water Polo	187	6,445		
Wrestling	7,587	265,039		

TABLE 4-2
1971–72 PER CAPITA PARTICIPATION IN HIGH SCHOOL SPORT BY MALES

Sport	National average for participation (one boy per X number of 14–17-year-old males)	Total number of participants	Leading states
Football	9	878,187	Minnesota, North Dakota, Idaho
Basketball	12	645,670	North Dakota, Nebraska, Montana
Track & Field	12	642,639	Nebraska, Kansas, Montana
Baseball	20	400,906	Oregon, Minnesota, Vermont
Wrestling	30	265,039	Iowa, Delaware, South Dakota
Cross Country	47	166,281	Alaska, South Dakota, Kansas
Golf	64	120,078	Iowa, Kansas, Minnesota
Swimming	86	91,309	Minnesota, California, Iowa
Tennis	87	91,279	Washington, Idaho, Arkansas
Soccer	101	78,510	Vermont, New Hampshire, New Jersey
Volleyball	125	63,544	Texas, Nevada, New Mexico
Gymnastics	195	40,530	North Dakota, Nebraska, Colorado
Hockey	350	22,656	Minnesota, Massachusetts, Alaska
Badminton	807	9,797	Arizona, Connecticut
Skiing	808	9,787	Vermont, Alaska, New Hampshire

basketball, tennis, and hockey. Data on trapshooting, road rallies, horseback riding, hiking, climbing, and a host of other activities can also be found. Breakdowns by states, regions and metropolitan areas, however, are almost nonexistent.

The most useful geographic sources on sports participation are the National Federation of State High School Athletic Associations and the *Blue Book of College Athletics*.[1] The Federation has compiled statistics on participation in all common types of high school sport. Information has been assembled for each state and includes the number of schools and participants for 24 sport activities (Tables 4-1 and 4-2).

Basketball is the number one game on the basis of the number of high schools involved (Table 4-1). The vast majority of the nation's high schools (nearly 20,000) field teams, and almost 800,000 athletes participate each year. Track and field, football, and baseball rank just behind basketball as measured by the number of participating institutions. However, football leads all sports in terms of the number of athletes who play the game (Table 4-1).

It is easy for small schools to field a basketball team. Once a suitable structure has been built, the game requires fewer players and more moderate costs than football. In fact, there are some schools playing without benefit of indoor facilities. However, many of these same small schools (over 1500 of them) also elect to field six- eight-, or nine-man football teams. Other common interscholastic sports, in order of their importance, are wrestling, cross-country, tennis, golf, and swimming. Ice hockey, soccer, volleyball, and gymnastics are also significant on a regional scale.

STATE-TO-STATE VARIATIONS IN PARTICIPATION

Meaningful analysis of the geographical variations in interscholastic sports requires per capita transformation of the data. This can be accomplished by measuring participation (number of players) relative to the number of males in the 14-17 age group in each state. The 14-17 age group, as identified by the 1970 census, was used in the calculation of each index. There were 3,612,029 boys participating in a total of 24 interscholastic sports during the 1971-72 school year. This means that one of every 4.39 persons in the 14-17 age group was participating in high school athletics. (The figure is inflated due to the fact that many boys participated in more than one sport; some participated in as many as five different activities.) Assigning

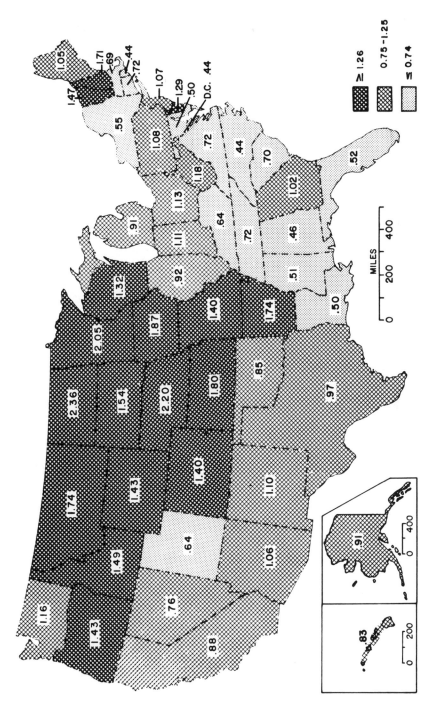

PER CAPITA PARTICIPATION IN ALL HIGH SCHOOL SPORTS - 1971 - 72

≥ 1.26

0.75 -1.25

≤ 0.74

Figure 4.2

AVERAGE PARTICIPATION = 1 PER 4.39 PEOPLE IN THE 14-17 AGE GROUP

this ratio a value of 1.00, the range of participation indices for all sports combined ranged from .44 in North Carolina, Rhode Island, and Washington, D. C., to 2.36 in North Dakota (Fig. 4-2).

FOOTBALL

More high school athletes are participating in football, including the six-, eight-, and nine-man varieties, than in any other sport (Fig. 4-3). Approximately one of every nine boys is playing the game. Per capita involvement is highest in the northern Middle West and Great Plains and throughout the lightly populated northwestern and Mountain States. Utah is the one notable exception. West Virginia, Texas, and Arkansas are the only states located outside of that region which exceed the national average by 50 percent. Extremely low participation is found in Maryland, New York, Rhode Island, and Connecticut. In addition, most of the southern United States is substantially below normal. Since football is now our most popular sport, it is surprising that so much variation exists. That Minnesota has nearly ten times the participation of Maryland, and that adjacent New York and Pennsylvania are so different is hard to explain.

The geographical variation in participation is a function of a host of variables, including population density, settlement patterns, climate, wealth, and social emphasis on given sports. In general, the highly urbanized states are characterized by low per capita participation. Cities like New York, Chicago, Philadelphia, Washington, and Boston have high schools with large enrollments compared to those in smaller cities and towns. In some cases there is not enough land available for football fields in the inner cities. In addition, there is only one varsity team per school regardless of the high school enrollment. It is easy to understand why a school of 200 students with a football team would generate a much higher rate of participation than one with 2000 students. The effect of high school size can be seen in the sparsely populated states west of the Mississippi River. Here with small towns dominating the landscape, participation is almost universally high.

The role of economic well-being is demonstrated in those states contained in the Appalachian Region. Many of the communities throughout Appalachia forego football because they simply cannot afford it. Small towns in eastern Kentucky, Tennessee, and the mountainous sections of Virginia and the Carolinas concentrate on the less expensive sports of basketball and baseball. On the other

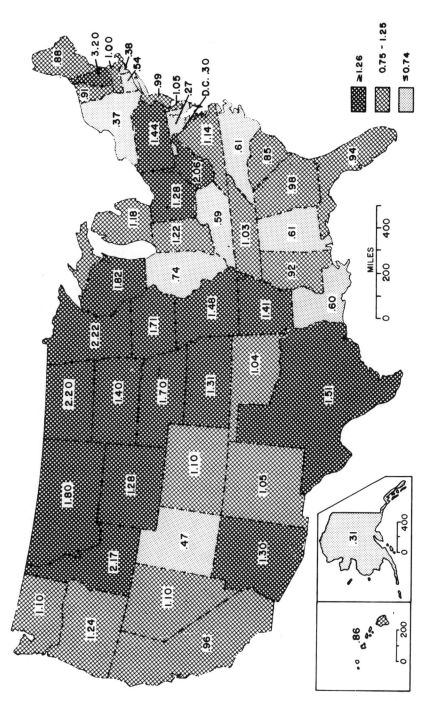

PER CAPITA PARTICIPATION IN HIGH SCHOOL FOOTBALL   -   1971 - 72

Figure 4.3

AVERAGE PARTICIPATION = 1 PER 18 PEOPLE IN THE 14-17 AGE GROUP

≥1.26

0.75 - 1.25

≤0.74

MILES

0   200   400

hand, the healthy economies of states such as Wisconsin and Minnesota allow even the small communities to field high school football teams. Providing the opportunity for high school boys to engage in football has traditionally been accorded high priority in both states.

Regional preferences for different sports also contribute to differences in the rates of participation. Because most Texans value football above all other games, even the very small and economically depressed communities support football teams. They must do it at the expense of other educational services, but nevertheless they do it. The glorification of basketball by residents of Illinois, Indiana, and Kentucky nets similar results in the depressed sections of those states.

The social role of sport also varies geographically and affects the number of athletes who are given a chance to play. Community prestige and winning teams are synonomous in some areas. Where this is the case, the most promising athletes are usually identified at an early age and groomed for their eventual place as a high school "regular." Those with less potential may be ignored and relegated to the cheering section. The overall impact of this type of "winning" emphasis is a lower rate of per capita participation. In those areas (Wisconsin and Minnesota seem to be reasonable examples) where the team is not viewed as a barometer of community prestige, sport functions more as a recreational outlet for players and spectators. Most boys who want to play are given the opportunity, and as a result, a much higher percentage participate.

BASKETBALL

The highest rates of participation in high school basketball are in the northern plains (Fig. 4-4). North Dakota and Nebraska, with indices of over four times the national average, are followed by Montana, Arkansas, and Wyoming. The abundance of small towns and the lack of cities in these states encourage a high degree of participation. A similar pattern of population distribution has produced above-average participation throughout the southern plains and in Minnesota, Missouri, and Iowa. The Midwest, centering on Illinois, is only slightly above average.

Low participation characterizes much of the South, the Atlantic Seaboard, California, and the Northeast. The former region has recently increased support for high school basketball, in response to the growth of the college game there. New York and New Jersey have participation rates of only .36 and .77, respectively. From this it is

PER CAPITA PARTICIPATION IN HIGH SCHOOL BASKETBALL - 1971 - 72

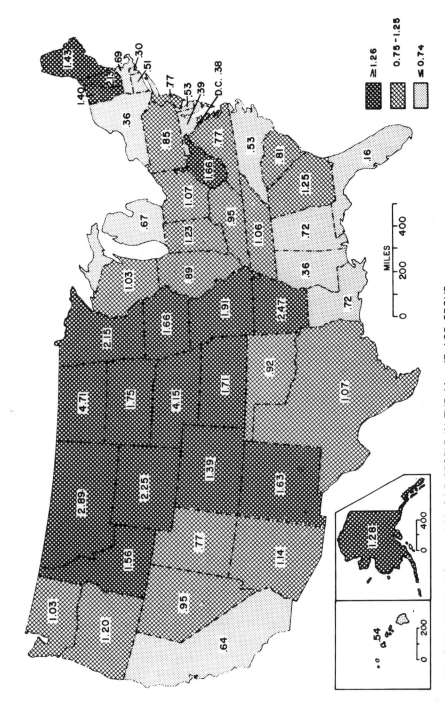

AVERAGE PARTICIPATION = 1 PER 24.5 PEOPLE IN THE 14 - 17 AGE GROUP

Figure 4.4

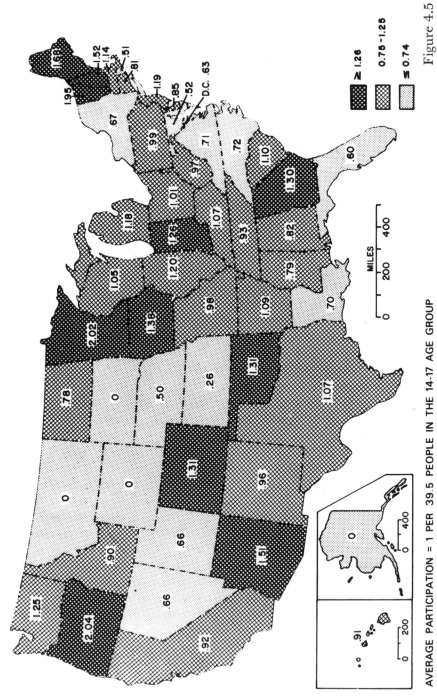

PER CAPITA PARTICIPATION IN HIGH SCHOOL BASEBALL   -   1971 - 72

Figure 4.5

≥ 1.26

0.75 - 1.25

≤ 0.74

MILES

0   200   400

0   200

0   400

AVERAGE PARTICIPATION = 1 PER 39.5 PEOPLE IN THE 14-17 AGE GROUP

apparent that only the best boys are playing high school basketball in Megalopolis. With very large schools and only one varsity team each, the competition is extreme. And among the few who play, the degree of success is very high.

High school basketball varies drastically between city and rural communities. The rural areas encourage a much higher rate of participation. At the extreme, thirteen times as many high school boys play basketball in Nebraska than in New York. As a result, high school basketball touches the lives of many more individuals in the small towns and has become a major focus of community attention. The "city game" is for a select few who are competing in what is generally a much tougher sport. It is only at the collegiate ranks that the two games begin to meld.

BASEBALL

Per capita participation in high school baseball does not exhibit the pronounced regional pattern characteristic of football and basketball. Minnesota, Vermont, and Oregon are the only states with as much as twice the normal participation level (Fig. 4-5). The Midwest is a region of above-average participation, as is the Southwest and Pacific Coast. The South and the Atlantic Coast states are uniformly low.

In most places baseball is not as important a sport in high school as football or basketball. Often the high school game is subservient to other forms of competitive organization such as American Legion, Babe Ruth, Pony, and similar types of summer leagues. The great concentration on Little League programs, typical in most American communities, has taken its toll on the players in the advanced age group (13-18). In general, the facilities, publicity, and attendance deteriorate after Little League. Hence players are faced with a less stimulating baseball environment after they have passed the ripe old age of twelve.

WHY THE VARIATION?

The geographical variations which characterize interscholastic participation in our trinity of national games defies simple explanation. As stated above, some of the key explanatory variables appear to be income, population density, settlement patterns, occupational structure, climate, and tradition. Except for the South, most of the agricultural states record high participation rates for the three "national sports" as well as for total participation in the 24 sports for which

data are available. The pattern of settlement in the northern Midwest, Great Plains, Rocky Mountain Region, and northern New
England more nearly approximates the classic central place model,
i.e., communities existing primarily to serve the needs of surrounding
rural population. The numerous small towns in these regions support
high schools which provide opportunities for participation in the basic sports of football, basketball, and baseball. School enrollments
of 150 to 600 students are common under these circumstances and
as a result almost anyone who wants to play, can. Contrast this to
the situation in New York City or Baltimore where with 3000 or
more students per school (many of which do not offer football programs), only a select few can participate. For these extremes the
relationship between settlement pattern, population density, and
participation is obvious. However, there are notable exceptions to
the settlement pattern explanation.

Pennsylvania and Ohio are two of the most highly urbanized
and densely populated states in the nation. But both are significantly
above normal in football participation. This is undoubtedly related
to a strong set of football traditions which exist there. A great number of Pennsylvania and Ohio communities are obsessed with winning
football and the development of highly skilled players. Due to this
kind of societal emphasis boys are being given the opportunity to engage in the sport at not only the varsity level but also as members of
"B" squads, freshmen-sophomore teams, etc.

The effect of state income differentials on high school participation is difficult to generalize. Many of the low income states of the
South have low overall participation rates (Fig. 4-2). Alabama,
Louisiana, Mississippi, and South Carolina are exemplary. On the
other hand, wealthy New York, Connecticut, Rhode Island, and Utah
are also low on the participation scale. Hence it would appear that in
the absence of a strong tradition surrounding a given sport such as
Pennsylvania football, Illinois basketball, and California swimming,
the arrangement of settlements and the density of the population are
more important than the level of wealth. For after all most states are
wealthy enough (if they choose to do it) to support adequate high
school programs in the basic sports activities.

INTERCOLLEGIATE ATHLETICS

The spatial organization of intercollegiate athletics in the United
States is the obvious result of a political organization which has tradi-

tionally placed a high value on individual state universities. Each
state has at least one major public institution; many have two; and a
significant number have groups of schools located so as to serve the
various regions within the state. And almost every state, regardless of
population or location, has elected to support "big time" athletic
programs in at least one of their universities.

Not only must the distribution of public universities be considered, but the locations of the private ones, which, by and large, can
be attributed to historical accident must also be taken into account.
Hence we would expect a greater number of private institutions to be
located in areas which have been settled for a longer period of time as
opposed to those which have been populated more recently. In addition the whereabouts of various religious groups has influenced the
sites of the denominational colleges.

It is possible to examine collegiate athletics in much the same
way as we have treated interscholastic sport. During the 1970–1971
season, there were 1022 colleges playing basketball and 660 playing
football. According to National Collegiate Athletic Association calcu-
lations, approximately 160 rated major status for basketball and
nearly 120 for football (Tables 4–3 and 4–4). New York, Pennsylvania, California, Illinois, and Texas are the leading states as far as total basketball playing opportunities are concerned. The leaders for
football are Pennsylvania, California, Ohio, New York, and Texas.
There is a relatively high rank–order correlation between total population and the number of playing opportunities.

However, when major college playing opportunities are considered, the relationship to population all but disappears.[2] As indicated
above, nearly all states are in the "big time" athletic business. Thus
while New York has 77 basketball teams, and 34 football teams, only
12 basketball teams and 6 football teams merit major college status.
Only 11 of California's 57 basketball schools and 10 of 40 football
schools are competing at the major college level. At the other end of
the population spectrum, Kansas has 20 basketball schools and 19
football schools. Only three in each sport are competing at the major
college level. Three of Idaho's five schools are competing in major
college football.

FOOTBALL

The spatial variation of collegiate playing opportunities is similar to
the interscholastic participation picture. Relative to their meager
population, the western states provide a greater number of playing

TABLE 4-3
PER CAPITA EMPHASIS ON COLLEGIATE FOOTBALL BY STATES (1970)

State	Number of major colleges	Index of emphasis (Average=1.00)	Total colleges	Index of emphasis (Average=1.00)
Alabama	2	.81	11	.99
Arkansas	1	.74	12	1.92
Alaska	0	.00	0	.00
Arizona	3	3.05	4	.70
California	10	.84	40	.62
Colorado	3	2.26	10	1.39
Connecticut	2	1.04	9	.91
Delaware	1	2.97	2	1.11
District of Columbia	1	1.73	6	2.46
Florida	3	.80	8	.36
Georgia	2	.67	7	.50
Hawaii	1	.38	2	.79
Idaho	3	5.97	5	2.17
Illinois	3	.39	24	.66
Indiana	3	.85	19	1.12
Iowa	2	.96	22	2.40
Kansas	3	1.82	19	2.59
Kentucky	2	.87	9	.86
Louisiana	2	.81	11	.93
Maine	1	1.37	5	1.55
Maryland	2	.85	6	.47
Massachusetts	5	1.29	16	.86
Michigan	3	.51	20	.69

Minnesota	1	.39	21	1.70
Mississippi	3	1.82	9	1.25
Missouri	1	.31	15	.99
Montana	2	3.92	8	3.56
Nebraska	1	.94	14	2.90
Nevada	0	00	2	1.25
New Hampshire	2	4.36	4	1.69
New Mexico	2	2.78	5	1.52
New Jersey	2	.44	10	.43
New York	6	.47	34	.57
North Carolina	6	1.74	20	1.21
North Dakota	2	4.17	7	3.53
Ohio	9	1.23	36	1.04
Oklahoma	3	1.71	13	1.56
Oregon	2	1.50	11	1.62
Pennsylvania	6	.70	49	1.28
Rhode Island	2	3.08	2	.64
South Carolina	4	2.22	8	.95
South Dakota	0	00	12	5.52
Texas	10	1.38	29	.80
Tennessee	3	1.11	17	1.37
Utah	4	5.94	6	1.75
Vermont	1	3.39	2	1.36
Virginia	5	1.67	16	1.06
Washington	2	.93	9	.81
West Virginia	2	1.42	13	2.29
Wisconsin	1	.34	20	1.40
Wyoming	1	4.01	1	.94

TABLE 4-4
PER CAPITA EMPHASIS ON COLLEGIATE BASKETBALL BY STATES (1970)

States	Number of major colleges	Index of emphasis (Average=1.00)	Total colleges	Index of emphasis (Average=1.00)
Alabama	2	.95	19	1.10
Arkansas	1	.63	15	1.55
Alaska	0	.00	2	1.33
Arizona	3	2.58	5	.56
California	11	.78	57	.57
Colorado	3	1.92	12	1.07
Connecticut	2	1.32	15	.99
Delaware	0	.00	3	1.07
District of Columbia	2	2.95	9	2.38
Florida	3	.68	19	.57
Georgia	2	.57	17	.73
Hawaii	0	.00	3	1.93
Idaho	1	1.68	6	1.69
Illinois	6	.67	44	.79
Indiana	4	.96	33	1.26
Iowa	2	.81	26	1.83
Kansas	3	1.54	20	1.77
Kentucky	6	2.21	19	1.18
Louisiana	3	1.03	16	.88
Maine	1	1.15	14	2.80
Maryland	2	.72	13	.66
Massachusetts	5	1.09	35	1.22

Michigan	4	.57	31	.69
Minnesota	1	.32	24	1.26
Mississippi	3	1.54	13	1.17
Missouri	2	.52	26	1.10
Montana	1	1.63	9	2.59
Nebraska	2	1.59	16	2.15
Nevada	0	.00	2	.83
New Hampshire	2	3.65	9	2.44
New Mexico	2	2.34	7	1.36
New Jersey	3	.55	19	.53
New York	12	.80	77	.84
North Carolina	5	1.23	33	1.29
North Dakota	1	1.77	8	2.60
Ohio	9	1.04	46	.86
Oklahoma	4	1.92	18	1.40
Oregon	3	1.90	15	1.43
Pennsylvania	7	.69	65	1.10
Rhode Island	3	3.88	6	1.26
South Carolina	4	1.88	14	1.09
South Dakota	0	.00	12	3.55
Texas	10	1.17	42	.75
Tennessee	3	.94	33	1.67
Utah	4	5.06	6	1.13
Vermont	1	2.82	9	4.00
Virginia	5	1.41	25	1.07
Washington	3	1.18	14	.82
West Virginia	2	1.20	16	1.83
Wisconsin	2	.56	24	1.08
Wyoming	1	3.44	1	.62

opportunities. Eight states and the District of Columbia provide over twice as many football playing opportunities as their population justifies (Fig. 4-6). South Dakota (with an index of 5.52), Montana (3.56), and North Dakota (3.53), are the leading overemphasizers. West Virginia, which has 13 football schools and its own intercollegiate conference, is exceptional for its region. Most of the states with the next highest level of playing opportunities are found west of the Mississippi River, where seven states have indices of 1.30 or higher. Also included in this group are Wisconsin, Tennessee, and northern New England.

As far as the total number of football programs is concerned, the underemphasizers include the densely populated northeastern states, Illinois and Michigan in the midwest, Georgia and Florida in the South, and Alaska. New Jersey, Maryland, Florida, and Alaska are the only states with less than 50 percent of the national average (Fig. 4-6).

The per capita distribution of major or "big time" football programs is somewhat different from the total distribution of programs (Table 4-3). Most of the western states overemphasize "big-time football." Arizona, with a population of slightly less than two million, can claim two universities that have become top flight national contenders in football as well as in basketball, baseball, and track. Arizona also features a third school that aspires to similar status. Most of the athletes needed to support these teams must be obtained outside the state. In Wyoming the same sports have been developed almost wholly through the procurement of athletes from the Midwest and Northeast. However, the state has probably gained more recognition in the past decade from its nationally ranked football team than from any other endeavor, and the team has provided considerable economic benefits to the city of Laramie.

Overemphasis is also characteristic of the smaller New England states, the South Atlantic belt, and the Great Plains states. Underemphasis is primarily confined to New York, New Jersey, and the Midwest, where the relatively populous states of Minnesota, Wisconsin, and Missouri each sponsor only one top-quality football team. In the midwestern states (excluding Ohio) which have Big Ten Conference members, there are only 15 major football teams, though the region has a population of more than 36 million. By contrast, the 16 Mountain and Basin state universities are supported by only nine million people.

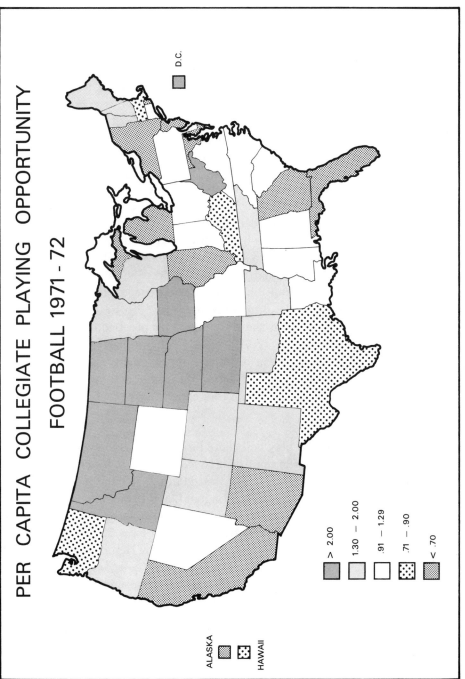

Fig. 4.6 Playing opportunities inlcude all NCAA and NAIA members competing on the intercollegiate level. "Club" football is not included.

There are many justifications given by universities that have developed, or aspire to, "big-time" football. Two reasons though seem paramount. One justification (perhaps it is subconscious) is to attract attention to *their* university and *their* place. How else can Nebraska, Wyoming, or Utah gain notoriety in New York or Chicago? The other reason for going "big time" is to provide a recognized form of entertainment to an area which, due to lack of sufficient population, could not support high-order forms of entertainment such as professional sport or theater. Collegiate athletics represent a quick route to both national attention and access to high quality entertainment.

The case of the University of Nebraska is an example of what can happen. Lincoln, Nebraska now claims the title of "football capital of the world." Under Coach Bob Devaney, the Cornhuskers football team won back-to-back national titles in 1970 and 1971. His eleven-year record, at a school which had been living in football obscurity for nearly a quarter century preceding his arrival, included 101 wins, 20 losses, and 2 ties. The recent success has produced a change in the life style of many Nebraskans. "It has been a tremendous shot in the arm for the state insofar as prestige, the human ego, and even the economy is concerned."[3] The improved fortunes of the university program have also spurred improvement and change in attitudes toward Nebraska high school football. Many other schools are striving to imitate the Nebraska experience.

BASKETBALL

The opportunity to play collegiate basketball is somewhat more evenly distributed than the opportunity to play football (Fig. 4.7).[4] Like football, overemphasis is concentrated in the sparsely populated northern plains, northern New England, and in Washington, D. C. Vermont leads the nation in per capita playing opportunities with an index of 4.00. It is followed by South Dakota, 3.55, Maine, 2.80, North Dakota, 2.60, Montana, 2.59, and New Hampshire, 2.44. There is no state with an index of below .53 (Table 4-4).

The Northeast emphasizes basketball to a significantly greater extent than football. It is much more common for the smaller schools in this region to forego football than it is in other areas. Major college basketball is more concentrated in the West, New England, and Middle Atlantic Region than is warranted by the population density of those areas. The biggest overemphasizers include Utah,

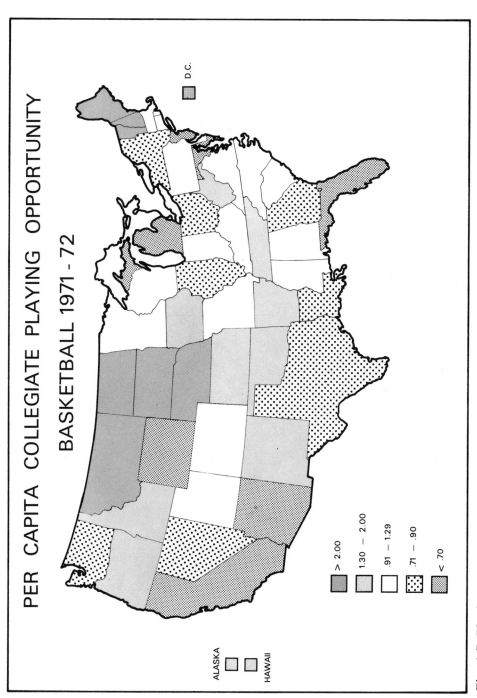

Fig. 4.7 Playing opportunities include all NCAA and NAIA members competing on the intercollegiate level. "Club" basketball is not included.

Fig. 4.8 This advertisement appeared in *The Wall Street Journal*, and other business publications. (Courtesy of the North Carolina Department of Conservation and Development.)

5.06, Rhode Island, 3.88, New Hampshire, 3.65, Wyoming, 3.44, and Vermont, 2.82. The Carolinas and Virginia are substantially above average as are New Mexico and Arizona.

The road to "big time" basketball is much easier and faster than the one that leads to football prominence. So many new schools are trying to develop basketball programs that any map of emphasis is quickly obsolete. Several states, like North Carolina, have tried and succeeded in basketball without a supply of local high school talent. North Carolina, though, has gone one step farther than most, using its collegiate basketball teams as the basis for major advertising campaign to attract new industry (Fig. 4–8). Thus sport can provide more than glory for a place and entertainment for the local residents. It can be a means to another end, and in this case, a supposedly better life through economic development.

THE CONFERENCE PATTERN OF ORGANIZATION

The athletic conference is an organization geared to increase the level of competition between universities located in the same region. The conference or league is also the major vehicle by which post-season contestants are selected for participation in national championship events and bowl games. At last count there were 149 athletic conferences in the United States![5] Many of them regulate competition in all sports, while others are organized around only one sport, such as bowling, baseball, skiing, or track and field. A total of 63 conferences crown football champions each year. They range from the prestigious Big Eight and Southeastern Conferences, with their big name institutions, to the Carolinas Intercollegiate Athletic Conference (CIAC), and the Midwest Collegiate Athletic Conference (MCAC), whose ranks include such relatively athletic unknowns as Catawba, Elon, Newberry, High Point, Ripon, Grinell, Knox, and Beloit.

There are 87 (even more if there are ties) basketball teams who annually claim the title of conference champion. Numerous associations of small colleges are organized for the purpose of basketball and "minor" sports competition. The conference affiliations form the basis for the identification of participants in the post-season tournaments of both the National Collegiate Athletic Association, University and College Division, and the National Association of Intercollegiate Athletics. Nonconference representatives are also selected for these tournaments but the bulk of the teams are league members.

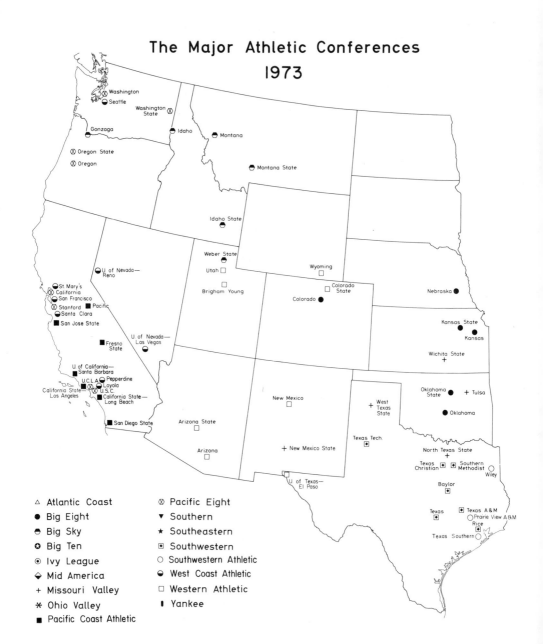

The Major Athletic Conferences 1973

△ Atlantic Coast
● Big Eight
◒ Big Sky
◎ Big Ten
◉ Ivy League
◈ Mid America
+ Missouri Valley
✳ Ohio Valley
■ Pacific Coast Athletic

⊗ Pacific Eight
▼ Southern
★ Southeastern
▣ Southwestern
○ Southwestern Athletic
◓ West Coast Athletic
□ Western Athletic
❘ Yankee

Figure 4.9

Organization and Location

Many of the more important athletic conferences conform broadly to traditional geographic concepts of the major regions of the United States (Fig. 4-9). The Corn Belt or Agricultural Midwest is very similar in extent to the Big Ten Conference. The Big Eight Conference is nearly synonomous with the Great Plains. The Southeastern Conference is confined to the Deep South, while the Ivy League and the Yankee Conferences represent the larger and more prestigious schools of the Northeast. Other conferences include the Pacific Eight, the Atlantic Coast, the Southwest, the Western Athletic, and the Missouri Valley. The geography of competition to a large extent reflects other forms of socio-economic and spatial interaction in the United States. Conference organization also carries over into other aspects of university life. Academic interaction and cooperation has been heightened as a result of conference organizations that owe their existence to the desire for controlled athletic competition. The Big Ten, with its interlibrary loan system, student and faculty exchange programs, symposia, clinics, debates, and other activities, provides a good example. Conferences also have a bearing on the way we think about a university—that is, whether it is an Ivy League or a Big Ten school.

There are, of course, many universities that have chosen to remain independent of the conference framework. Notre Dame, Georgia Tech, Miami, Tulane, Penn State, Pittsburgh, and the National Service Academies are the most notable football "independents." Notre Dame football is a national institution. Alumni and fans are located in all sections of the United States, and the university's radio network beams the games to most major cities. In addition, the television network carries Sunday "playbacks" to the same areas. Notre Dame has established long-standing rivalries with Army, Navy, Southern California, Pittsburgh, Miami, and Purdue; rivalaries which flourish without formal conference affiliations. As a privately funded school, Notre Dame is now the exception where major college football is concerned. However, it was not long ago that Fordham, Detroit, Marquette, Georgetown, and Santa Clara, were thriving in the big-time football arena. These and most of the other Catholic universities have dropped football to the club sport level and confine their efforts to basketball and the less expensive sports. It is unlikely that the era of the great independents will ever return, but it was certainly fun for the big city fan while it lasted.

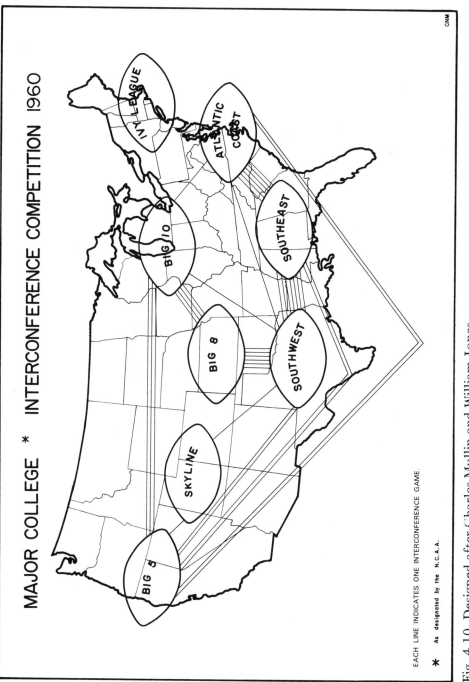

MAJOR COLLEGE * INTERCONFERENCE COMPETITION 1960

EACH LINE INDICATES ONE INTERCONFERENCE GAME.

* As designated by the N.C.A.A.

Fig. 4.10 Designed after Charles Mullin and William Jones.

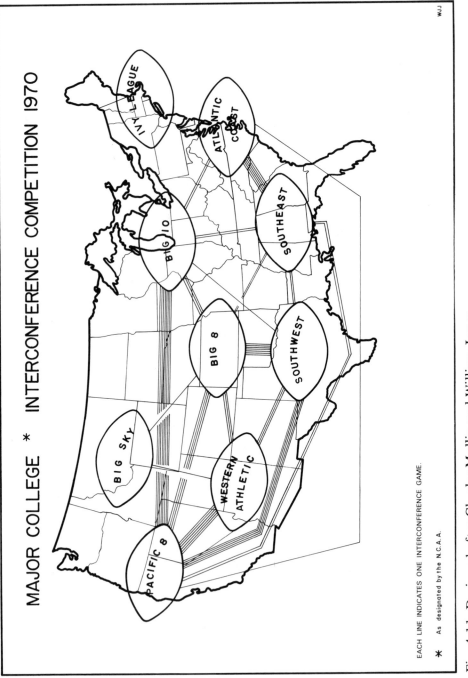

Fig. 4.11 Designed after Charles Mullin and William Jones.

SPATIAL INTERACTION BETWEEN CONFERENCES

Although the major conferences are organized on a sectional scale to promote intrasectional competition, considerable intersectional competition has developed. The football contests between member institutions of the Big Ten and Pacific Eight Conferences are illustrative of the type of spatial interaction which has evolved between diverse sections of the country. (Fig. 4–10). Spatial interaction between the major conferences increased substantially during the 1960–1970 period. The number of intersectional football games jumped from 33 in 1960 to 54 in the 1970 season. Most of the 1960 intersectional activity involved teams from adjacent conferences, for example Southeast *vs.* Atlantic Coast and Southwest, and Big Eight, *vs.* Southwest. The Pacific Coast schools, then in the Big Five Conference, had the greatest geographical range, competing against teams in all major conferences except the Big Eight and the Ivy League. The latter group engaged in no intersectional competition. Southeastern Conference members were spatially confined almost exclusively to their immediate cultural region.

By 1970 the intersectional play had taken on a much more encompassing geographical dimension (Fig. 4–11). Adjacent regions were competing less with one another and more with far-distant areas. The Pacific Coast schools were the leaders, participating in games with all the other prestige conferences. Even the Southeast moved out to schedule games with Big Eight and Big Ten members.

THE JUNIOR COLLEGES

Junior colleges in some areas have emerged as significant athletic entities. They now serve as pipelines to many of the major colleges, grooming athletes who for one reason or another are not deemed ready to attend a four-year school. Almost all junior colleges support some kind of athletic program. However, those which field football teams, or take their basketball seriously, are confined to just a few regions (Fig. 4–12).

California is the citadel of junior college football. Of the 176 junior college football teams, 72 are located there. California junior college football is a major sporting attraction. And as might

THE DISTRIBUTION OF JUNIOR COLLEGE FOOTBALL AND BASKETBALL TEAMS , 1972

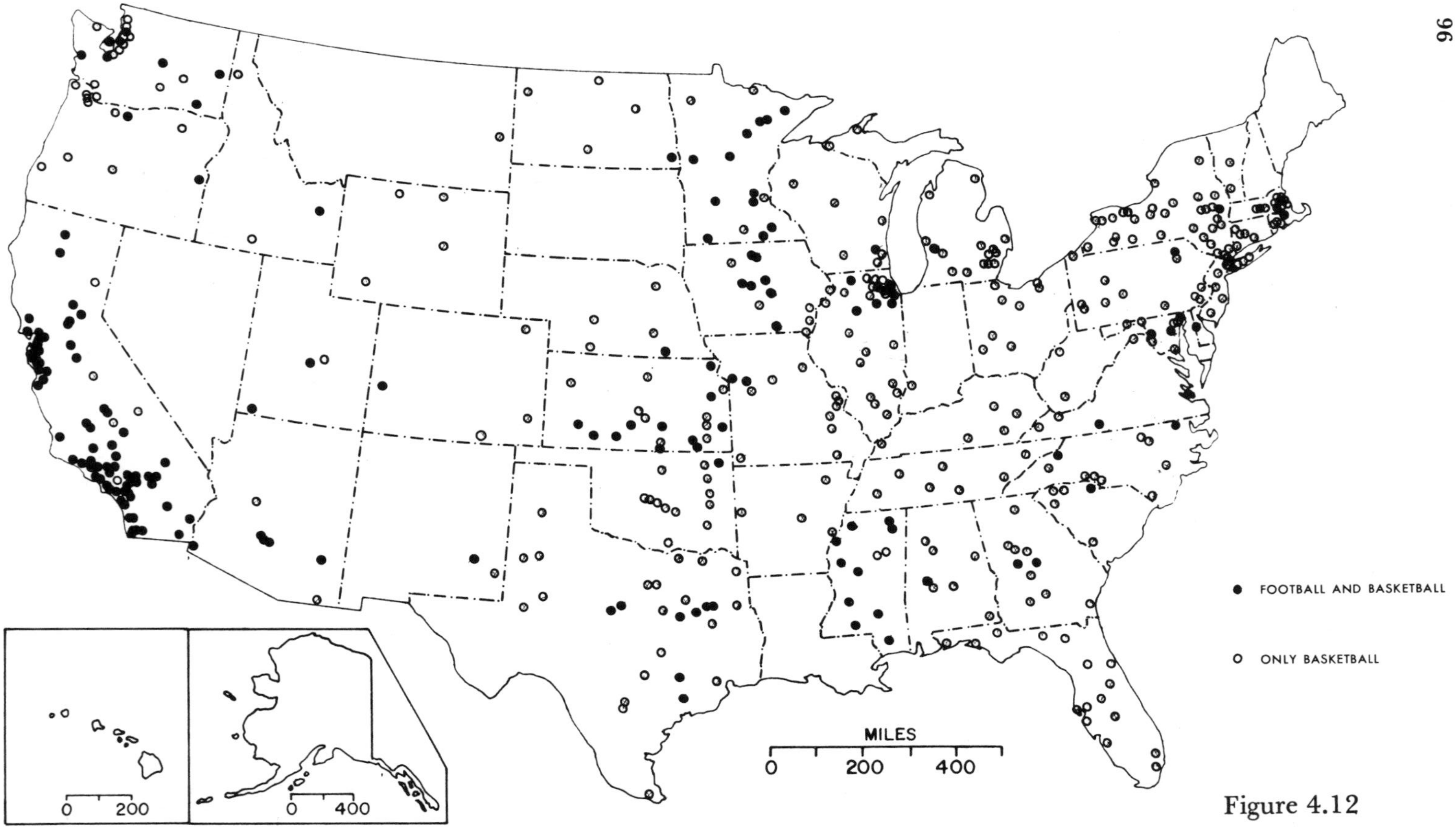

● FOOTBALL AND BASKETBALL

○ ONLY BASKETBALL

MILES

0   200   400

0   400

0   200

Figure 4.12

be expected the products of these institutions are widely sought by recruiters from all parts of the country.

Other states which take junior college football seriously include Kansas, Minnesota, Texas, Iowa, Illinois, and Mississippi, though none of them have more than 12 teams. One noteworthy anomaly in the world of junior college football is Northeastern Oklahoma A & M. As the only Oklahoma junior college which plays football, the school has a national schedule and qualifies regularly for post-season bowl games.

Nearly three times (478) as many junior colleges play basketball as play football. For example, 41 of New York's schools play basketball, while only three play football. All of Florida's junior colleges play basketball, while none play football, a situation that is repeated in many other states. The great majority of the junior colleges are commuter institutions designed to serve the educational needs of a small geographical area. In this setting athletics are offered primarily as a recreational outlet for the students and in most cases are not as important as they are in the university environment. The fact that the junior college concept is indigenous to California probably accounts for the more complete athletic programs there.

PROFESSIONAL SPORT

The location of professional sport franchises is primarily governed by profit motivation. Professional teams are businesses first and entertainment media second. For this reason their location corresponds closely to the distribution of the largest population concentrations (Fig. 4–13). The present distribution of football, baseball, and basketball franchises is a good approximation of the distribution of people. During the past twenty years, with better transportation and less conservative ownership, professional teams have decentralized from the Northeast to all the populous sections of the country.

Although the locational pattern of the Major League professional teams makes sense, many of the alignments within the leagues, conferences, and divisions are far from optimal. Assuming that the sports fan has difficulty separating the difference between his psychological identification with his team and with his city, we must conclude that those who control professional sport are failing to take advantage of many natural place-to-place rivalries. Baseball is most illustrative of this situation.

MAJOR LEAGUE CITIES: BASEBALL, BASKETBALL AND FOOTBALL

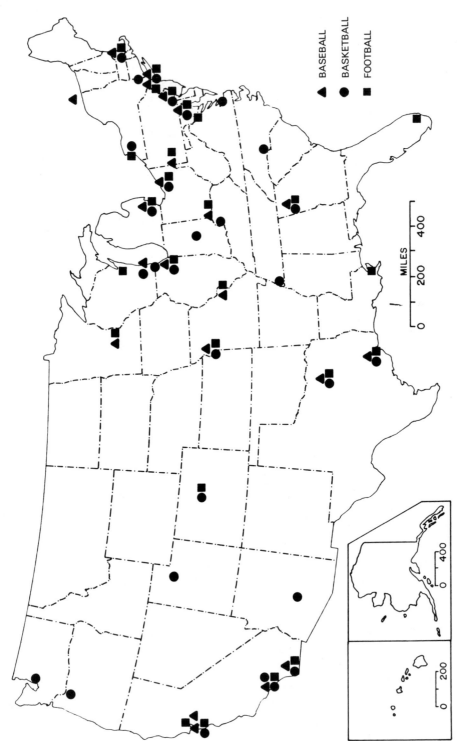

Fig. 4.13 The location of the Big League franchises during the 1973 season.

Major League baseball consists of two twelve-team divisions known as the National and American Leagues. Except for spring training, the All-Star Game, and the World Series, there is no competition between the two. As a result, such attractive rivalries as New York—New York, San Francisco—Oakland, Los Angeles—Anaheim, Chicago—Chicago, Chicago—Milwaukee, Houston—Dallas and Pittsburgh—Cleveland are being ignored completely. Similar examples exist in football and basketball, but to a lesser extent.

It seems as though the United States has failed to profit from the very successful organization of professional sport in Britain. Place-to-place rivalries are much more intense throughout Britain, where the "glory-of-the-town" motivation is stronger. The close proximity of the perennial football powers to one another has produced finely demarcated fan regions. A great many of the British football contests are of the Green Bay—Chicago variety.

It is doubtful that such an intensity is feasible in the United States, but a better spatial organization of competition is both possible and necessary.

ANOTHER FORM OF SPATIAL ORGANIZATION

Golf, tennis, and bowling are the only American sports which lack a home turf. Golfers must move to a new tournament location every week. The 1971 tour is illustrative of the general pattern of events. There were a few changes in 1972, and there may be a few in the future, but the migratory behavior will probably remain essentially unchanged. The golfers begin play in Los Angeles during the first week in January (Fig. 4-14). They stay in California, Arizona, and Hawaii for the first seven tournaments. The tour then moves to Florida, for a month, stops in New Orleans and North Carolina in preparation for the Master's tournament at Augusta, Georgia. By now it is mid-April and the road show soon wanders west again, this time to Texas and Nevada. Since the geographical organization of professional golf is motivated by the hope of drawing good weather at the tournament location, play moves north from Texas through Memphis and Atlanta. After October, it jumps around—Texas, California, South Carolina, Nevada—in response to the weather and the whim of wealthy sponsors.

Americans living in the Southwest and South have much more accessibility to professional golf than their northern neighbors. Over

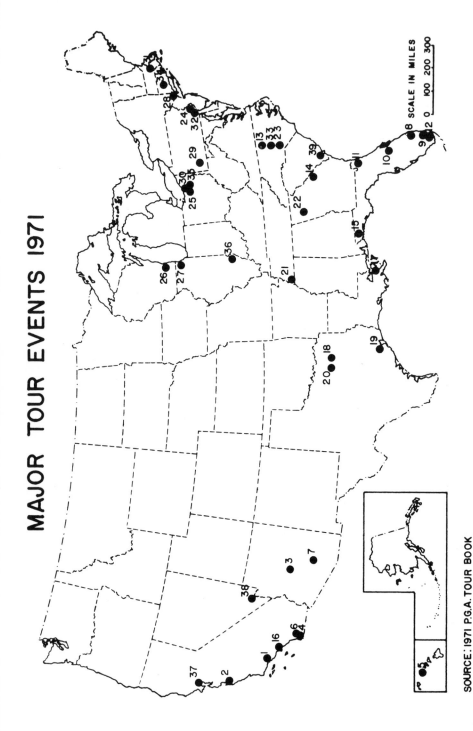

MAJOR TOUR EVENTS 1971

SCALE IN MILES
0   100 200 300

SOURCE: 1971 P.G.A. TOUR BOOK

Fig. 4.14 The numbers indicate the progression of the tour from January to December. The first event was in Los Angeles and the tour culminated at Hilton Head Island, South Carolina.

50 percent of the 1971–1973 tournaments were held in only five states, California, Florida, Texas, North Carolina, and Pennsylvania. Most of the midwest, plains, and far west were completely void of tournament activity.

Tennis is similar to golf although traditionally it has had a stronger international dimension. Competition between professionals from the United States, Great Britain, Australia, Western Europe and India has been sponsored on a regular basis for many years, and may have set the stage for the emergence of an international golf tour. Both sports have moved in part to a stable locational pattern, in the form of the mini golf tours for young professionals and the city tennis teams composed of a combination of men and women players.

NOTES

1. *Official Handbook 1970–71*, National Federation of State High School Athletic Associations, Chicago, Illinois, pp. 65–75.

2. The term major college is based on a rating system devised by the NCAA, one of two regulatory organizations for college athletics in the United States. There classification of a school as major or small college division has been based on its schedule, number of athletic scholarships, and performance against other universities. A new NCAA system inaugurated in 1973 allows for three divisions instead of two.

3. Milton Richman, "Nebraska Football Capital of the World," United Press International, June, 1972.

4. *Blue Book of College Athletics* (Cleveland: Rohrich Corp., 1970–1971), pp. 350–399.

5. *Ibid.* pp. 350–399.

5 / Identifying Sports Regions

As discussed earlier there are several possible ways to identify and establish boundaries for different kinds of sports regions. It was decided that the best way to analyze the problem was to rely on the regional variations in the production of high-quality athletes.

To answer the primary "where" questions concerning the origins of athletes and their migratory behavior, a representative sample of college and professional athletes was assembled. The rating system of the National Collegiate Athletic Association was used as a basic guideline for selecting the schools contained in the football and basketball samples. Virtually all of the colleges and universities to which the N.C.A.A. accords University Division, or Major, status were included (Table 5-1). A few, which in the writer's opinion, were no longer competing successfully at that level, or for which data could not be gathered, were excluded from the sample. Several top-class N.C.A.A. College Division teams were added on the merits of their performance during the last six years (Table 5-1). Most of the additions were made to the basketball sample where the frequency of small college victories over university opponents is much higher than in football. Selection was governed by a team's long-term performance and one "upset" was not enough to merit a small school's inclusion.

A total of 136 universities from 46 states and the District of Columbia make up the football sample. Each school included the products of six years' recruiting (two mutually exclusive rosters from the years 1961–1967), a total of approximately 14,500 players. For example, rosters were dispersed over a minimum of three-year intervals, i.e., 1962–1965 or 1961–1964 to eliminate the possibility of an individual's being represented more than once. In the rare case where duplication did occur, it was eliminated by dropping the player from one roster. The basketball statistics were taken from 161 teams containing nearly 4200 players and was also based on a six-year period. Data on the hometown high school that each athlete attended were assembled from the rosters contained in university sports publicity booklets and in some cases from game programs. From this information, it was possible to categorize athletic productivity for the United States and for individual cities, counties, metropolitan areas, states, and county regions. Production was calculated from both a total output (number of players from any area) and on a per capita basis.

Generalizations about the origin of baseball players were derived from the geographical data contained in the 1968 major league rosters. Each team's spring training roster was used to provide the largest sample possible. This included approximately twenty players per ball club who spent a part of the season in the minor leagues.

Because such a large number of athletes was utilized, it is assumed that differences in player ability have been canceled out. This assumption was tested in the case of the football sample by comparing professional player origins to those of the much larger university group. The results were very similar with two exceptions. If we can use the geographical distribution of professional player home towns as a guide, then some of the southern states have been slightly under represented (see Figs. 6–1, 6–2) at the collegiate level. This is due chiefly to the exclusion of the area's numerous, but small, black schools, which are classed as college division by the NCAA, in spite of their large contributions to the professional ranks. For example Grambling University is second only to Notre Dame in sending players to the pros. On the other hand, several northeastern States (particularly in New England) seem to be over-represented. The number of universities in that region playing marginal quality football is undoubtedly responsible for padding the figures there. In addition, graduates of the region's prestige universities have a greater range of job selections than graduates from other sections of the United States.

In general though, during the sampling period, most of the states contained college teams of both high and mediocre calibre. For example, of the ten Texas schools, Texas, S.M.U., Houston and Texas Tech had significantly better records than their local competitors.

TABLE 5.1
COLLEGES AND UNIVERSITIES INCLUDED IN THE SAMPLE

Region	University	Football	Basketball
EAST	Army	x	x
	Boston College	x	x
	Boston University	x	
	Brown	x	x
	Buffalo	x	x
	Colgate	x	x
	Columbia	x	x
	Connecticut	x	x
	Cornell	x	x
	Dartmouth	x	x
	Fordham		x
	George Washington	x	x
	Georgetown		x
	Harvard	x	x
	Holy Cross	x	x
	Lasalle		x
	Maine	x	x
	Manhattan		x
	Massachusetts	x	x
	Navy	x	x
	New Hampshire	x	x
SOUTH	Alabama	x	x
	Auburn	x	x
	The Citadel	x	x
	Clemson	x	x
	Davidson	x	x
	Duke	x	x
	Florida State	x	x
	Florida	x	x
	Furman	x	x
	Georgia Tech	x	x
	Georgia	x	x
	Kentucky	x	x
	Kentucky Wesleyan		x
	Western Kentucky		x
	Louisiana State	x	x
	Louisville	x	x
	Loyola (New Orleans)		
	Maryland	x	x
	Memphis State	x	x
	Miami University, Florida	x	x
	Mississippi	x	x

EAST

School		
New York University		
Niagara		x
Pennsylvania	x	x
Pennsylvania State		
Pittsburgh	x	x
Princeton	x	x
Providence		x
Rhode Island	x	x
Rutgers	x	x
St. Bonaventure		
St. John's		x
St. Joseph's		x
Seton Hall		x
Syracuse	x	
Temple		x
Vermont	x	x
Villanova	x	x
Yale	x	x

SOUTH

School		
Mississippi State	x	x
Morehead State		x
Murray State		x
North Carolina	x	x
North Carolina State	x	x
Richmond	x	x
South Carolina	x	x
Southern Mississippi	x	x
Tennessee	x	x
Tulane	x	x
V.P.I.	x	x
Vanderbilt	x	x
Virginia	x	x
V.M.I.	x	x
Wake Forest	x	x
West Virginia	x	x
William & Mary	x	x

TABLE 5-1 CONTINUED

Region	University	Football	Basketball
MID-WEST	Bowling Green	x	x
	Bradley	x	x
	Cincinnatti	x	x
	Colorado	x	x
	Creighton		x
	Dayton	x	x
	Depaul		x
	Detroit		x
	Drake		x
	Evansville		x
	Illinois	x	x
	Southern Illinois		x
	Indiana	x	x
	Iowa	x	x
	Kansas	x	x
	Kansas State	x	x
	Kent State	x	x
	Loyola		x
	Marquette		x
	Marshall	x	x
	Miami University, Ohio	x	x
	Michigan	x	x
	Michigan State	x	x
SOUTH-WEST	Arizona	x	x
	Arizona State	x	x
	Arkansas	x	x
	Baylor	x	x
	Houston	x	x
	New Mexico	x	x
	New Mexico State	x	x
	Northern Arizona	x	
	North Texas State	x	x
	Rice	x	x
	S.M.U.	x	x
	T.C.U.	x	x
	Texas	x	x
	Texas A&M	x	x
	Texas Tech	x	x
	Texas Western	x	x
WEST	Air Force	x	x
	Brigham Young	x	x
	California	x	x
	Colorado State	x	x
	Fresno	x	x
	Gonzaga		x
	Idaho	x	x

MID-WEST		
Minnesota	x	x
Missouri	x	x
Nebraska	x	x
North Dakota State		x
Northwestern	x	x
Notre Dame	x	x
Ohio State	x	x
Ohio University	x	x
Oklahoma	x	
Oklahoma City		x
Oklahoma State	x	x
Purdue	x	x
St. Louis		x
Toledo	x	x
Tulsa	x	x
Western Michigan	x	x
Wichita State	x	x
Wisconsin	x	x
Xavier	x	x

WEST		
Long Beach		x
Los Angeles State	x	x
Montana State	x	x
Oregon	x	x
Oregon State	x	x
Portland		x
San Francisco		x
San Jose State		x
Santa Clara		x
Seattle		x
Stanford	x	x
U.C.L.A.	x	x
U.S.C.	x	x
University of the Pacific	x	
Utah	x	x
Utah State	x	x
Washington State	x	x
Weber State	x	x
Wyoming	x	x

Similarly Purdue and Notre Dame outperformed the University of Indiana, and Kansas was better than Kansas State and Wichita.

The distribution of institutions which are not engaged in the expensive business of scholarship-subsidized athletics, but which nevertheless house a number of good athletes on their campuses is assumed to be geographically constant. One needs only to glance at the rosters of the professional teams to appreciate the contributions of the country's smaller colleges. Amherst, Williams, Tufts, Catawba, Western Illinois, U.C. Santa Barbara, Florida A & M, South Dakota State, and Augustana are but a few. On the other hand, the sheer number (over 500) of these schools which are playing intercollegiate football should result in the production of a respectable number of expert players.

The utilization of six-year roster samples has the advantage of balancing out good and bad seasons. Furthermore, the universal trend toward multiplatoon and specialty unit football and "strong bench" basketball justifies the use of complete traveling rosters as opposed to "first stringers" or lettermen. Thus, it is believed that the players on which the following maps, tables and other generalizations are based are an accurate representation of place-to-place *variations* in athletic production.

Among the most outstanding football teams of the period during which the sampling was conducted were Alabama, Louisiana State, Arkansas, Texas, Tennessee, Ohio State, Michigan, Michigan State, Notre Dame, Purdue, Penn State, Nebraska, Air Force, Oklahoma, and Wyoming. This was the era dominated by quarterbacks such as Joe Namath, John Huarte, Terry Hanratty, Bob Griese, Gary Beban, Roger Staubach, and Terry Baker. Other outstanding players included Jack Snow, Jim Seymour, Alan Page, Clinton Jones, Carl Eller, Duck Butkus, Tommy Nobis, Leroy Jordan, Merlin Olsen, Gale Sayers, and Mel Farr.

The basketball parade was led by U. C. L. A., Ohio State, Kentucky, Texas Western (UTEP), Michigan, Davidson, Duke, St. John's Santa Clara, Marquette, Tennessee, Miami of Florida, North Carolina, Houston, St. Joseph's, Kansas, Wichita, Loyola, Princeton, and Dayton. Dominant players of the period included Jerry Lucas, John Havlicek, Lew Alcindor, Gail Goodrich, Edgar Lacy, Bill Bradley, Willis Reed, Walt Frazier, Cassie Russell, Billy Cunningham, Rick Barry, Lew Dampier, "Bad News" Barnes, and Elvin Hayes.

The data for football and basketball players are examined from the standpoint of total output or production and also that of per capita production. Regarding total output we can compare football

player production in the Los Angeles metropolitan area (596) with
Chicago's (439) and Pittsburgh's (544) production. Or we can contrast the number of hoopsters from the Denver metropolitan area (30),
Atlanta (22), or from metropolitan Salt Lake City (22). These statistics
are fine for coaches or scouts who want to know how many potential
college players they are likely to find in any given city or area and
whose objective is to maximize their recruiting effort while minimizing
travel and expenses. However, none of the figures make allowance for
differences in population. We cannot, in all fairness, compare Pitts-
burg's output with Chicago's because we are dealing with different
population bases.

In order to assess the *relative* producing capacities of various
places, we have to compensate for variations in population. Based on
a 1960 total of nearly 180 million United States residents, the 14,500
football players represented roughly one person in 12,500. This type
of rating system assumes similar age structures of the population for
the areal units which are being compared, whether they are states,
counties, or cities. Knowing that age structures do vary slightly at the
city and county level, we can use these differences to help explain differences in production for certain areas. Hence a county with a large
retirement-age population would have fewer males in the football-age
playing group and would not be expected to generate as many players
as one with a younger age structure. Extreme differences in age structure are rare and after testing, it was decided that the use of total population for per capita measurements was the best method.

A ratio of one player per 12,500 people represents the national
average of production. If a state or county is supplying players at a
rate of one per 25,000 total population, it would be operating at only
50 percent of the national norm. A ratio of one per 6250 would
amount to twice the production characteristic of the nation as a whole.
Normal output of 1 per 12,500 can be represented as an index value of
1.00 and by using this simple formula

$$\text{Index value} = \frac{\text{number of players}}{\text{total population}} \div \frac{1}{12,500} ,$$

we can establish an index for any area, which can be used for all kinds
of comparative purposes.

For basketball the national norm for the period was one player
per 42,500 population, which is assigned an index value of 1.00. In
baseball, the relatively small professional sample is composed of only

TABLE 5-2
SAMPLE COMPARISONS OF ATHLETIC OUTPUT

Metropolitan area	Standard Metropolitan Statistical Area Population, 1960	Football players	Ratio one player per	Per capita index	Basketball players	Ratio one player per	Per capita index
Atlanta	1,017,188	112	9,082	1.38	22	46,236	.92
Chicago	6,220,913	439	14,171	.88	170	36,594	1.16
Denver	929,383	66	14,080	.89	30	30,979	1.37
Los Angeles	6,038,771	596	11,313	1.11	178	37,880	1.12
Pittsburgh	2,405,435	544	4,422	2.83	93	25,866	1.64
Salt Lake City	447,795	35	10,940	1.14	22	17,410	2.44

TABLE 5-3
RANKING OF PER CAPITA PERFORMANCE

Performance grade	Description	Per capita ratio (norm=1.00)	Equivalent to one football player per population of	Equivalent to one basketball player per population of
A+	Spectacular	3.00	4,170	14,150
A	Outstanding	2.50-2.99	4,171- 5,000	14,151- 17,000
B	Commendable	1.50-2.49	5,001- 8,330	17,001- 28,290
C	Average	0.75-1.49	8,331-16,670	28,291- 56,590
D	Poor	0.40-0.74	16,671-30,125	56,591-106,000
F	Lousy	0.40	30,126	106,001

one player per 250,000 people. This ratio can also be assigned a value
of 1.00. From these ratios, we can also calculate the chances of any
athletically-minded boy making the grade in either college football
or basketball or in professional baseball.

Now let us return to the six metropolitan area examples and
compare their relative strengths as producers of football and basketball talent (Table 5-2). We can see that although Los Angeles and
Pittsburgh were the source of similar numbers of footballers, the
latter's per capita rate was nearly three times higher. Chicago's 439
players and Denver's 66 figure out to virtually the same per capita
index. The per capita indices are the true measure of a place's ability
to produce and, to a large extent, are indicative of the emphasis placed
on a given sport. The only apparent weakness of per capita comparisons is at the very small county level, where the production of only
one or two players can give a distorted and sometimes misleading
picture of a place's importance. This difficulty can be overcome by
combining the small counties into county groups.

A letter-rating system has been devised to make comparisons
between places even easier (Table 5-3). It can be used to categorize
output from any kind of areal unit. The categories range from A,
for those with 2.5 or more times average production, to F, for areas
which are providing less than 40 percent of the average. Producers
in category A are very rare except at the county level, and there are
many states which can claim only a few A counties for a given sport.

6 / Football: Where They Come From

Football has become an American institution. The players, fans, traditions, anecdotes, and legends are an intrinsic part of the American scene, to say nothing of the game's massive economic and social impact. Football is a game played, watched, or discussed heatedly, and sometimes intelligently, by a substantial proportion of our population. Attendance at college and professional games now surpasses 34 million annually.[1] High school play is even more popular as evidenced by the ten million who watched in Texas, the state where "football mania" is perhaps strongest.[2] Television now brings an average of five games a week into American homes from early September to mid-January. Even prime Monday evening viewing time has been taken by the professionals, and an avid fan can see two to four professional games on a single Sunday afternoon. In addition, the season has been extended, through post-season bowls and play-offs and pre-season exhibitions to the point that competition occurs in every month but February, March, April, and May.

Football is a national game, but the ability to play is not equally distributed throughout the United States. Some areas stand out in terms of high school programs sponsored and the quality and amount of college-bound talent which they produce. As expected, most of the larger cities are reasonable sources of major-college and university football talent (Fig. 6–1). Los Angeles, Chicago, Pittsburgh, Houston, Cleveland, and Dallas are particularly conspicuous on the map of player origins. However, there are exceptions, such as New York, Philadelphia, and Detroit, which are supplying far less than the per capita norm.

112

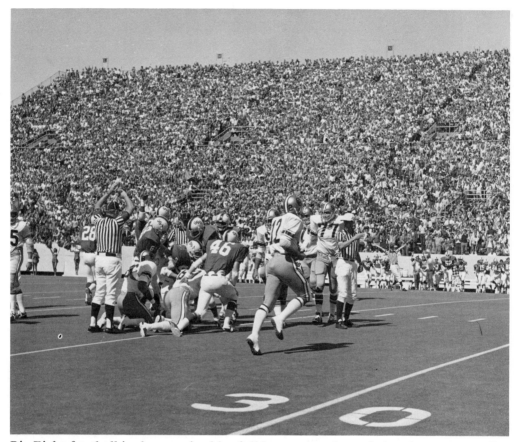

Big Eight football is characterized by full house crowds, and abundant press, radio, and television coverage. (Photo courtesy of Oklahoma State University Department of Public Relations.)

There is a high level of rural production throughout sections of the Southeast, Texas, and the Southern Plains. On the other hand, a paucity of players is coming from the lower Midwest, Northern Plains, and the Rockies. The careful observer might note a surprisingly large cluster of players (in terms of population) in northern Utah, west Texas, western Pennsylvania, and southern New Hampshire, or the small map symbols that represent the contributions of Baltimore, Milwaukee, Kansas City, and Indianapolis.

Professional football player origin is geographically similar to the college player sources (Fig. 6-2). One exception is the Southeast, particularly Mississippi and Louisiana (primarily due to the many

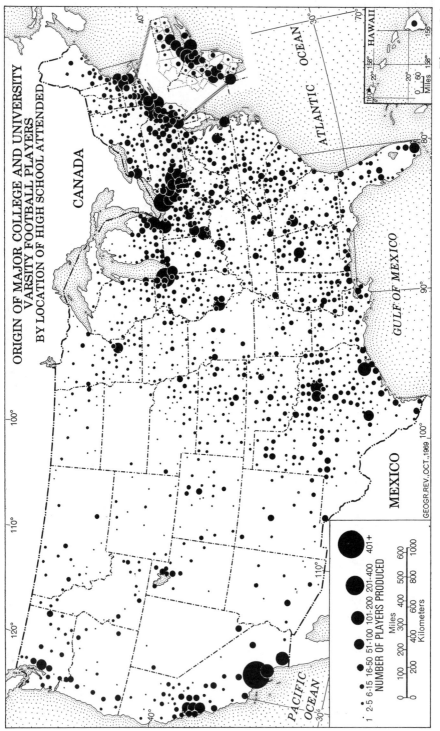

ORIGIN OF MAJOR COLLEGE AND UNIVERSITY
VARSITY FOOTBALL PLAYERS
BY LOCATION OF HIGH SCHOOL ATTENDED

Figure 6.1

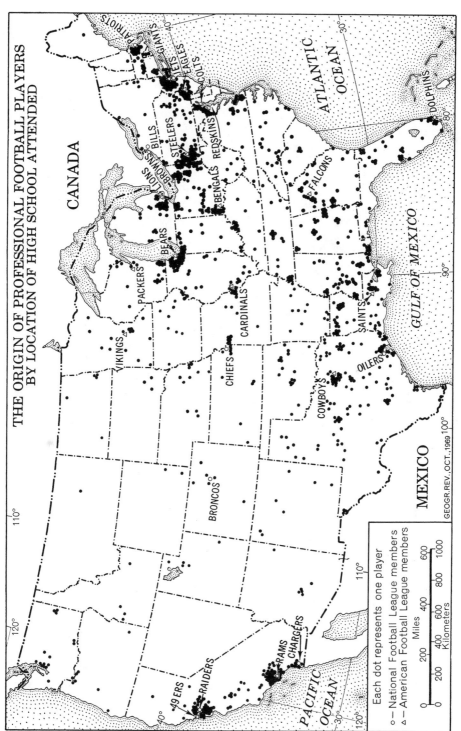

THE ORIGIN OF PROFESSIONAL FOOTBALL PLAYERS
BY LOCATION OF HIGH SCHOOL ATTENDED

Each dot represents one player

o — National Football League members
▵ — American Football League members

GEOGR.REV.,OCT.,1969

Figure 6.2

Football and other sports are influenced more and more by advancing technology. Note the oxygen equipment in this photo. (Courtesy of Oklahoma State University.)

small-college black players who make the pros, but are not included in the major university sample), which has a *relatively* high professional output compared to its college player production. The same can be said for Texas. Conversely, the Northeast is *relatively* low on the professional scale.

An examination of the per capita output of players compensates for the variation in population density throughout the country and allows for valid state, regional, and city comparisons. Using the system described in Chapter 5 (normal production = 1.00), we find that the state range extends from Ohio's 1.74 to New York's 0.47 (Fig. 6–3). The county range for those which sent at least one player is from 26.00 for Morgan, Utah to 0.10 for Queens, New York. Several large counties like Potter (Amarillo), Texas, and

Cheerleaders and pom-pom girls are an integral part of the collegiate sports scene. (Photo courtesy of Oklahoma State University.)

Harrison (Biloxi), Mississippi (Table 6-1) have indices of over 3.00, which means that on a per capita basis, they are providing more than 30 times the number of players that Queens does.

By mapping the per capita county yield, a somewhat different player source pattern can be seen (Fig. 6-4). Big city dominance has all but disappeared, with the exception of Pittsburgh, Cleveland, Dallas, Cincinnati, and Atlanta. Most of the leading cities on a total supply (or quantity) basis (Los Angeles, Chicago, Houston, San Diego, Seattle, and Miami) are only sending forth gridiron talent in numerical proportion to their large populations. On the negative side, the five boroughs of New York City, which accounted for only 80 players, are operating at the incredibly low rate of 13 percent of the national norm. Other major cities which are contributing at rates of less than 60 percent of the norm are: Detroit, Boston, St. Louis, San Francisco, Baltimore, Kansas City, Philadelphia, and Milwaukee.

Many of the suburban areas surrounding these large cities are in marked contrast. For example, the counties adjacent to New York City (Nassau, Westchester, and Rockland) are breeding many more

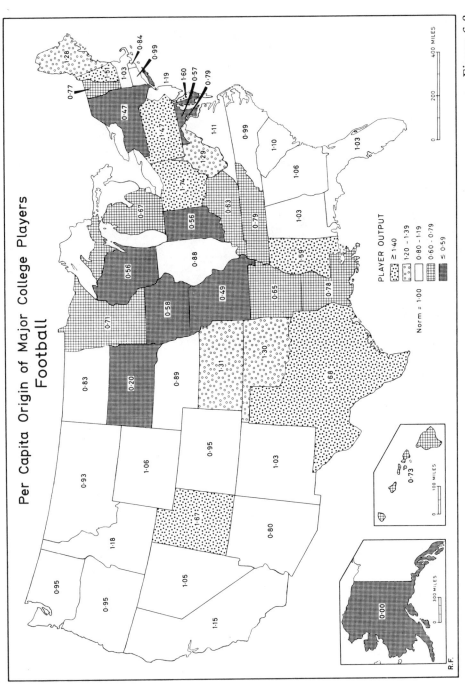

Per Capita Origin of Major College Players
Football

Figure 6.3

TABLE 6-1
THE LEADING FOOTBALL COUNTIES FROM A TOTAL AND PER CAPITA STANDPOINT

Counties	Production one per	Per capita index	Number of players	Major city or cities
1. Jefferson, Ohio	2680	4.66	37	Steubenville
2. Beaver, Pennsylvania	3130	3.99	66	Aliquippa
3. Potter, Texas	3052	3.57	33	Amarillo
4. Harrison, Mississippi	3734	3.35	32	Biloxi, Gulfport
5. Galveston, Texas	3794	3.30	37	Galveston, Texas City
6. Westmoreland, Pennsylvania	3870	3.23	91	Pittsburgh, SMSA
7. Washington, Pennsylvania	4020	3.11	54	Washington
8. Fayette, Pennsylvania	4130	3.03	41	South of Pittsburgh, Uniontown
9. Lucas, Ohio	4440	2.81	109	Toledo
10. Trumbull, Ohio	4850	2.58	43	Warren
11. Allegheny, Pennsylvania	4890	2.56	333	Pittsburgh
12. Hillsboro, New Hampshire	5090	2.46	35	Manchester, Nashua
13. San Joaquin, California	5100	2.45	49	Stockton
14. Peoria, Illinois	5110	2.45	49	Peoria
15. Mahoning, Ohio	5270	2.37	60	Youngstown
16. Henrico, Virginia	5270	2.37	64	Richmond
17. Cambria, Pennsylvania	5350	2.34	38	Johnstown
18. Arlington, Virginia	5653	2.21	45	Arlington, Washington D.C., SMSA
19. Schuylkill, Pennsylvania	5760	2.17	30	Pottsville
20. Contra Costa, California	5761	2.17	71	Richmond
21. Stark, Ohio	5770	2.17	61	Canton, Massillon, Alliance
22. New Castle, Delaware	5800	2.16	53	Wilmington
23. St. Joseph, Indiana	6120	2.04	39	South Bend
24. Hamilton, Ohio	6700	1.86	129	Cincinnati
25. Bucks, Pennsylvania	6710	1.86	46	Philadelphia SMSA, Bristol, Middletown

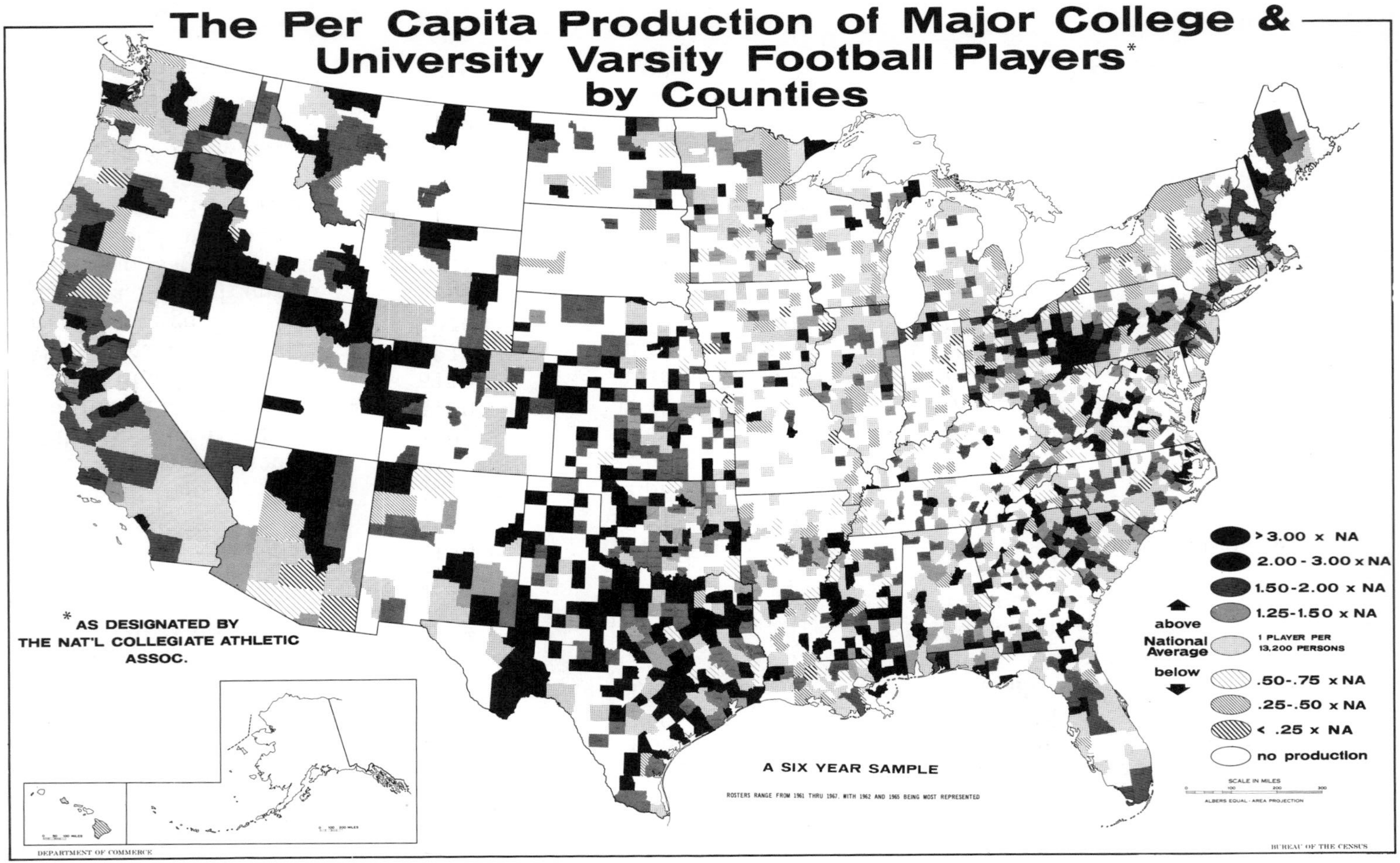

The Per Capita Production of Major College & University Varsity Football Players* by Counties

* AS DESIGNATED BY THE NAT'L COLLEGIATE ATHLETIC ASSOC.

Legend:

Above National Average:
- >3.00 × NA
- 2.00 - 3.00 × NA
- 1.50 - 2.00 × NA
- 1.25 - 1.50 × NA

1 PLAYER PER 13,200 PERSONS

Below National Average:
- .50 - .75 × NA
- .25 - .50 × NA
- < .25 × NA
- no production

A SIX YEAR SAMPLE

ROSTERS RANGE FROM 1961 THRU 1967 WITH 1962 AND 1961 BEING MOST REPRESENTED

SCALE IN MILES

ALBERS EQUAL AREA PROJECTION

BUREAU OF THE CENSUS

DEPARTMENT OF COMMERCE

Figure 6.4

A GENERALIZED PATTERN OF ABOVE AVERAGE PER CAPITA PRODUCTION OF MAJOR COLLEGE & UNIVERSITY VARSITY FOOTBALL PLAYERS*

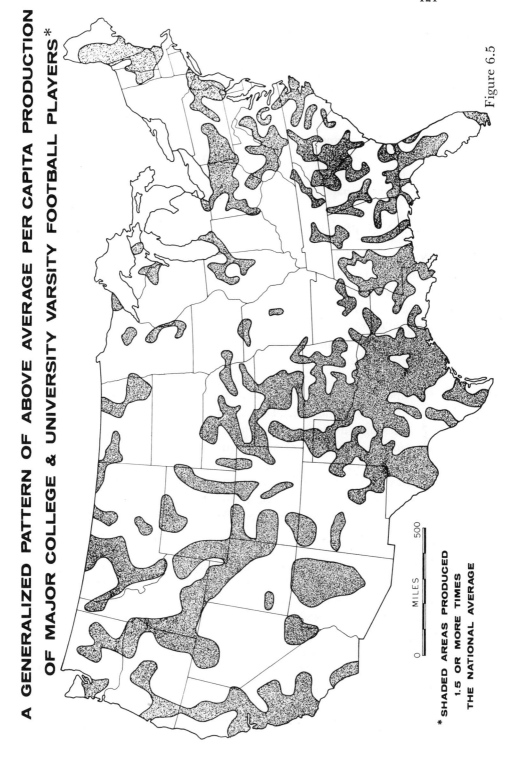

0   MILES   500

* SHADED AREAS PRODUCED
1.5 OR MORE TIMES
THE NATIONAL AVERAGE

Figure 6.5

players per capita than the city. The cities to the east of San Francisco (San Jose and Richmond), the Orange county complex south of Los Angeles, and the western Boston suburbs (Waltham, Newton, and Lexington) are all generating football players at a significantly higher rate than their adjacent central cities. The Philadelphia area is another such case. Extremely high per capita output is confined to a few sections only, but above-average performance is fairly widespread (Fig. (Fig. 6-5). Low and spotty output is found in much of the Midwest, New York, Appalachia, and the Mid-South.

REGIONAL PRODUCTIVITY BASED ON CITY-COUNTY UNITS

From the standpoint of total player origins, the leading city-county regions are Los Angeles, Chicago, Pittsburgh, and Cleveland (Table 6-2). Even though Los Angeles and Chicago develop an enormous amount of football talent, they are each within 15 percent of the national average when per capita production is considered. Pittsburgh and Cleveland, however, support schoolboy football programs which are churning forth college players at a rate much higher than the national norm, as shown by their respective per capita indices of 2.56 and 1.83. Other large cities which rank high in per capita production are Cincinnati, Dallas, Toledo, Atlanta, and San Jose.

Throughout the country, there are several areas which are outstanding developers of quality football players. Western Pennsylvania, eastern Ohio, southern Mississippi, four regions in Texas, the east Bay area near San Francisco, and the Wasatch Valley of Utah are among regions which have two to four times the quantity of athletes which their population warrants. "PenWevO" is such a region.

PENWEVO

Of the one-hundred largest metropolitan areas in the nation, only three merit an A rating. Pittsburgh, Toledo, and Youngstown-Warren are all situated in the western Pennsylvania-eastern Ohio region. In this area, characterized by heavy manufacturing (steel, metals, glass, chemicals, and mining), are located seven of the country's ten best overall per capita producers (counties sending forth five or more players per year) (see Table 6-1). Four of these rare counties are situated in western Pennsylvania, and three are in Ohio. Steubenville (Jefferson county), Ohio and Aliquippa (Beaver county), Pennsylvania, the two leaders, are less than fifty miles apart. This belt, stretching from Johnstown, Pennsylvania through the Pittsburgh district, across the

TABLE 6-2
THE LEADING FOOTBALL COUNTIES ON THE BASIS OF TOTAL PLAYER OUTPUT

Counties	Total produced	Production, one per	Per capita index	Leading city or cities
1. Los Angeles, California	492	12,270	1.02	Los Angeles
2. Cook, Illinois	354	14,490	0.86	Chicago
3. Allegheny, Pennsylvania	333	4,890	2.56	Pittsburgh
4. Cuyahoga, Ohio	247	6,840	1.83	Cleveland
5. Harris, Texas	130	9,565	1.30	Houston
6. Hamilton, Ohio	129	6,700	1.86	Cincinnati
7. Wayne, Michigan	127	20,970	0.60	Detroit
8. Middlesex, Massachusetts	122	10,150	1.23	Waltham, Newton, Lexington
9. Dallas, Texas	112	8,495	1.47	Dallas
10. Bergen, New Jersey	109	7,160	1.75	Bergenfield, Teaneck, Fairlawn Hackensack
11. Lucas, Ohio	109	4,440	2.81	Toledo
12. Orange, California	104	6,770	1.85	Anaheim, Santana
13. Nassau, New York	104	12,500	1.00	Long Island
14. San Diego, California	102	10,130	1.23	San Diego
15. Dade, Florida	94	9,950	1.26	Miami
16. Westmoreland, Pennsylvania	91	3,870	3.23	Pittsburgh SMSA, Latrobe Irwin, Monessen
17. Essex, New Jersey	83	11,130	1.12	Newark
18. Fulton, Georgia	82	6,780	1.84	Atlanta
19. Santa Clara, California	79	8,130	1.54	San Jose
20. Fairfield, Connecticut	79	8,270	1.51	Bridgeport, Stamford, Norwalk
21. Westchester, New York	78	10,370	1.20	New York suburbs, Yonkers
22. Erie, New York	76	14,000	0.89	Buffalo
23. Contra Costa, California	71	5,761	2.17	Richmond
24. St. Louis, Missouri	71	20,470	0.61	St. Louis
25. King, Washington	71	13,170	0.95	Seattle

panhandle of West Virginia, and on to Cleveland via Youngstown is the same area where the professional game was spawned.

During the period of the study, this area accounted for 1250 football players, representing production of two and one-half times the national average (see Fig. 6-4). From a population of slightly over six million came nearly nine percent of the nation's major college recruits and they are recruited by colleges in all areas of the country. Western Pennsylvania players have been the most widely sought, and they are competing at virtually every "big time" football school. Recent players who strayed from the region to play college football elsewhere include such standouts as Joe Namath, Mike Lucci, Doug Buffone, Bruce Gossett, John Unitas, Dick Shiner, Dick M Molzelewski, Charley Scales, Fred Biletnikoff, Jim Ringo, and Myron Pottios. There are almost as many football luminaries from eastern Ohio, but they have had a lower propensity to leave the home region.

Whereas the majority of Pennsylvania gridders come from the southwestern part of the state, Ohio makes a more balanced contribution. It contains seven of the nation's B level metropolitan areas. Ohio is reputed to have the best high school coaching system in the country, with nearly 40 percent of its counties at B level or above (Table 6-3).

Stark County, Ohio provides an excellent example of what takes place in the heart of a football region. Both Massillon, which is frequently mentioned in any enlightened discussion concerning high school football, and Canton, the home of the Professional Football Hall of Fame, are located in Stark County. Massillon, or "Tigertown," has amassed over 300 football victories during the past forty years. Excellence on the gridiron is manifested by a high school stadium seating over 21,000, a coaching staff which has grown to number ten men, better facilities and equipment than many colleges have, and a very productive junior high school "farm" system. Football and Massillon are synonymous. Tradition at the community's general hospital has established that each newborn male shall have a toy football in his crib.[3]

Community support for the game is, by any measure, high. Annual home attendance in Massillon regularly exceeds 100,000, and at least 4000 rooters accompany the team on each of its road engagements. Portraits of past heroes grace the walls and windows of the downtown area, and the local citizens are most eager to spread the Massillon story to any receptive listener.

Massillon is only one of many communities in Pennsylvania,

TABLE 6-3
PRODUCTION CONSISTENCY BASED ON THE PERCENTAGE OF "A"
AND "B" COUNTIES IN THE MAJOR SOURCE STATES

State	Number of A counties	Number of B counties	Percentage of A and B counties for each state (national norm = 19.5%)
Texas	72	47	47
Mississippi	13	18	38
Ohio	6	26	38
Pennsylvania	9	15	36
Oklahoma	10	17	35
Utah	8	2	35
Kansas	17	17	32
West Virginia	9	8	31
South Carolina	3	10	28
Washington	3	8	28
California	3	12	26
Oregon	4	4	22
Nebraska	9	11	22
Colorado	6	7	21
Virginia	4	16	21
North Carolina	6	14	20
Georgia	11	19	19
New Jersey	0	4	19
Florida	2	11	18
Alabama	1	12	18
Tennessee	0	10	11
Massachusetts	0	1	7
Michigan	1	5	7
Illinois	0	6	6
Indiana	0	3	3

Ohio, and West Virginia where football is more than a game. The situation is similar in nearby Steubenville, the major power in Jefferson County. In the place of the "Tigertown" signs and traditions, there are banners proclaiming the invincibility of the "Big Red," the Steubenville High School gridiron representative. The annual battles with the despicable Massillon Tigers or the equally evil Canton Bulldogs are a topic of conversation throughout the other fifty weeks of the year. Steubenville, Toronto, Martins Ferry, and East Liverpool, Ohio; Wierton and Wheeling, West Virginia; and McKeesport, Washington, Beaver Falls, and Aliquippa in Pennsylvania are all in the Massillon class. The Upper Ohio Valley is a region devoted to quality high school athletics, and community support there is epitomized by a booster group known as the "Dapper Dan" Club. Each year the organization honors the region's outstanding high school athletes as well as the "Valley's" professional athlete of the year. The club routinely promotes schoolboy sporting activity and serves to centralize the great support and enthusiasm which exists throughout the entire area. Groups like the "Dapper Dan" serve to encourage continued levels of high athletic productivity, whether they are in PenWevO, Texas, Illinois, or Mississippi.

THE MIDDLE ATLANTIC REGION

The Middle Atlantic region (excluding Maryland) is providing players at a pace consistent with the national output. It can be viewed as normal or neutral territory. Noteworthy B sources include Richmond, Arlington, and Roanoke, Virginia, Wilmington, Delaware, Winston-Salem and Charlotte, North Carolina. Significantly, all of these communities except Arlington are highly dependent on manufacturing. Their occupational structures are very similar to the major producers of western Pennsylvania and eastern Ohio and provide further documentation of the relationship between manufacturing and football.

THE NORTHEAST

As a whole, the northeastern United States is not a good source of football talent. New York, the dominant state, developed less than one-half the number of college players that its large population should have sent forth, and both Vermont and Rhode Island were substantially below the national norm. If there is a football "hotbed" in the area, it is in the cities and suburbs of New Jersey, Connecticut, Massachusetts, and New Hampshire. New York City is an incredibly low supplier, but as mentioned earlier, many of the surrounding cities are in sharp contrast. To the northwest, Bergen County, New Jersey rates a strong B for production 75% above normal. The Newark–Jersey City metropolis provided twice as many players as New York City and had a per capita rate that was ten times greater. Even suburban Nassau County on Long Island rates a good C. Northeast of the city in Westchester County (Yonkers), per capita output exceeds the national norm by 20%. In Connecticut, the Bridgeport-Norwalk–Stamford metropolitan area generated nearly 100 players and rated a B in per capita production.

The other major northeastern supplier of football talent is the Boston suburban ring. Middlesex County (Waltham, Lexington, Newton) stands out as a particularly good source. The Merrimac

Valley to the north of Boston, including the cities of Manchester and Nashua, New Hampshire, is an A producer, and Hillsboro county, New Hampshire, ranks highest among the populous counties of New England (Table 6-2).

THE SOUTH

Southern Mississippi is conspicuous in a highly capable football state which contains a total of 13 A counties. The zone centering on Biloxi-Gulfport and trending northward to Medenhall in Simpson County accounted for 101 players, for a per capita index of 3.20. The Simpson County index was an amazing 6.90! This is a region that is growing rapidly, particularly by southern standards. Despite the growth, it is still characterized by low per capita incomes and a small percentage of the labor force working in manufacturing. However, there is no denying its football prowess. Forrest County (Hattiesburg) provided 18 players at a per capita rate of over 4.20. Lauderdale (Meridan) and Adams (Natchez), among counties with ten or more players, were also in the A category. The geographical consistency of Mississippi football is demonstrated by the fact that 38 percent of its counties ranked B or better (Table 6-3).

The rest of the South does not match Mississippi's output, although there are several important metropolitan sources. Most notable among them are Atlanta and Miami (C+). The city of Atlanta itself is a B source, with poor production in the suburbs resulting in the lower overall rating. Of the region's larger metropolitan areas, Birmingham, Memphis, Nashville, Knoxville, Jacksonville, and Fort Lauderdale are each characterized by an above-average contribution. Among the smaller centers, Talladega County (Talladega, Sylacauga), Alabama and Grady County (Cairo), Ware County (Waycross), and Wayne County (Jesup), in southern Georgia, rate A.

TEXAS AND THE PLAINS

Texas includes four highly productive regions. The northeastern Texas region, with a per capita index of 2.90 (A), had an output of 162 players (Fig. 6-4). The area is composed of small cities north and east of Dallas-Forth Worth, such as Kilgore, Sherman, Longview, McKinney, Gainesville, Palestine, and Rockwall. Rockwall is the second leading county in the United States with a per capita rating of 15.00. Dallas and Fort Worth are both B suppliers and rank very high among cities in their size category.

Another noteworthy district is located on the Pecos, centering on the oiltowns of Midland and Odessa. This district includes the sparesely populated counties south of the river and stretches northward through Big Springs, Lamesa, and up to Denver City. In this "football-happy" section, college players have been developed at a rate of 3.5 times the national norm.

An eight-county area in the Texas panhandle, centering on Amarillo and Borger, accounted for 71 players, representing production at a pace exceeding four times the national average (over 40 times that of Queens, New York or Anderson, Indiana). This region, characterized by 5000- to 20,000-acre ranches encompasses Dalhart, Dumas, Hereford (Deaf Smith county), and Tucumcari, New Mexico.

The central Texas zone includes a part of western Oklahoma and contains 32 counties. It extends from Eldorado to Abilene through Graham and Wichita Falls, and the latter three are the major foci of contribution. The locations in Oklahoma include Enid, Hobart, Clinton, and Elk City. This sprawling section sent forth 153 players and registered a per capita index of 3.25.

The high standards of Texas high school football are not confined to these four regions. The totality of the region is evident from the percentage of A and B counties contained within the state (Table 6-3). Using this statistic, both Texas and Oklahoma rank very high. This consistency is largely attributable to the ability of the small towns to turn out football players, a feat which is not common in most other sections of the country. The relative importance of football in Texas is illustrated by game attendance, the number of coaches, and the expenditures on the athletic (football) program (Table 6-4). Many of the smaller Texas communities have football seating capacities as large or larger than their populations. Even the medium-sized cities can accomodate twenty to thirty percent of their population for high school contests. The towns of Plano and Palestine, in the northeastern part of the state, both average over one-third of their total population in attendance at home games, as compared to less than one percent attendance at basketball games. Annual expenditures amount to $200 to $300 per athlete, not including dollars spent for the facilities which compare to many at the college level. Palestine High School has eight football coaches, and Plano has six.

Outstanding high school football is a way of life for many Texans. During personal interviews, numerous school administrators echoed one another in stating that the people just would not stand for anything less than highly competitive football, and that they are

TABLE 6-4

COMMUNITY SUPPORT FOR TEXAS FOOTBALL

Selected cities	High school enrollment	Percent of males trying out for sports	Seating capacity percent of city population		Attendance, percent of city population		Expenditure per athlete	Coach-athlete Ratio	Number of coaches	
			Football	Basketball	Football	Basketball			Football	Basketball
Decatur	320	50	70	13	84	8	$150	1/27	3	2
Jacksboro	300	50	54	21	104	10	$160	1/25	3	2
Rockwall	325	61	92	14	94	7	$185	1/20	5	3
Wilmer-Hutchins	460	30	280	56	112	17	$114	1/14	5	2
Athens	825	19	64	14	28	7	$304	1/13	6	3
Lewisville	820	43	150	40	101	10	$171	1/25	7	3
Vernon	730	46	41	4	33	2	$154	1/21	8	1
McKinney	1040	29	47	7	36	3	$228	1/19	8	3
Palestine	1275	16			36	3	$300		8	3
Plano	1050	23	35	5	30	1	$200	1/20	6	2
Irving	2600	25	26	5	20	1	$188	1/27	8	3
Longview	1600	25	16	5	16	3	$349	1/22	9	2

TABLE 6-5
ATHLETIC OUTPUT OF TEXAS AND OKLAHOMA
STANDARD METROPOLITAN STATISTICAL AREAS

SMSA	Football number	Per capita index	Letter rating	Basketball number	Per capita index
Houston	130	1.31	C	35	1.20
Dallas	140	1.61	B	37	1.45
San Antonio	51	1.09	C	7	0.43
Fort Worth	72	1.57	B	24	1.78
Oklahoma City	43	1.05	C	17	1.41
Tulsa	50	1.49	C	13	1.32
El Paso	25	1.00	C	5	0.68
Beaumont-Pt. Arthur	45	1.84	B	4	0.56
Corpus Christi	31	1.75	B	1	0.19
Austin	12	0.71	D	2	0.40
Lubbock	11	0.88	C	8	2.18
Brownsville-Harlington-San Benito	12	0.99	C	0	0
Waco	18	1.50	B	2	0.57
Amarillo	33	3.57	A	4	1.47
Galveston-Texas City	37	3.30	A	3	0.91
Wichita Falls	24	2.31	B	1	0.33
Abilene	20	2.08	B	1	0.33
Texarkana	8	1.09	C	2	0.93
Odessa	23	3.16	A	3	1.40
Lawton	10	1.38	C	1	0.47
Tyler	18	2.56	A	1	0.49

willing to pay for it.[4] Over eighty percent of the "on the street" respondents claimed football to be their favorite sport, but few were sure of the reasons for their choice. Many of the coaches held the firm belief that football unites a community and solidifies the bonds between people.

Football also has its effect on intercommunity relations. After considerable delay, several west Texas towns decided that they could cooperate on an industrial park venture in spite of the fact that their allegiances were to different high school football teams.

Most of urban areas are also sponsoring productive high school football programs. Of the 21 metropolitan areas, 18 have indices of

1.00 or better (Table 6-5). Four of the ten A metropolitan areas in the United States are in Texas, and seven of 36 B metropolitan areas are contained in the two-state area. Amarillo, Galveston–Texas City, and Odessa are among the five outstanding suppliers in the nation. Among the larger centers, Dallas, Forth Worth, Tulsa, and Houston rank high and compare favorably to cities in their size categories, with the exception of Pittsburgh, Cincinnati, Toledo, Dayton, and Youngstown. In Oklahoma, Tulsa rates a B, and Oklahoma City and Lawton are each C sources. The dominance of football over basketball is indicative of the degree to which one sport can grip a geographic region.

In the central plains area, Wichita and Topeka, Kansas are also average producers, but in football-happy Nebraska, Omaha is a C–, and Lincoln, the "football capitol of the world" is a D source. Outstanding smaller counties in the region include Douglas, Kansas, the home of Kansas University (14 players for a per capita index of 4.03), Cole, Missouri (11 players for a per capita index of 3.4), and Dawson, Nebraska (7 players for a per capita index of 4.5).

UTAH

Another football stronghold in the West contains northern Utah, southeastern Idaho, and southwestern Wyoming. Total yield here amounted to only 83 players, but the per capita index was 3.20. The bulk of the players originated from the northern suburbs of Salt Lake City and from the Ogden–Logan area. Kemmerer and Evanston, Wyoming, and Idaho Falls, Idaho accounted for most of the remainder.

THE FAR WEST

The last area of national consequence, on the basis of per capita productivity, is located east of San Francisco and includes Contra Costa County (El Cerrito, Richmond), Stockton, and Modesto. It has a per capita index of 2.34, well above the California average of 1.15. Nearly half of the region's 157 players came from the northeastern Bay section.

The west coast is providing slightly more than its share of collegiate footballers. As a state, California ranks 15% above the national average, while Oregon and Washington are each 5% below it. Aside from the prolific East Bay region, San Jose, Bakersfield, and Orange County are strong B sources. Most of the other large centers (Los Angeles, Fresno, Sacramento, Santa Barbara, and San Bernadino) are average. Further north, Portland and Eugene, Oregon, and Seattle, Spokane, and Tacoma, Washington also rate C. Of the small number of A counties in the Pacific states, Madera, California (10 players, per capita index, 3.09), Jackson (16 players, per capita index, 2.70) and Malheur, Oregon (7 players, per capita index, 3.8), and Chelan, Washington (11 players, per capita index, 3.40) deserve mention.

STATE PERFORMANCE

California, Ohio, Pennsylvania, and Texas, respectively, are the leading states from the standpoint of gross production; they account for nearly 38 percent of the national total (Table 6-6). Illinois heads a second group, which includes New York and New Jersey, with outputs of about one-half that of the four leaders. A third cluster, producing approximately one-third as many, contains Massachusetts, Michigan, and Florida.

In general, the most populous states provide the bulk of the football talent; however, there is by no means a perfect correlation between a state's population and its ability to grow football players. New York, with a population approximately equal to that of California, accounted for less than half as many players, and Michigan, with slightly fewer people than Texas, had less than one-third of the Lone Star contribution. Thus, at the per capita level, the ranking of states is considerably different (Table 6-6). The leading states are Ohio, Texas, Utah, Delaware, Mississippi, New Hampshire, and Pennsylvania. Completing the top ten are Kansas, Oklahoma, and West Virginia. Only Ohio, Pennsylvania, and Texas rank in the top ten for both total and per capita output.

At the other end of the scale, the worst per capita producers are New York, Missouri, Indiana, Wisconsin, Maryland, and Iowa, with indices representing a player yield of just 30 to 35 percent of the leaders. Allowing for population differences, players are being developed in Ohio and Texas at three times the rate they are being developed in New York and Missouri.

Professional players come from the states and cities that one would expect, relative to the collegiate pattern. The five leading college states are among the leading professional ones (Table 6-7). The South, however, does much better at the per capita level. Mississippi is the standout, but Louisiana and Alabama, which are mediocre college producers, have outstanding records in matriculating athletes to the professional ranks. This situation seems to reflect both the

TABLE 6-6
THE ORIGIN AND PER CAPITA PRODUCTION OF MAJOR COLLEGE FOOTBALL PLAYERS

State	Number of players	Per capita index (norm=1.00)	State	Number of players	Per capita index (norm=1.00)
1. Ohio	1350	1.74	26. Oregon	134	.95
2. Mississippi	204	1.69	27. Washington	217	.95
3. Texas	1290	1.68	28. Montana	50	.93
4. Utah	119	1.67	29. Nebraska	101	.89
5. Delaware	57	1.60	30. Illinois	707	.88
6. New Hampshire	78	1.51	31. Rhode Island	58	.84
7. Pennsylvania	1333	1.47	32. North Dakota	42	.83
8. Kansas	228	1.31	33. Alaska	0	.80
9. Oklahoma	242	1.30	34. Arizona	83	.80
10. West Virginia	192	1.29	35. Dist. of Columbia	48	.79
11. Maine	99	1.28	36. Tennessee	225	.79
12. New Jersey	579	1.19	37. Louisiana	203	.78
13. Idaho	63	1.18	38. Vermont	24	.77
14. California	1443	1.15	39. Hawaii	38	.73
15. Virginia	353	1.11	40. Minnesota	193	.71
16. South Carolina	210	1.10	41. Michigan	420	.67
17. Georgia	333	1.06	42. Arkansas	93	.65
18. Nevada	24	1.05	43. Kentucky	154	.63
19. Alabama	270	1.03	44. Iowa	228	.58
20. Florida	409	1.03	45. Maryland	142	.57
21. Massachusetts	426	1.03	46. Indiana	209	.56
22. New Mexico	78	1.03	47. Wisconsin	177	.56
23. North Carolina	361	.99	48. Missouri	169	.49
24. Connecticut	200	.99	49. New York	625	.47
25. Colorado	134	.95	50. South Dakota	11	.20

TABLE 6-7

PROFESSIONAL FOOTBALL PLAYERS: THE LEADING STATES

Rank	Total production	Rank	Per capita production	Per capita rate
1.	Texas	1.	Mississippi	2.94
2.	California	2.	Louisiana	2.44
3.	Pennsylvania	3.	Texas	2.11
4.	Ohio	4.	Alabama	1.74
5.	Illinois	5.	Georgia	1.40
6.	Louisiana	6.	Pennsylvania	1.39
7.	Mississippi	7.	District of Columbia	1.38
8.	Michigan	8.	Arkansas	1.34
9.	Florida	9.	California	1.25
10.	Alabama	10.	Ohio	1.25

standard of coaching in the South, and the role of the region's black colleges.

WHY FOOTBALL FEVER

The extent to which many communities become involved with football, or any other sport, cannot be easily explained. Something intangible—perhaps we can call it sociocultural emphasis—accounts for the great interest and prolific output of talent in certain parts of the United States. What causes this emphasis to evolve? To what degree is it related to the economic and occupational structure of the community or region? Are manufacturing and mining towns more apt to develop good players than rurally oriented service centers? What role does climate play? How does the ethnic or racial makeup of a community affect the production of athletes?

These are a few of the factors that are most likely to be related to a place's ability to generate high-calibre athletes. Most obvious, perhaps, is the degree to which a community supports its schoolboy athletic program, in terms of money and time and enthusiasm. The question now becomes: What set of conditions is conducive to a strong community-support situation? Is community size, wealth, and occupational structure important? Or are other factors responsible?

When the origins of football players are used as a measure, there is no significant statistical difference between the per capita contributions of Standard Metropolitan Statistical Areas (SMSA's) and cities of less than 50,000. However, there are proportionately many more cases of smaller counties that are very high suppliers (more than 2.5 times the national average) than is the case with their larger counterparts. Areas characterized by poor economic health, such as the hardcore poverty counties of Appalachia, the Ozarks, and the northern parts of Michigan and Wisconsin, are generally poor sources of football players. Many high schools in these sections do not even field football teams. Conversely, there are very few wealthy counties that are producing substantially above the national average.

Perhaps an in-depth look at the socioeconomic conditions which characterize a few of the most prolific source areas of college football players will provide some answers concerning the high levels of production. The following examination of the situations in western Pennsylvania, eastern Ohio, the West Virginia panhandle (PenWevO), the Texas districts, Southern Mississippi, and northern Utah provides some clues regarding the character of a football region.

PENNSYLVANIA-WEST VIRGINIA-OHIO

The core area of PenWevO focuses on the Pittsburgh Metropolitan area and encompasses part of the West Virginia panhandle and three counties in eastern Ohio, which include the cities of Steubenville, Alliance, Canton, and Massillon. This region is most noted for its fine football, but it has also produced basketball talent at a rate which is nearly double the national norm.

The PenWevO area is primarily engaged in the business of manufacturing steel and other heavy industrial products. All but one of the counties have above-average employment in manufacturing, ranging from 25.7 percent for Ohio County to 61 percent for Hancock County. The norm for the entire region exceeds 40 percent in manufacturing activity. Contrary to popular belief, income levels also range from average to slightly above average. There is little evidence to substantiate the frequently held belief that athletes from the region are trying to escape from substandard economic and social environments. Nor is the desire to "escape" evidenced by the statistics on population change. During a period (1950–1970) which saw over half of the nation's counties lose population, all but one of the PenWevO counties gained. With regard to education, the population in this region has about one year less formal education, on the average, than its national counterparts. Historically, the need for a vigorous emotional and physical outlet was responsible for the birth of professional football in this area. Even today, when relatively high incomes prevail, the nature of mine, mill, and factory workers undoubtedly stimulates rugged athletic endeavor.

The heavily industrialized counties, centering on Pittsburgh, contain substantially more people of foreign stock than the nationwide percentage. In accordance with expectations, a substantial portion of the athletes are of East European and Italian descent. The black population is relatively small, but it has provided more than its share of athletes to the area total.

Settlement density is high throughout the area. Superimposed upon this is a political system that has divided the population up into a large number of corporate units. Because of this density, a substantial population of medium-sized high schools in close proximity to one another has been created. The schools are large enough to consistently field high calibre teams, but not so large as to preclude the participation of many worthy boys. The proximity of the many large high schools to one another has also served to stimulate local rivalries and generally upgrade the quality and intensity of competition.

In summary, PenWevO is a densely settled industrial district whose residents earn a decent living. The area contains more people of foreign stock and fewer blacks than the United States as a whole. But the area is not unlike several of the other industrial concentrations which dot this country. It does, however, have a greater tradition involving athletic pursuits.

PenWevO has many large football stadiums, and for many games there is standing room only. Capacities generally exceed high school enrollments by five or more times, with one school in Beaver County, Pennsylvania, having fifteen stadium seats for every member of its student body.[5] Schools in western Pennsylvania and eastern Ohio generally have excellent athletic facilities and generous financial support for coaching staffs.

The quality of facilities and coaching personnel are tangible measures of community support. It is the degree to which people identify with sports and their local teams which is difficult to measure accurately, much less compare from place to place. Field study in the area did uncover unmistakable evidence of intense community identification with the local team. The previously described Massillon situation is a case in point.

TEXAS

The Texas–Southern Plains region has little in common with PenWevO in occupational structure. The possible exceptions are the Dallas–Fort

Worth and the Houston areas. Much of the outstanding football is
played in rather sparsely populated sections of the state. Rural-ori-
ented service communities tend to dominate the football scene. These
are towns that have very little which could be construed as manufacturing activity. The only prominent exceptions are the oiltowns of
Midland and Odessa, both characterized by outstanding football production. It would appear that the relatively strong showings of
Houston and Dallas–Fort Worth are just a product of the overall
Texas mania for football.

Economically, the people are relatively wealthy. After adjust-
ments for cost-of-living differences, they have a standard of living similar to the PenWevO residents.[6] They also average nearly two more
years of formal education. They are primarily native Americans; less
than 5 percent are of foreign stock. The proportion of blacks is low
here, as in PenWevO, Fort Worth again being the only exception.

Many of the Texas counties are experiencing a rapid rate of
population growth. Climatic amenities have been important in attracting people to the state and have certainly not hurt the advancement of
outdoor sporting activity. As a result of in-migration, the importance
of manufacturing activity to local economies is also increasing.

The Texas–Oklahoma area is the epitome of successful "small–
town" high school football, since much of the area's talent comes
from communities like Graham, Borger, Andrews, Rockwall, Cald-
well, Elk City, and Clinton. Texas might best be described as the
"holyland" of the high school game, with over 1000 high schools
fielding teams, backed by over 2000 junior high elevens and a multitude of elementary squads. In many towns, football is life's biggest
diversion, which is in no small way related to the absence of other
game-destroying temptations. Football is a way of life, and in the
autumn, the scheduling of games actually *controls* the tempo of activity from Friday evening through Sunday afternoon.

It is clear that different sets of socioeconomic and physical environments are associated with the successful programs of Texas and
PenWevO. And it is easy to say that football prowess is the result of
some type of sociocultural emphasis and that good football programs
are likely to be associated with high levels of community support.

Several hypotheses concerning Texas and, to some extent, Oklahoma football excellence need testing. They are as follows:

1. There is an above-average emphasis on rugged individualism or
    "ruggedness" here which finds expression on the gridiron, either

through direct participation or an intense identification with the participants.

2. There is an above-average emphasis on militarism which is reflected in an attraction for games which demand considerable self-discipline, i.e., football.

3. The state-related "nationalism" which seems to reach a zenith in Texas and Oklahoma finds a micro-expression at the local level so that community prestige is more vital than in other sections of the country. The football team is a tangible instrument by which prestige is judged. This state-oriented nationalism is reflected in the great reverence for such songs as "The Eyes of Texas," "Deep in the Heart of Texas," and "Oklahoma."

4. The fine autumn weather provides ample time for a long season including "playoffs."

5. There is an absence of intervening opportunity so that greater emphasis is placed on football. (In other words, there is little else to do.)

6. There are numerous local opportunities to play major college football.

Some of these hypotheses are documented by the voting behavior of Texas and Oklahoma congressmen and a casual observation of editorial comments in the region's newspapers. This is a part of the nation where the individual believes himself to be more self-reliant than many of his fellow Americans. It is an area where provincialism supercedes nationalism on many fronts, where support for the war effort in Vietnam was strong, where the fraternity-sorority system still thrives, where D. A. R. membership is high, and where urban problems are less acute, or occupy a very low position on the priority list. The great involvement with football is a clue to the character of Texas and Oklahoma and other places which have so completely embraced the game. Hypothesis three can be reduced to cover the community as well as the state scale. At the local level, football may be the only outward manner by which a town can demonstrate its superiority over another town and show its character. Bob Wright, a veteran high school coach, remarked about his hometown of Ballinger in west Texas:

I remember every night before a game, I'd get a call from one of the matriarchs of the town. "Bob," she'd say.

"Yeh, Big Mamma" (we all called her that).

"How y'all doin Bob? Want you to know we are behind you in the game—win, lose or draw. But I know you'll do it all right, Bob." And Big Mamma'd call the quarterback and half the team just to let them know how important that game was.[7]

The sentiment was reiterated recently by Charlie Krueger, the 37-year-old veteran All-Pro tackle of the San Francisco '49ers in an attempt to explain what it took to be a success in the professional game. In describing the kinds of players who made it, he stated "They were, for the most part, good old boys from Texas and Southern towns where spectral lights did not shine on their farms and factories. I guess that we were the last completely goal-directed group to enter the pros, and I tell you we were scared to death to fail."[8]

It would appear that there is a thread that ties Pennsylvania and Texas football together. Texas high school football got its start during the oil boom, and many of the oil towns still rank at the top of the state's high school football ladder. A significant number of the oil field workers migrated to Texas from the PenWevO region, bringing with them a great lust for the game. It is quite possible that the football mania spread throughout the state, and into Oklahoma as well, with the spread of the oil boom and has since thrived in the community pride environment that is so characteristic of the area.

UTAH

The situation in northern Utah is similar to that in PenWevO and Texas only in terms of the general characteristics of the population. It is similar in size, distribution and degree of urbanization, but it has a miniscule black population. Only 0.5 percent of the total population of the state is black.

In educational achievement, Utah ranks quite high, relative to the regions already discussed. In contrast to the PenWevO area, Utah has a low percentage of its work force engaged in manufacturing, but is on a par with Texas.

Incomes in Utah reflect greater affluence than the other two areas. Four of the five Utah counties have median family incomes exceeding $6100 per annum, while only a few of the PenWevO or Texas counties approach this figure. Utah housing is similarly indicative of more affluent ownership, and expenditures on education are very high compared with most of the other counties in the United States.

It has been suggested that there are particular reasons for the high generation of football players in PenWevO and Texas, but such suggestions or hypotheses do not seem appropriate, nor can they be substantiated in the Utah case. Perhaps success here is due in part to the high socioeconomic standards present, but it is also possible that this success is the result of the Latter Day Saints' emphasis on physical well-being. Since this is a predominantly Mormon region, and since part of the Mormon philosophy includes an emphasis on a sound healthy body, religious influences could indeed be the underlying cause of Utah football and basketball success. This is not to say that athletic success is not stressed, but that the source of the emphasis is quite different.

MISSISSIPPI

The Mississippi story is the most difficult to explain. In virtually every economic category, Mississippi lags far behind the other areas. If there is any place where athletics can be viewed as an "escape route" from economic and social disadvantage, that place is Mississippi. It should be pointed out, however, that while the best football counties have large black populations, they are not the blackest counties in the state, so perhaps the "escape" is not available to everyone.

GENERALIZATIONS

There is clearly a multivariate explanation for athletic success, whatever the sport or the location may be. The high quality of western Pennsylvania or Texas football, Indiana basketball, or Long Island lacrosse have similar causes. When local athletes attain fame at the college or professional level, they become heroes with whom young boys and parents identify. Lads, encouraged by their parents, seek to duplicate these performances, and an increasing number of them are fortunate in attaining their goals. Many of them return to the home region and assume coaching positions, with the result being the intensification of rivalries and the expansion or growth of an "athletic region."

Whatever the local sport or sports may be, they generally have tremendous social significance to the community. The degree to which a town's population becomes involved or identifies with a team or group of teams varies greatly. Such variation is generally related to the size of the community and the availability of other attractive forces. Based on a state-to-state comparison of the per capita yield of major college football players and the number of boys engaged in high school football, it appears that there are two types, or at least two outcomes, of community support. Given a high level of community involvement, the ability of an area to turn out college football material seems closely related to the density of population and the average enrollment in the region's individual high schools. Very large or very small schools are less likely to be good producers than those with 500 to 1000 students. The very small schools generally do not give one another very stiff competition, have marginal facilities and coaching staffs, and encourage their best athletes to participate in a variety of sports. The very large schools provide one another with tough competition, but discourage all but the best athletes from participating, thus failing to give many of the "late bloomers" a chance. The medium-sized schools provide the best of both worlds to the young athlete. In summary, sparsely populated areas are likely to have a large number of very small schools, large cities, a small number of very big schools. From a population density standpoint then, the ideal situation is somewhere in between.

Per capita participation in high school football was discussed in Chapter 4 (see Fig. 4–3). There, it was found that the pattern of participation is much lower throughout the South and the East, with the exceptions of Pennsylvania and Delaware. Surprisingly high participation is also found in Minnesota, Wisconsin, Iowa, and Michigan.

The correlation between per capita high school involvement and college player contribution is weak. Texas, Kansas, and Pennsylvania rank high in both categories, whereas New York, Kentucky, and Maryland rank low. On the other hand, with a great amount of schoolboy involvement in Iowa, Michigan, and Minnesota, there is little matriculation to university competition. Utah, Oklahoma, and New Hampshire are illustrative of the other extreme.

What can be concluded from this data? One possibility is that having a large number of high school players in some areas results in watered-down competition, which is not geared to bringing out the best in the available talent. This seems to be the case in Iowa, Minnesota, and Wisconsin, where each small town elects to field a football team. They also elect to support teams in all of the other major sports, which are likely to be staffed by the same personnel. In such a situation, only the very best all-around athletes, and a few specialists, perfect their skills to the level required for university competition. Thus these states tend to rank low in the output of college-bound athletes.

Another conclusion to be drawn is that specialization in high school and junior high athletic programs tends to result in a proportionately greater number of university-calibre athletes. Texas and Indiana provide good examples in football and basketball, respectively.

THE DEFICIT AREAS

An examination of the deficit areas sheds more light on the question of what high school football excellence is related to. The low per capita producers can be generalized into three broad groups. They include several of the large eastern–central cities, the Midwest, and areas of rural poverty, such as the Ozark-Quachita region and much of Appalachia.

Eastern Cities

The five major eastern seaboard centers of megalopolis are poor hunting grounds for football talent. Of the nine inner city counties, six are in the F category, and only the District of Columbia merits a C production rank (Table 6–8). When one considers that little Westmoreland County, to the east of Pittsburgh, was the source of more players than the five boroughs of New York City combined, the realization of just how bad our premier metropolis is in the football department becomes strikingly apparent. The fact that the suburban counties around New York, Boston, Washington, and Philadelphia are much better player sources also points out something about the type of school environment which is conducive to the development of good footballers. The sheer size of many city institutions, the lack of practice and playing space, and the financial crisis which has struck so hard at out giant urban high school systems, all operate to the disadvantage of creditable football programs. Athletes in this type of situation are not given sufficient opportunity to develop their potential, and the student body is deprived of an experience which is an integral part of high school life in most places throughout the United States. This is just one more piece of evidence which demonstrates that the most serious recreational crisis is in the cities.

The remainder of the below-average eastern cities are confined to upper New York State and eastern Pennsylvania. Albany, Schenectady, Utica, Rome, Rochester, Lancaster, and York are each D performers.

TABLE 6-8
FOOTBALL PERFORMANCE OF THE FIVE MAJOR URBAN
CENTERS OF MEGALOPOLIS

Central county	City	Number of players	Central county per capita index	Total metropolitan area per capita index
Suffolk	Boston	42	0.67	1.51
Bronx	New York	12	0.11	0.38
Kings	New York	30	0.14	0.38
Queens	New York	15	0.10	0.38
New York	New York	17	0.13	0.38
Richmond	New York	6	0.34	0.38
Philadelphia	Philadelphia	54	0.33	0.87
District of Columbia	Washington	48	0.79	1.15
Baltimore city	Baltimore	37	0.49	0.41
		261		

The Midwest

On the basis of its substantial population, the land of the "Big Ten"
is a surprisingly meager source of football players (Table 6–9). With
such long-term exposure to high-class college performers, it is hard to
believe that so few schoolboys from this region have been recruited
into major college programs. Of the midwestern states, only Illinois
is performing at a rate approaching the national norm, in spite of the
fact that its southern half is much below average. Production is low
in both the very large cities and throughout the sprawling countryside, generously dotted with many potential suppliers of top-flight
players. The major cities of Detroit, St. Louis, Indianapolis, Milwaukee, and St. Paul can achieve only D-level output, but even this is considerably better than some of their smaller neighbors (Table 6–9).

It is difficult to account for the poor showing. Perhaps the same
problems which tend to bog down many of the big eastern metropolises are at work in places like Detroit, St. Louis, and Milwaukee.
Large schools and high densities of population seem to result in dis-
economies of scale, where the grooming of college gridiron aspirants
is concerned. But this does not explain the poor performance of the
smaller cities and towns around the Midwest. An example is Indiana,

TABLE 6-9
THE MIDWESTERN DEFICIT REGION—FOOTBALL

State	Number of players	Per capita index	Worst cities or metropolitan areas	Number of players	Per capita indices
Michigan	420	0.67	Detroit	189	0.63
			Grand Rapids	13	0.45
			Kalamazoo	6	0.44
			Jackson	7	0.66
			Muskegon	5	0.42
Wisconsin	177	0.56	Milwaukee	46	0.48
			Racine	7	0.62
			Kenosha	3	0.37
Minnesota	193	0.71	St. Paul	22	0.65
Iowa	128	0.58	Waterloo	1	0.11
			Clinton	1	0.23
			Council Bluffs	1	0.15
			Ames	1	0.26
			Fort Dodge	1	0.27
Indiana	209	0.56	Indianapolis	27	0.49
			Fort Wayne	4	0.22
			Muncie	1	0.11
			Anderson	0	0.10*
			Marion	1	0.15
			Terre Haute	3	0.35
Kentucky	154	0.63	St. Joseph	1	0.14
			Louisville	110	0.67
			Bowling Green	1	0.28

*Calculated on the basis of one player.

the home of Notre Dame, Purdue, and Indiana Universities. The state has a per capita index of just 0.56, slightly more than one-half the national average. Of its important urban concentrations, only South Bend, Gary–Hammond, and Evansville have been worthwhile sources of players from a per capita standpoint. The majority of counties are providing players at a rate of far less than one-half the United States output. Muncie, Anderson, and Fort Wayne exhibit results far below average. With the exception of Louisville, the same is true for Kentucky.

Why is that so? In the case of Indiana and Kentucky, meager output of football players coexists with an extremely high production of basketballers. Emphasis on the hardwood sport has seemingly been at the expense of football excellence, particularly at the great majority of small schools in these states. However, concentration on one sport does not preclude the existence of balanced athletic programs in Pennsylvania, Ohio, Illinois, and Utah, so perhaps we must search for other explanations. It could be the *degree* of one-sport concentration which is most critical, with both states, Indiana and Kentucky, in this instance sending forth more than twice as many hoopsters as their population would warrant. There is probably some point of single sports emphasis which produces diminishing returns where other sports are concerned, and it may be that Indiana and Kentucky have reached such a point.

The basketball excuse cannot be put forward for the other deficit states in the Midwest. Heavily industrialized Michigan does not begin to match the output of nearby Ohio and Illinois. Wisconsin, Minnesota, and Iowa are much below their economically similar neighbors to the west and south. The presence of only one major football playing institution in each of the former may help to explain the low production. In addition there is a relatively low propensity to migrate from these states, due to the strong cultural ties between the people and the land, which have developed over the years. However, even if some boys opt to play ball at one of the local state colleges instead of going to an out-of-state "major," this would not explain the very small per capita yield.

Missouri's two major centers, St. Louis and Kansas City, are both considerably above the state average, but even they are far from being adequate suppliers. The minor contribution of the state is definitely related to the poverty which grips its south central portion. Many of the school districts cannot afford the expense of worthwhile football programs. Good football and substandard living conditions do not mix well. This is illustrated by the paucity of players from the hill lands of Missouri and Arkansas and also from the hard-core poverty counties of Virginia, Kentucky, and Tennessee.

NOTES

1. For information on attendance at college and professional sporting events, see the section on sporting records in *The World Almanac*, (New York: Doubleday, 1972), p.

2. Wayne E. Green, "Big Time Small Fry: Schoolboy Football is Serious Business in Texas," *Wall Street Journal*, Dec. 1, 1967, p.1.

3. Douglas B. McDonald, *Geographic Variation in Athletic Production: An Axiomatic or Accidental?*, unpublished Master's Thesis, Southern Illinois University, 1969, pp. 49–53. See also Walter Bingham, "Football from the Cradle," *Sports Illustrated,* vol. 15, Nov. 13, 1961, pp. 46–51.

4. Personal interviews were taken at twelve randomly selected cities in the northeastern Texas football region during the fall of 1970.

5. McDonald, *op. cit.,* p. 35.

6. For comparative data on cost of living variations, see U. S. Bureau of Labor Statistics, *City Worker's Family Budget for a Moderate Standard of Living,* Bulletin 1570–1, Washington, D. C., 1966.

7. *The Christian Science Monitor,*

8. Morton Sharnik, "The Last of the Old Leather," *Sports Illustrated,* Vol. 39, Sept. 17, 1973, p. 86.

7 / Basketball: Where They Come From

Like football, there appears to be a strong relationship between the sources of basketball players and large urban agglomerations (Fig. 7-1). The metropolitan area of New York City, containing nearly 6 percent of the United States population, provided roughly the same proportion of the country's "major" college players. But even though nearly six out of every 100 players come from New York, the total metropolitan region merits only a middle C rating for production intensity. Three other metropolitan areas which are conspicuous for the large number of players they send forth are Los Angeles, Chicago, and Philadelphia. Each has a high C ranking, and together they account for 12 percent of the national total. Although none of these SMSA's has an extremely large output in relation to population, the huge mass of capable prospects in such close proximity makes each a prime recruiting territory. The struggle to attract their best athletes has been extremely heated, as the cases of recent luminaries Wilt Chamberlain, Tom Gola, Rick Barry, Billy Cunningham, Kevin Loughery, and Guy Rogers (all from Philadelphia), indicate.

Other noteworthy metropolitan areas are San Francisco-Oakland, Pittsburgh, Washington, D.C., St. Louis, and Newark. Each of these warrants a B ranking, which is unusually high for large cities. The only A metropolitan area of over 500,000 is Louisville, Kentucky, located in the heart of the nation's small town basketball region.

147

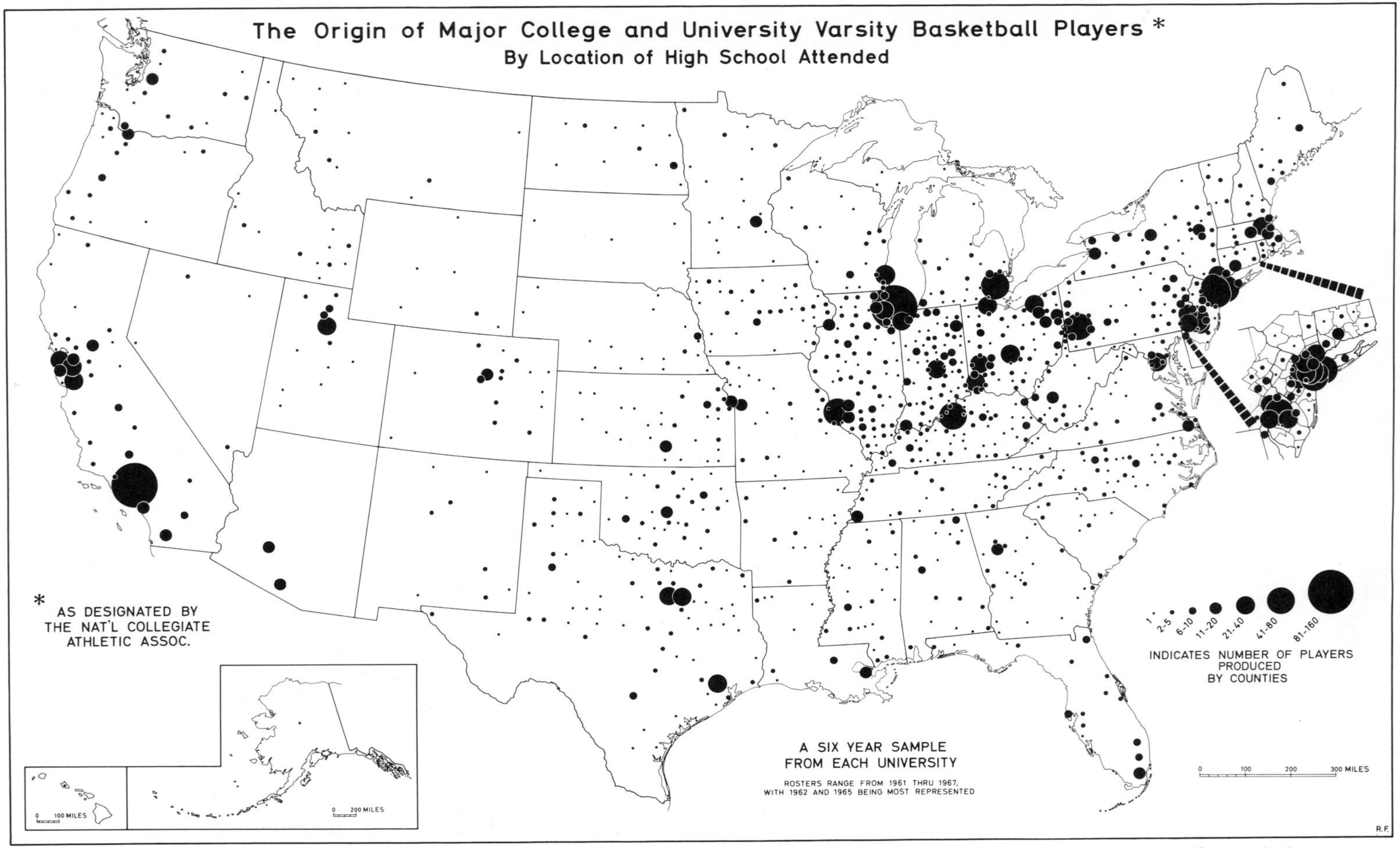

The Origin of Major College and University Varsity Basketball Players *
By Location of High School Attended

INDICATES NUMBER OF PLAYERS PRODUCED BY COUNTIES

81-160
41-80
21-40
11-20
6-10
2-5
1

A SIX YEAR SAMPLE FROM EACH UNIVERSITY

ROSTERS RANGE FROM 1961 THRU 1967, WITH 1962 AND 1965 BEING MOST REPRESENTED

* AS DESIGNATED BY THE NAT'L COLLEGIATE ATHLETIC ASSOC.

Figure 7.1

Basketball is the leading spectator sport in the United States.

TABLE 7-1
THE ORIGIN AND PER CAPITA PRODUCTION OF MAJOR COLLEGE BASKETBALL PLAYERS

State	Net production	Rank, production	Rank, population	Production per capita one per	Per capita index, norm=1.00	Rank
1. Alabama	40	27	19	81,670	0.52	42
2. Alaska	1	50	51	226,000	0.19	50
3. Arizona	33	29	35	39,450	1.08	20
4. Arkansas	24	36	31	74,420	0.57	40
5. California	392	1	2	40,510	1.05	22
6. Colorado	52	24	33	33,370	1.26	13
7. Connecticut	29	33	25	87,410	0.49	43
8. Delaware	7	47	47	63,710	0.67	36
9. Dist. of Columbia	32	31	40	23,880	1.78	4
10. Florida	68	17	10	72,820	0.58	39
11. Georgia	52	24	16	75,800	0.56	41
12. Hawaii*	1	50	44	633,000	0.07	51
13. Idaho	19	38	43	35,110	1.21	14
14. Illinois	359	2	4	28,080	1.51	6
15. Indiana	234	6	11	20,270	2.10	3
16. Iowa	63	20	24	43,780	0.97	23
17. Kansas	69	16	28	31,580	1.35	10
18. Kentucky	163	9	22	18,750	2.27	2
19. Louisiana	30	32	20	108,560	0.39	46
20. Maine	29	33	36	33,410	1.27	12
21. Maryland	18	41	21	172,670	0.25	48
22. Massachusetts	91	12	9	57,580	0.74	31
23. Michigan	109	10	7	71,770	0.59	38
24. Minnesota	33	29	18	103,450	0.41	44

25.	Mississippi	36	28	29	60,500	0.70	33
26.	Missouri	93	11	13	46,450	0.91	25
27.	Montana	19	38	42	35,530	1.20	17
28.	Nebraska	26	35	34	54,270	0.78	29
29.	Nevada	8	45	50	35,630	1.19	18
30.	New Hampshire	15	43	46	40,470	1.05	21
31.	New Jersey	201	8	8	31,110	1.37	9
32.	New Mexico	16	42	37	59,440	0.72	32
33.	New York	354	3	1	47,400	0.90	27
34.	North Carolina	73	14	12	62,410	0.68	35
35.	North Dakota	23	37	45	27,480	1.55	5
36.	Ohio	303	5	5	32,030	1.33	11
37.	Oklahoma	76	13	27	30,630	1.39	8
38.	Oregon	50	26	32	35,380	1.20	15
39.	Pennsylvania	310	4	3	36,630	1.16	19
40.	Rhode Island	8	45	39	107,370	0.40	45
41.	South Carolina	19	38	26	125,420	0.34	47
42.	South Dakota*	4	49	41	175,000	0.24	49
43.	Tennessee	54	22	17	66,060	0.64	37
44.	Texas	214	7	6	44,770	0.95	24
45.	Utah	54	22	38	16,500	2.58	1
46.	Vermont	11	44	48	35,450	1.20	16
47.	Virginia	72	15	14	55,100	0.77	30
48.	Washington	57	21	23	50,050	0.85	28
49.	West Virginia	64	18	30	29,060	1.46	7
50.	Wisconsin	64	18	15	61,750	0.69	34
51.	Wyoming	7	47	49	47,140	0.90	26
	Total	4163					

*No university in the sample.

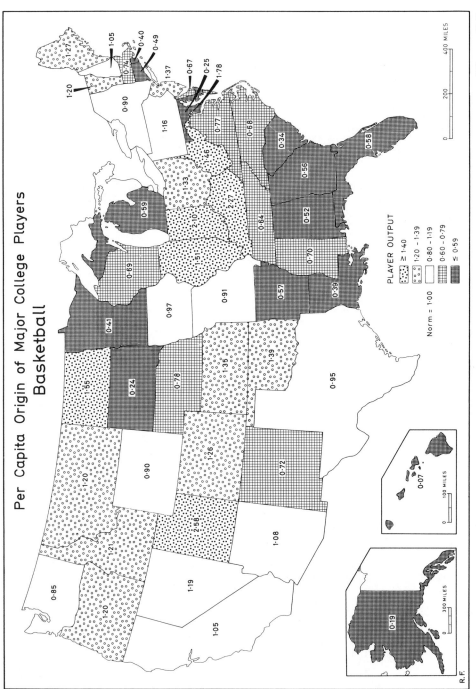

Per Capita Origin of Major College Players
Basketball

Figure 7.2

TOWARD A STATE-BASED REGIONALIZATION

A number of generalizations can be made from a comparison of basketball player origin on a state-to-state basis (Table 7–1). There is a strong tendency toward regional groupings of states with high and low player output.

The large industrial states account for a great percentage of the athletes. The five most populous ones (California, New York, Pennsylvania, Illinois, and Ohio) are responsible for over 41 percent of the total. All but New York have per capita rates in excess of the national average, and Illinois and Ohio are substantially above it. Most of the players from the large northeastern states and from California originate in or around the largest urban areas.

A region composed of Illinois, Indiana, Kentucky, Ohio, and the southern section of West Virginia accounted for over 26 percent of the national total, some of which would be included in the area referred to above. Kentucky, Indiana, and Illinois, excluding Cook County (Chicago), are the source of a great number of players in relation to their population, many of whom are from small communities in which basketball is the major form of entertainment, and in repeated instances, represents the focal point of the area's social life.

Impressive production is also characteristic of several of the less urbanized states. In the southern plains, both Oklahoma and Kansas place high on the per capita scale, and there are many high-producing counties in north Texas. Farther west, Utah rates as the country's outstanding contributor, with an output nearly three times above the norm (Fig. 7–2).

Four deficit areas can be identified. They include the Deep South, the Middle Atlantic States, Southern New England, and the Northern Middle West (Fig. 7–2). The South is consistently low, with most states contributing only between 35 and 60 percent of the expected total relative to their population. Some of the region's major cities, such as Birmingham, Charleston, Greenville, and Mobile, have sent out fewer than three players in the six-year sample period. Of the major centers, only Atlanta, Memphis, Miami, and Fort Lauderdale have attained a low C rating.

The Middle Atlantic states, particularly Maryland, are producing far less than the amount their population justifies. Maryland is performing at a rate only 25 percent of the national norm, and the city of Baltimore failed to provide a *single* player during the period of the study! North Carolina, a state whose universities consistently field top-class teams, and Virginia, with five major colleges, each ranks considerably below the national mean.

In the northern Middle West, Michigan, Minnesota, and Wisconsin have generated few players from their relatively large populations. Some of the area's large cities (Detroit, Milwaukee, and Madison) are contributing their share, but most are not. Minneapolis and St. Paul have done quite poorly, as has Duluth and most of the medium-sized cities in Michigan. The majority of rural areas have sent out no players at all. Southern New England is very similar to the upper Midwest. The Boston area rates a low C, while the other metropolitan areas lag behind with D and F ratings.

THE MAJOR SOURCE REGIONS

THE NORTHEAST

Although a tremendous number of players come from New York, New Jersey, Pennsylvania, and California, relatively few of their counties rank high from a per capita standpoint. In New York, Schenectady is the only county with an A grade (Fig. 7–3). It is surrounded by two smaller B counties, Montgomery and Fulton, and a number of other fairly productive ones in the upper Hudson and Mohawk Valley region. Union County is the New Jersey leader and also ranks as the highest producing suburban county in the United States. It sent forth 38 players for a per capita rating of 3.20. The leading towns included Union, Elizabeth, Cranford, and Plainfield. Other major New Jersey producers include Bergen, Hudson, and Somerset counties, all at the B level.

Pennsylvania players tend to come from either the Philadelphia or Pittsburgh areas. The former region focuses on the city proper and the ring of suburbs to the west that are contained in the B counties of Delaware and Montgomery. Camden, New Jersey, which is a part of Philadelphia metropolitan area is also a major contributor. The Pittsburgh region is located in the midst of a high-producing, three-state, thirteen-county section with an overall A rating (not including Allegheny County itself). This is the same area that was identified as an intense football region. The most outstanding counties include Hancock, Ohio and Brooke, West Virginia along with Columbia and Stark, Ohio and Armstrong, Beaver, and Washington in Pennsylvania. Mercer county, to the north of this region, is the only one in Pennsylvania with an A rating.

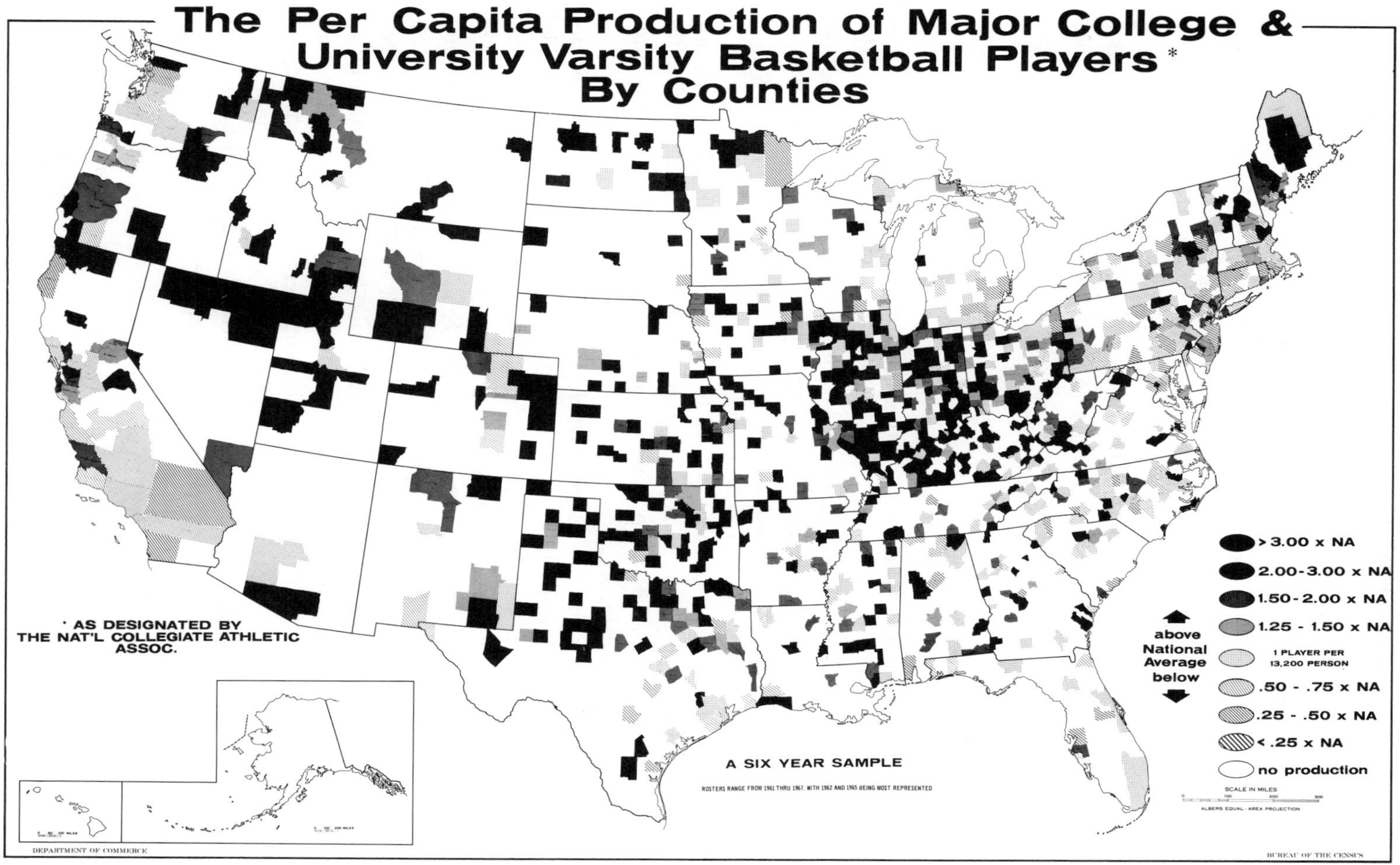

The Per Capita Production of Major College & University Varsity Basketball Players* By Counties

* AS DESIGNATED BY THE NAT'L COLLEGIATE ATHLETIC ASSOC.

A SIX YEAR SAMPLE

ROSTERS RANGE FROM 1967 THRU 1967 WITH 1962 AND 1965 BEING MOST REPRESENTED

> 3.00 x NA
2.00 - 3.00 x NA
1.50 - 2.00 x NA
1.25 - 1.50 x NA
1 PLAYER PER 13,200 PERSON
.50 - .75 x NA
.25 - .50 x NA
< .25 x NA
no production

above National Average below

SCALE IN MILES

ALBERS EQUAL AREA PROJECTION

DEPARTMENT OF COMMERCE

BUREAU OF THE CENSUS

Figure 7.3

CALIFORNIA

The California output is not excessive, relative to its large population. Only two of the state's smallest counties rank at the A level. Little Siskiyou county on the Oregon border is particularly impressive, having turned out players at a pace nearly seven times the national average. Relative to its population, the San Francisco Bay area (B) has been more successful than Los Angeles. San Francisco, Oakland, El Cerrito, and Richmond are making nearly equal contributions.

ILLINKY

The region encompassing Illinois, Indiana, Kentucky (IllInKy), and spilling over into several adjacent states is truly phenomenal as a player source region. Unlike other areas where output is scattered and inconsistent, the majority of counties are providing some basketball talent, and many of them merit A ratings. Small-town basketball, with the fan loyalties and hysteria that accompany it, finds its greatest expression here. The analogy with Texas football is inescapable.

Of the nation's 346 A counties, forty are in Kentucky, thirty-four in Illinois, and thirty-two in Indiana. Most of the IllInKy counties have meager populations and contain settlements of less than 10,000, but far from all of the productive communities are in the village and small town category.

The metropolitan zones which dot the countryside are also contributing substantially more players per capita than their nationwide counterparts. Only fourteen of the largest 200 United States metropolitan areas can claim an A production rating, and eleven of them are located here. The stalwart is Louisville, Kentucky which has the most impressive per capita rating of the major American cities (2.81). Jefferson, the central county, has performed at a pace more than three times above the United States norm (Table 7-2). Several other Ohio River cities are equally impressive. Evansville ranks even higher than Louisville, and Wheeling and Huntington, West Virginia, Ashland, Kentucky, and Cincinnati and Dayton, Ohio are also outstanding sources. The Ohio River counties that stretch from Parkersburg, West Virginia, to Aliquippa, Pennsylvania, comprise an area with an overall A rating (Fig. 7-2).

It is probably more than coincidence that two of the nation's long-time college basketball giants (Louisville and Cincinnati) are located on the Ohio River and that many other perennial powers, beginning with the University of Kentucky, are in the immediate vicinity.

TABLE 7-2
COUNTIES WHICH RANK VERY HIGH ON BOTH A PER CAPITA AND TOTAL
OUTPUT BASIS

County	State	Major City	Number of players	Per capita efficiency rating (average=1.00)
Pima	Arizona	Tucson	17	2.70
Dupage	Illinois	Elmhurst	22	2.98
Kane	Illinois	Aurora–Elgin	13	3.35
Kankakee	Illinois	Kankakee	6	2.85
Marion	Illinois	Salem	6	6.50
Perry	Illinois	Pinckneyville	7	17.10
Rock Island	Illinois	Rock Island–Moline	17	4.50
Allen	Indiana	Ft. Wayne	16	2.65
Delaware	Indiana	Muncie	18	3.12
Elkhart	Indiana	Elkhart	8	3.64
Henry	Indiana	New Castle	9	6.12
Madison	Indiana	Anderson	8	2.73
Porter	Indiana	Portage	8	4.24
Tippecanoe	Indiana	Lafayette	6	2.91
Vandeburgh	Indiana	Evansville	14	3.64
Vigo	Indiana	Terre Haute	8	3.10
Wyandotte	Kansas	Kansas City	11	2.53
Boyd	Kentucky	Ashland	9	7.32
Fayette	Kentucky	Lexington	9	2.91
Floyd	Kentucky	Prestonburg	8	8.24
Hopkins	Kentucky	Madisonville	6	6.60
Jefferson	Kentucky	Louisville	44	3.09
Kenton	Kentucky	Covington	8	2.78
Marshall	Kentucky	Benton	6	15.17
Penobscot	Maine	Bangor	8	2.69
Union	New Jersey	Elizabeth, Plainfield	38	3.22
Schenectady	New York	Schenectady	12	3.33
Cass	North Dakota	Fargo	9	5.74
Allen	Ohio	Lima	7	2.93
Belmont	Ohio	Martins Ferry	8	4.07
Greene	Ohio	Xenia	6	2.70
Washita	Oklahoma	Cordell City	7	17.03
Mercer	Pennsylvania	Sharon, Forrell	9	2.99
Davis	Utah	Bountiful, Layton	8	5.31
Clark	Washington	Vancouver	10	4.62
Cabell	West Virginia	Huntington	10	3.88

Kentucky Wesleyan at Owensboro and Kentucky State at Frankfort
have dominated NCAA college division and NAIA tournament play in
recent years. Evansville, the school that helped to put small college
basketball on the map, is also in the "Valley." Recruiters from these
and nearby colleges need seldom travel far to staff their teams, but
they are facing increasingly heavy competition from adjacent states for
the region's huge supply of players (see Chapter 10).

In upstate Indiana, the cities of Fort Wayne, Gary–Hammond,
Terre Haute, and Muncie are also grade A sources. The other Hoosier
metropolitan areas, Indianapolis and South Bend, provide a massive
number of players and merit B ratings. Additional A centers in IllInKy
include Rock Island–Moline, Illinois, and Lexington, Kentucky. A
national examination of counties which rank high on both total output and per capita counts serves to confirm IllInKy supremacy (Table
7–2). Over 73 percent of these counties are in the region.

Although the metropolitan zones provide many players, the
small towns dominate the area basketball scene. There are literally
hundreds of donors to the university coffers. In spite of their numbers, it is possible to identify six regions which substantially exceed
the IllInKy average. In some cases, the areas are separated only by a
few counties, but each seems sufficiently different to warrant individual consideration. Moving from east to west, they include the Miami
Valley of western Ohio, the Hatfield–McCoy territory of eastern Kentucky and southern West Virginia, the western Kentucky horseshoe,
central Indiana, north central Illinois, and southern Illinois (Fig. 7–3).

1. The Western Ohio (Miami Valley) Region

This district is composed of ten counties. It sent forth sixty-two players for a 2.58 per capita rating, compared to 1.33 for the state of Ohio.
High productivity extends from north of Lima and includes the small
towns of Sydney, Piqua, and Eaton. It focuses on the Dayton metropolitan zone and also encompasses the eastern suburban fringe including such places as Xenia, Franklin, and Wilmington. The entire
complex is probably an eastern extension of the central Indiana zone.
This region is more industrialized and better off economically than most
of IllInKy.

2. Appalachia (The Hatfield–McCoy Territory)

Appalachia contains only fifteen counties which produced thirty-five
players at a 3.00 per capita rating. It is an amorphus territory centering on Bluefield and Beckley in West Virginia and characterized by

some of the most extreme rural poverty in the United States. Such places as Oakhill and Mullens, West Virginia and Jenkins (which lost over half its population between 1950 and 1960) and Prestonburg, Kentucky are representative. Kentucky's Floyd County was the source of eight players, which amounts to a per capita performance of over ten times the national norm. Although the basketball facilities befit the area's economic state, fan interest and support is not lacking. Many of the area schools do not field football teams, a fact which has helped to make basketball the focus of community attention.

3. Western Kentucky–Southern Indiana

Focusing on Evansville, this region includes twenty-seven counties that accounted for sixty-five players and a 3.80 per capita rating. It is a typical small-town basketball area encompassing a horseshoelike zone in western Kentucky and southern Indiana. The principal donors are Glasgow, Bowling Green, and Madisonville in Kentucky and Evansville, Jasper, Huntingburg, Loogootee, and Paoli, Indiana. This contiguous group of counties has the highest per capita ranking in the United States, and continues to succeed in spite of widespread school consolidation efforts.

4. Central Indiana

The central Indiana region comprises thirty-four counties which produced 121 players, for a rating of 3.10. The Hoosier basketball area extends northwest from Louisville, Kentucky almost to Gary and contains a large proportion of Indiana's medium-sized cities. Previously cited Muncie, Anderson, and Lafayette, as well as smaller Columbus, Newcastle, Seymour, and Peru have all made significant contributions. Henry County (New Castle) and even smaller Dearborn (Aurora and Greendale) are averaging in excess of six times the national rate. This section of Indiana is characterized by sectors of strong agricultural production, considerable industrialization, and above-average incomes. It is in marked contrast to Appalachia and western Kentucky–southern Indiana.

5. North Central Illinois

This is an expansive territory composed of twenty-eight counties, which sent forth 130 players. Its 2.90 rating is nearly double the Illinois average of 1.51. The region actually extends into southwestern Michigan, bisecting the Gary-Hammond metropolitan area and spreading out across central Illinois, including four counties in east-

ern Iowa. Urbanization is more characteristic here than in any of
the other five identifiable districts. A high proportion of the players
come from the industrialized suburban fringe of Chicago which bor-
ders the southern end of Lake Michigan. The medium-sized industrial
centers of Illinois also make large contributions. The most significant cities include St. Joseph and Benton Harbor, Michigan, Gary–
Hammond, Michigan City, Portage, and LaPorte, Indiana. The Illinois stand-outs are Kankakee, Ottawa, Rock Falls, Sterling, Peoria,
Pekin, Rock Island, Moline, Bloomington, and Quincy. Rock Island–
Moline, is the premier source with a per capita rating exceeding
five times the national average.

6. *Southern Illinois*

Southern Illinois contains thirty-one counties that accounted for
ninety players. It has a per capita rating of 3.40, which is well over
twice the Illinois level. The area includes much of the Illinois mining
region, and the economy has been in a state of labor decline for many
years. It also encompasses a section of marginal farming land, the Illinois suburbs of St. Louis, and a few counties in southern Indiana
and Kentucky. There is a strong resemblence to the western Kentucky
region, and from a socioeconomic standpoint, they could almost be
included together.

The nine-county mining district of southern Illinois, centering
on West Frankfort, Harrisburg, Benton, Pinckneyville, Herrin, Carbondale, Mount Vernon, and Centralia, was responsible for one-third of
the total output, at a per capita rate of *six* times the national norm.
Heavily industrialized East St. Louis, Alton, and Granite City were
major sources also but at substantially lower per capita levels. Marshall
County, Kentucky (county seat Benton) provided six players and had
a production rating of 15 times that which its population of 16,000
would suggest.

TOWARD EXPLANATION

The majority of these small communities have a great deal in common.
Therefore comments about one should have some application to most
of them. By federal standards, Perry County, in the heart of the
southern Illinois mining district, is economically sick. It has a median
family income 30 percent below that of the rest of the United States,
and nearly one-third of its breadwinners earn less than $3000. Almost

half of the county's housing is classed as unsound, and since 1940, people have been leaving the county at a rate of nearly 2 percent per year.

Where basketball is concerned, Perry is far from ill. The county can claim the most impressive per capita record in the nation. During the period of the study, its two major communities, Pinckneyville and Du Quoin (the site of the annual Hambiltonian Harness Racing Events) were the source of seven players, seventeen times the number expected from a county population of 19,000. In fact, just one player every twelve years would have been sufficient to fulfill the county quota.

Through the years, Pinckneyville has been the dominant basketball partner. Most of its success has come under the tutelage of a man called Duster Thomas, who was the high school coach for nearly 35 years. His teams have made numerous trips to the Illinois state tournament, a feat that can be accomplished only after head-to-head competition with many larger high schools, since until 1970, Illinois, like Indiana, conducted a state elimination tournament in which each of the schools, regardless of enrollment, competed for a single title. The dream goal of beating the state's best teams, some with very large student bodies, has provided a great incentive for the small entries. In 1952, the Illinois title went to Hebron, a tiny northern community with only 95 high school students. Cobden, a very small town between Carbondale and Cairo, advanced to the final game in 1964, only to be beaten by a team from the much larger community of Pekin.

The geography of present-day player production is undoubtedly related to a basketball tradition which has evolved over a long period of time. By looking at the Indiana State High School Tournament from its inception in 1911, we can get another measure of the geographical differences in basketball ability, emphasis, and hysteria.

Indiana State Tournament competition is organized to enable over 600 schools to play for one of 64 sectional titles, against teams in their immediate vicinity. The 64 winners are divided into 16 regional groups. The regional champions are then dubbed as the state's "sweet sixteen." After semi-State competition, four teams square off for the state title.

We have examined the "sweet sixteen" teams from 1911 to 1973 to determine the effect team success, particularly long-term success, has on the generation of college-bound players (Fig. 7–4). As expected there is a strong relationship between the two. For example the metropolitan areas which were the most prolific suppliers of basketball

APPEARANCES IN INDIANA SWEET SIXTEEN

HIGH SCHOOL BASKETBALL TOURNAMENT

1911 - 1972

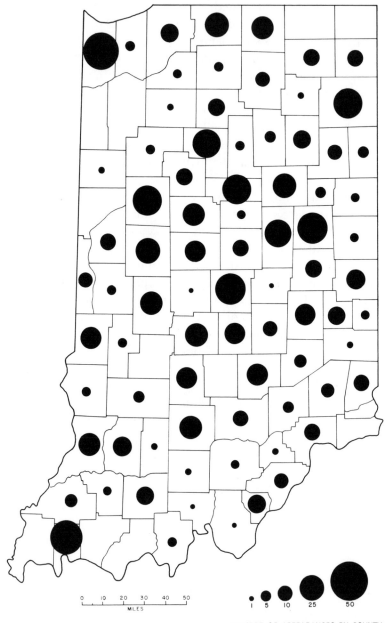

NUMBER OF APPEARANCES BY COUNTY

Figure 7.4

Marion Crawley with two young dribblers at the Don Odle-Taylor University basketball camp. (Photo courtesy of Taylor University.)

talent frequently made it to the "sweet sixteen." Evansville, Gary, Muncie, Kokomo, Fort Wayne, Lafayette, and Indianapolis qualified with the greatest regularity.

The most successful high school from a state-title standpoint has been Muncie Central with five championships. Lafayette Jefferson, which has claimed four, is not far behind. Muncie was the scene of a school-splitting struggle which lasted for more than a decade. The basketball forces in the community prevented Muncie Central from being divided into three high schools, essentially on the argument that the division would greatly reduce the city's chances of winning the state title. Thus the total educational program was sacrificed for the sake of basketball excellence.

The extreme community pressure to win and go to the state tournament is conducive to the production of great players, just as its absence is likely to produce a mediocre bunch. This can be seen in counties like Newton, Jasper, Brown, and Owen which have never sent a team to the "sweet sixteen." The same counties failed to produce either a major or small college player during the last ten years.

Indiana high school basketball has, like that of Illinois, spawned its share of heroes who serve to maintain a high level of interest in the game. Perhaps the most famous is Marion Crawley, who is considered by most to be the Dean of the Indiana high school game. Operating in the shadow of Purdue University, Crawley has guided his Lafayette Jefferson team to four state titles, 23 consecutive sectional tournament crowns, and 21 regional titles. His clubs have reached state finals on 13 occasions, not to mention his 734 career wins. Crawley like many other coaches in the state and region has used his basketball success to good advantage in a number of business ventures.

Another product of the intense interest that Hoosiers have in the game is the boy's basketball summer camp. The czar of this business is Don Odle, basketball coach and athletic director of Taylor University, located in Upland. Odle has promoted the game and improved the quality of play by attracting thousands of boys to his camps over the past twenty years. He could do this only because parents were willing to invest their money to improve their son's basketball. To have a good player in the family is so important that parents have sent Odle many more "young dribblers" than he could possibly handle. His success has prompted many others to organize similar camps in the Illinky region and throughout the United States.

Boys throughout Illinky are indoctrinated early to the fine points of the game. Those with potential are playing organized basketball in the fourth grade. They don't just play a "run and shoot" game but are carefully tutored in the system that prevails in the local high school. The coaching of the district elementary students is closely coordinated, so that by the time the lads reach high school they have been playing the accepted style of ball for as long as six years. With this kind of experience, accompanied by encouragement, and even pressure in the home, it is little wonder that successful teams evolve.

What then is responsible for the concentration of so much ability in small places like these? It can be confidently stated that basketball has become a community focus for many people, perhaps even a way of life. And like football in Texas or Ohio, the point where community pride, and not just a game is at stake, is often reached. It would seem that the degree of interest which people have in the sport has been the result of a long-term and increasingly intense exposure. Excellent teams and players create more interest and excitement and produce local heroes with whom the town can identify. Eventually a group of fans develop loyalties strong enough to persist through adversity. This group struggles with the coach and squad in the "building" years and celebrates their success when the fruit has been harvested. Gathering places and watering spots around the community are the scenes of discussions concerning the fortunes of the team during the off-season. One Indiana high school coach put it this way in trying to explain why basketball was so important, and of such high quality in his southern Indiana region:

> The majority of our basketball players live on farms or in small communities. Just about every one of our boys (varsity down to 5th and 6th grade) has some type of basketball goal on his barn, garage, etc. These boys, and especially those in grades 10, 11, and 12, play basketball *every day* of the year. Maybe ten minutes a day, or maybe a couple of hours. They seem to thrive on playing basketball. Therefore, our coaching staff does very little prodding of them to practice some basketball in the summer months; instead it seems to be a natural instinct for them.[1]

Illinky basketball appears to thrive best in small-town environments, where incomes and education levels are relatively low, and where the sport may very well be viewed as a social necessity. This profile fits Perry and the majority of its neighbors in southern Illinois, Indiana, Kentucky, and West Virginia. It is in these areas that high school basketball reigns supreme as the winter entertainment attraction, perhaps because there has been little else from which to choose. The development of major college powers in this region such as Kentucky, Louisville, Southern Illinois, Indiana, West Virginia, Cincinnati, Western Kentucky, and others has only added to the excitement.

Good coaches and intense community spirit have produced good teams and outstanding individual players. This in turn has created a massive supply of athletes wanting to be coaches, many of them returning to the home area after college. Gradually a few good teams have expanded geometrically, and more and more players are available to college recruiters. Thus the cycle is continuous and "social emphasis" tends to diffuse outward from the original stimulus, whether it is a Duster Thomas, a great individual player, or a new university on its way up the ladder of basketball success.

The extent of community support in Indiana is summarized in Table 7–3. Indiana, Illinois, and Kentucky have long emphasized

TABLE 7-3
COMMUNITY SUPPORT FOR INDIANA BASKETBALL—1970-1971*

Selected cities	High school enrollment	Percent of males out for basketball	Seating capacity, percent of city population		Attendance, percent of city population	
			Football	Basketball	Football	Basketball
Veedersburg	550	5.5	75	140	60	136
Paoli	495	5.1	22	80	18	72
Aurora	600	4.2	30	25	22	32
Mt. Vernon	975	2.5	10	32	9	30
Green Castle	750–	4.0	8	28	6	25
Washington	1000	2.5	8	37	10	36
Shelbyville	1300	2.3	8	33	6	31
Valparaiso	1145	1.3	17	13	14	12
Kokomo	1800	2.4	5	10	6	9
Columbus	2500	3.2	5	16	6	15

*This information is based on a questionaire which was processed in May, 1971.

basketball to the detriment of their football programs.[2] Most of
the communities have fieldhouses with capacities which substantially
exceed their outdoor facilities. In many cases, the gymnasiums are
larger than the schools and serve as centers for community activities

THE ROLE OF PARTICIPATION

As is the case for football, per capita participation in high school basketball is not a grood indicator of collegiate player production (compare Figs. 4-3 and 7-2). The highest rates of participation are in
Nebraska, the Dakotas, Montana, Minnesota, and Wyoming. Of these,
only North Dakota is a high producer of college players, and South
Dakota, Nebraska, and Minnesota are significantly below normal.

The production heartland surrounding the Ohio Valley records
slightly higher-than-normal participation. This results primarily because only the best prospects are encouraged to play basketball. The
most promising candidates are singled out early, usually at age ten or
eleven, and are groomed from then on. Thus even with over 750 Illinois schools and 640 Indiana schools playing the game, per capita
participation remains relatively low.

Much of the South has both low participation and production.
In recent years, though, participation has increased, probably in response to greater emphasis on the college game.

The character of the city game is aptly demonstrated by the
situation in New York and New Jersey. The production rate in New
Jersey is 1.37 as opposed to a participation rate of only .77. New
York is producing at a .90 rate with participation of only .36. Many
quality players have emerged from both states during the last decade,
and a large portion have been recruited away from the Northeast. It
is apparent that only the best boys are playing high school basketball,
particularly in the metropolitan areas. With very large schools and
only one varsity team, the competition is extreme. But among the
few who play, the degree of success is very high.

According to Axthelm,

> Basketball is the city game. Its battlegrounds are strips of as-
> phalt between tattered wire fences or crumbling buildings; its
> rhythms grow from the uneven thump of a ball against hard sur-
> faces. It demands no open space or lush backyards or elaborate
> equipment. It doesn't even require specified numbers of players;
> a one-on-one confrontation in a playground can be as memorable
> as a full-scale organized game. Basketball is the game for young

athletes without cars or allowances—the game whose drama and action are intensified by its confined spaces and chaotic surroundings.

Basketball is more than a sport or diversion in the cities. It is a part, often a major part, of the fabric of life. Kids in small towns—particularly in the Midwest—often become superb basketball players. But they do so by developing accurate shots and precise skills; in the cities, kids simply develop "moves." Other young athletes may learn basketball, but city kids live it.

Basketball has always been something special to the kids of New York's bustling streets. Two decades ago, it fed the dreams of the Irish athletes on famous playgrounds such as the one on 108th Street in Rockaway, Queens. Those playgrounds produced Bob Cousy and Dick McGuire and other superb playmakers and brilliant passers; they also spawned countless athletes who were almost as accomplished but never made it to college and didn't achieve public recognition. On Kingsbridge Road in the Bronx, tough, aggressive Jewish youths grew into defense-minded, set-shooting stars; some led the colleges of the city to national prominence in the 1940's, but still others faded before the public ever learned their names. With money available for cars and sterios and surfboards, the hunger vanished from many white playgrounds, and so did the top-caliber basketball. But the blacks of Harlem and Bedford-Stuyvesant more than filled the void. Some made it to colleges and into the pros, helping to reshape the game with their flamboyant moves. Many more collapsed, victimized by drugs or the lure of the ghetto streets. Still others failed to find a niche in college or the pros, but endured as playground heroes, facing the challenges of the best of each new generation of players, occasionally proving themselves against pro players who return to the parks for summer games.[3]

Axthelm's view of the city game coincides with my remarks about the role of basketball in the towns of IllInKy. The sport has been more of a community focus in the small towns but there are signs that it is developing a similar function in the city ghettos. Neighborhood tournaments and leagues attract large followings to the outdoor playgrounds, and demand for more asphalt spaces, hoops, nets, and lighting facilities continues to grow.

It is difficult to substantiate Axthelm's contention that the city players develop different skills from those developed by the small-town boys. However, it is probable that playground basketball hastens the participants to perfect "moves" and encourages improvision, relative to the more structured environment associated with the small-town gymnasium. The hypothesis could certainly be tested by comparing players who had grown up in the city with those from the small towns.

THE ROLE OF CLIMATE

Another explanation for the concentration of basketball excellence in the mid-section of the country centers on climatic patterns. The basketball heartland has a winter climate, intermediate between the frigid and snowy northland and the rainy, mild South. Snow-cover in the northern states (Minnesota, Wisconsin, and Michigan, northern New York, and New England) is reliable enough to assure a good environment for outdoor sports activity. Skiing and ice hockey are extremely popular. Hockey has recently become a very important interscholastic sport and is in direct seasonal competition with basketball.

Throughout the South, outdoor activity thrives during all seasons of the year. The per capita indices of the southern states decrease as winter temperatures rise. For example, Virginia, Tennessee, and North Carolina are much better producers than Alabama, Louisiana, and South Carolina. North Texas is a much better basketball area than South Texas.

The mid-section of the United States does not possess a climate conducive to sustained outdoor winter sporting activity. Snow cover is inconsistent from year to year, and ice is seldom dependable for more than a few weeks of skating. The weather is bad enough to have driven most people indoors. Hence basketball has been embraced as the major cold-season sport.

OTHER IMPORTANT AREAS

High-caliber play in the Plains States appears to be a westward extension from the heartland source. The intense interest in the former area seems to have leapfrogged over the states of Missouri and Iowa, but their lower-than-average ratings are misleading. Between them they possess a total of 25 A counties and four contiguous sections of counties characterized by higher-than-average production. Each state, however, contains great spaces which are subnormal or totally unproductive. A near-mania for girls' basketball in Iowa and in some parts of Missouri may account in part for the lack of emphasis. Poverty, and the subsequent shortage of athletic funds which goes with it, provides some explanation for poor performance in the Missouri Ozarks.

Oklahoma and Kansas are each among the top ten states in production efficiency. Wichita and Topeka are B level producers, while Oklahoma City and Tulsa rate a high C. There are fifteen A counties in Kansas and sixteen in Oklahoma, including Washita county, which was the home of seven players for a rating of sixteen times the United States norm. Small-town basketball is also very important in northern Texas where most of the states' 26 A counties are located. Interest in the game throughout the Plains region has probably stemmed from the long-term success of the University of Kansas and Oklahoma State University programs. The presence of coaches "Phog" Allen and Henry Iba has had a great influence on high school development in the Great Plains region and on game strategy throughout the country. Emphasis on basketball has also increased tremendously among their "Big Eight" conference rivals and in the football-dominated Southwest conference. A number of the Missouri Valley Conference schools and several major independents are also located in this area.

Most of the sparsely populated western states have provided basketball players at a rate slightly in excess of the national norm. The game has flourished in a number of cities, the most prominent being A level Tucson and Salt Lake City. Portland and Eugene are B sources, while Denver and Phoenix rate a high C. The improvement in the quality of western competition is probably related to the continual migration of basketball enthusiasts from the East and the gradual emergence of quality college teams in the region. Staffing the multitude of teams cannot be accomplished with local players, but high school competition has improved noticeably with better coaching and the "social elevation" of the game.

Utah is undoubtedly the most rabid basketball state in the Mountain West. On a per capita basis, the state is the nation's leading source of college players, nearly all of whom play for one of the state's four major teams, three of which have frequently ranked among the best in the country. The fourth, Weber State, has gained national recognition during the last few years and has advanced to the NCAA Western regionals in 1968, 1969, and 1972. Utah basketball has attained its elevated status by importing from other areas, particularly California. Brigham Young University has gone as far as Yugoslovia in search of quality players. Nonetheless, many of the best players have been of local origin, a high percentage of whom are

Mormons. They have been the beneficiaries of the high priority which the Mormons accord to physical fitness and competitive sports. The production core of Utah encompasses Salt Lake City, Ogden, and the northern rural counties, Box Elder and Cache. It also extends into Mormon-dominated southern Idaho, where Pocatello and Idaho Falls stand out, and into northern Nevada's lightly populated Elko and Humbolt counties.

THE DEFICIT AREAS

Emphasis on basketball decreases drastically to the south of the Kentucky-Illinois core area. Virginia ranks first among states south of the Mason-Dixon line with a production index of 0.78, 22 percent below the national average. The others range from Maryland's 0.25, which is only 11 percent of the Kentucky figure, through 70 percent for Mississippi (Table 7-4). There are, however, several widely scattered regions within the great southern vacuum which may have reached the takeoff stage as far as high school basketball is concerned. In North Carolina, where the high quality of college ball is a major advertising theme of the state's industrial development department, a concerted effort is now under way to improve the high school programs. Raleigh and Durham are B sources and have undoubtedly benefited by their proximity to Duke, Wake Forest, and the University of North Carolina, with interest in the college sport extending gradually to the high school level.

TABLE 7-4
BASKETBALL PRODUCTION IN THE SOUTHERN DEFICIT REGION

State	Number of players	National rank	Per capita rate	National rank
Virginia	72	15	0.78	30
Mississippi	36	28	0.70	33
North Carolina	73	14	0.68	35
Tennessee	54	22	0.64	37
Florida	68	17	0.58	39
Arkansas	24	36	0.57	40
Georgia	52	24	0.56	41
Alabama	40	27	0.52	42
Louisiana	30	32	0.39	46
South Carolina	19	40	0.34	47
Maryland	18	41	0.25	48

Even with marked improvement in the high schools, the vast majority of talent must still be pulled in from Pennsylvania, New Jersey, New York, and the midwestern core area (Chapter 10). In fact, all of the universities in the Atlantic Coast conference recruit the bulk of their players from outside the conference area. South Carolina and Maryland are the worst states in the country, in terms of the per capita supply of players. Maryland does not contain a single county of better than C level, and there are only three of those. Baltimore, with a successful National Basketball Association team, has to be the worst basketball city in the country with not one major college player during the period of the study, from a population of over 900,000. Suburban Baltimore County had only two players, for an F per capita rate of one per 246,000. The entire metropolitan area produced only six players instead of the forty that their population would justify. This is a metropolis with successful major league franchises in three sports, and what appears to be the most under-developed big-city high school athletic program in the United States. It is possible that the emphasis on lacrosse has overshadowed the traditional major sports.

Association with superior college basketball has apparently had little effect in South Carolina. Only the Columbia area can claim even C level production on a scale large enough to mention. Most of the major universities in the Deep South are affiliated with the Southeastern Conference, which has not been noted for its basketball prowess. All this is changing, mostly due to the efforts and accomplishments of one man, Adolph Rupp. By fielding teams at the University of Kentucky which consistently humiliated his conference rivals, Mr. Rupp has served as a geographical diffusion agent, thereby stimulating the development of the game at many of these schools. Perhaps at first from self-defense, but later from genuine interest, the quality of competition in the conference has been strikingly elevated. Mammoth new fieldhouses have replaced or are replacing crackerbox gymnasiums. The ascension of basketball has been most noticeable in Tennessee and Mississippi, but all of the conference members have made tremendous gains.

The improvement has so far been largely underwritten by high schools in the Midwest core, and to some extent in the Northeast, though some progress among the region's high schools is apparent. The production of A level Jackson county (Scottsboro, Bridgeport) and B level Tuscaloosa and Dothan, Alabama are indicative. Mississippi's Hattiesburg area rates an A and Jackson a B+. Above-average

TABLE 7-5
D AND F METROPOLITAN AREAS IN THE SOUTH

SMSA	Population	Number of players	Percent of national average	Letter rating
Birmingham	635,000	1	0.07	F
Mobile	314,000	3	0.41	D
Shreveport	224,000	3	0.45	D
Monroe	102,000	0	—	F
Lafayette	85,000	0	—	F
Nashville	400,000	3	0.32	F
Orlando	319,000	3	0.40	F
New Orleans	907,000	12	0.59	D
Jacksonville	455,000	6	0.56	D
Chattanooga	284,000	3	0.45	D
Augusta	217,000	2	0.39	F
Lake Charles	145,000	2	0.58	D
Albany, Georgia	76,000	0	—	F

output in Georgia and Louisiana is very limited and confined to rural sections. The South's two largest cities, Atlanta and Miami, rate a low C for production intensity. The progress is overshadowed by the presence of numerous laggards, of which Birmingham and Nashville are the worst (Table 7-5).

THE NORTHERN MIDWEST

High school basketball mania also decreases abruptly north of the IllInKy core. Wisconsin (.69), Michigan (.59), and Minnesota (.41) are all the source of substantially fewer athletes than expected on the basis of their population. Wisconsin's poor showing stems from the almost total absence of players from the state's small towns. Madison and Racine are B sources, and Milwakee (C) is contributing its fair share. Michigan's problem seems related to the relatively unproductive programs characteristic of its larger cities. Detroit proper has held its own and merits a low C, but the suburban fringe of Oakland (F) and Macomb (F) counties were the source of only nine players from a population of 1.1 million. Nearby Ann Arbor, Jackson, Flint, and Bay City also rate F. Flint had but one player from a popu-

lation of nearly 400,000. Among the other cities, Lansing and Kala-
mazoo are average sources. The low output in Minnesota is uniform,
including the Minneapolis–St. Paul area (the latter with no production)
and the majority of the small counties. High-calibre small-town basketball is confined to the northernmost section and a small area in
the southwest.

The decline in the quality of small-town basketball northwest
from IllInKy is best explained by the climate hypothesis. Basketball
must contend with many more diversions in the north. When autumn
recedes throughout the nation, most high schools (virtually all the
small ones) turn their attentions to the hardwood. Hockey now
challenges the supremacy of basketball in the Northeast, Midwest and
in New England, and the reliable winter snow cover provides for
many other recreational opportunities. Wrestling is also growing in
popularity. To invert the argument, the small IllInky schools have
had little else to catch their interest, and hence, the position of basketball has constantly been enhanced.

Southern New England is very similar to the northern Midwest.
Basketball output is low except in Boston and Worcester. Hartford
(F), Providence (F), Bridgeport (D), and New Haven (D) rank far below average. Hockey is very popular, and skiing is readily available
throughout the region.

NOTES

1. From a letter written by Al Harden, head basketball coach at Fountain
    Central High School, Veedersburg, Indiana, May, 1970.

2. Based on a questionnaire sent to a large sample of high school basketball
    coaches in a selection of high- and low-producing states during 1970.

3. Peter Axthelm, *The City Game* (New York: Harper & Row, 1970), pp. 1–3.

8 / Baseball: Where They Come From

Baseball has claimed the title of "America's national pastime" for many years. Like basketball, it is a game which was developed and perfected in the United States, and like football, it has roots in England. It is a game which never became firmly established in collegiate circles. Therefore, it has been played by professionals from its infancy. Baseball is a summer sport, and until recently, summer provided *much* more leisure time than other seasons of the year. Partially for this reason, baseball quickly rose to a place of supremacy on the national sporting scene, though the fact that it predated football and basketball has undoubtedly had some effect. Baseball scholars delight in pointing out its scientific and statistical nature. By comparison to the other major American sports, its pace is slow and relaxed, with hitting and running action confined to only a small percentage of the time devoted to playing the game and to a small space on the playing field. Because baseball is not as strenuous as many other sports, there are significantly more games played in a single season. In addition, much emphasis has been placed on record keeping. Only over the long pull can a player demonstrate his true worth. Thus, batting averages, home runs, runs batted in, stolen bases, assists, pitching victories, and other statistics have taken on far greater significance for baseball and the baseball fan. Immortals like Babe Ruth, Joe Dimaggio, Lou Gerhig, Walter Johnson, Roger Hornsby, and Cy Young established records over long competitive careers which serve as standards for today's players. They are remembered most for their seasonal and career performances and not so much for single-game feats. This aptly demonstrates the sanctity of the baseball record-keeping system.

THE ORIGIN OF PLAYERS

Baseball talent is spatially concentrated to a greater extent than is the case for football and basketball. The degree of concentration is such that only a few cities and states are significant contributors to the major league clubs. Since the professional baseball sample is small when contrasted to the collegiate football and basketball samples, meaningful generalizations are only possible at the state, regional, and metropolitan scale.

REGIONAL AND STATE PRODUCTION

On a total output basis, there is a strong correlation between population and the production of baseball talent (Fig. 8-1). California, the leading state, is in a class by itself and accounts for over 17 percent of the current player crop (Table 8-1). Another major concentration comes from the northeastern industrial region, including the states of Massachusetts, New York, New Jersey, Pennsylvania, Ohio, and Illinois, representing nearly 29 percent of the national total. A region consisting of Missouri, Oklahoma, and Texas provided another 12 percent, while the Deep South, particularly North Carolina, Alabama, Florida, and Louisiana sent forth the bulk of the remainder (13 percent).

Production can be regionalized to an even greater extent from a per capita standpoint (Fig. 8-2). California is the leading state with a per capita index of 1.97. The California output is not confined to any section of the state. Los Angeles, San Diego, San Francisco, Sacramento, and Fresno are all producing in excess of twice the national average (Table 8-2). Adjacent Nevada and Idaho are also high per capita producers. However, the impact of the "Sun Belt" ends abruptly in Arizona, New Mexico, and Utah, a curious occurrence since these states are known for their outstanding collegiate programs.

Another leading baseball region includes Oklahoma, Missouri, and Arkansas. Oklahoma is very close to California in per capita output. Missouri, particularly the St. Louis area, has traditionally been a baseball stronghold and a principal source of professional players. The South as a region is not uniformly strong. Alabama, North Carolina, and Louisiana are prolific suppliers, while Georgia and Tennessee are significantly below the national average.

The Origin of Major League Baseball Players*

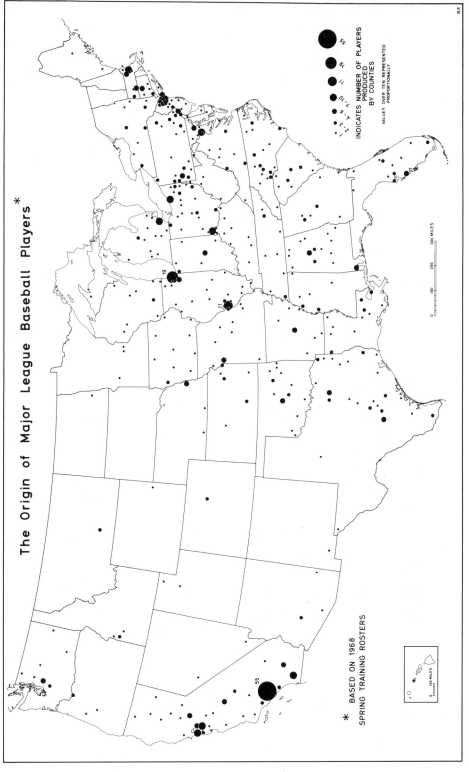

INDICATES NUMBER OF PLAYERS
PRODUCED
BY COUNTIES

VALUES OVER TEN REPRESENTED
PROPORTIONALLY

55
19
11
7-10
4-6
2-3
1

0   100   200   300 MILES

* BASED ON 1968
SPRING TRAINING ROSTERS

0   100 MILES

Figure 8.1

TABLE 8-1
THE ORIGIN AND PER CAPITA PRODUCTION OF MAJOR LEAGUE BASEBALL PLAYERS

State	Number of players	Per capita index	State	Number of players	Per capita index
Alabama	25	1.91	Mississippi	8	1.03
Arizona	3	0.60	Missouri	26	1.51
Arkansas	10	1.40	Montana	2	0.74
California	124	1.97	Nebraska	7	1.16
Colorado	3	0.43	Nevada	2	1.75
Connecticut	9	0.88	New Jersey	21	0.86
Delaware	2	1.12	New Mexico	1	0.26
District of Columbia	8	2.63	New York	39	0.58
Florida	21	1.06	North Carolina	27	1.47
Georgia	10	0.63	North Dakota	1	0.39
Hawaii	1	0.38	Ohio	41	1.05
Idaho	4	1.50	Oklahoma	18	1.94
Illinois	41	1.02	Oregon	5	0.71
Indiana	11	0.59	Pennsylvania	41	0.91
Iowa	11	1.00	South Carolina	11	1.16
Kansas	9	1.03	Tennessee	11	0.78
Kentucky	10	0.82	Texas	37	0.96
Louisianna	17	1.30	Utah	2	0.56
Maine	2	0.52	Virginia	13	0.72
Maryland	10	0.81	Washington	13	1.14
Massachusetts	23	1.12	West Virginia	4	0.53
Michigan	23	0.74	Wisconsin	11	0.69
Minnesota	3	0.22	Wyoming	1	0.76

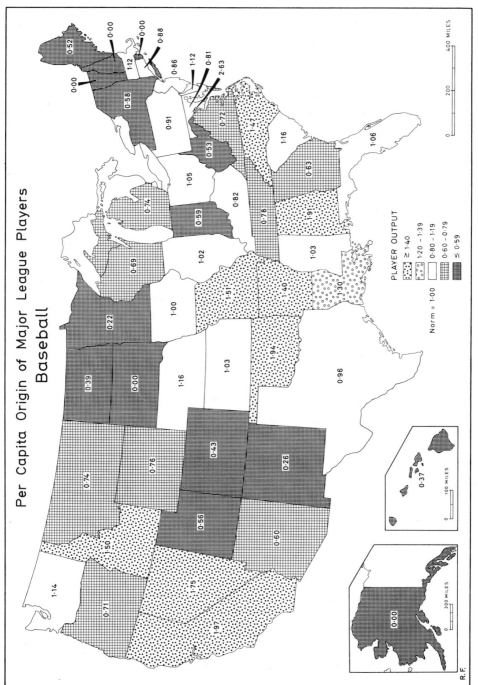

Per Capita Origin of Major League Players
Baseball

PLAYER OUTPUT

≥ 1·40
1·20 – 1·39
0·80 – 1·19
0·60 – 0·79
≤ 0·59

Norm = 1·00

Figure 8.2

TABLE 8–2
LEADING BASEBALL COUNTIES

State	County	Major City	Number of players	Per capita index (Norm=1.00)
Alabama	Mobile	Mobile	6	4.81
Arkansas	Pulaski	Little Rock	4	3.97
California	Fresno	Fresno	5	3.42
	Los Angeles	Los Angeles	55	2.27
	Sacramento	Sacramento	5	2.49
	San Diego	San Diego	9	2.17
	San Francisco	San Francisco	7	2.36
	Alameda	Oakland, Berkeley	7	1.92
	Tulare	Tulare	3	4.47
Connecticut	Hartford	Hartford	4	1.44
District of Columbia	District of Columbia	District of Columbia	8	2.63
Florida	Sarasota	Sarasota	4	13.16
Georgia	Bibb	Macon	3	5.32
Illinois	Cook	Chicago	19	0.93
	Madison	East. St. Louis	3	3.33
	Will	Joliet	4	5.21

State	County	City		
Indiana	Marion	Indianapolis	4	1.43
Louisianna	Caddo	Shreveport	3	3.42
Maryland	Baltimore City	Baltimore	5	1.32
Massachusetts	Hampden	Springfield	4	2.34
	Middlesex	Lexington,Waltham	5	1.02
	Suffolk	Boston	9	2.84
Michigan	Wayne	Detroit	9	0.85
Missouri	St. Louis City	St. Louis	11	3.68
Nebraska	Douglas	Omaha	4	2.90
New York	Kings	Brooklyn	7	0.67
	New York	Manhattan	6	0.88
	Richmond	Richmond	3	3.36
North Carolina	Martin	Williamston	3	27.78
Ohio	Cuyahuga	Cleveland	8	1.21
	Hamilton	Cincinnati	7	2.04
Oklahoma	Oklahoma	Oklahoma City	4	2.27
Pennsylvania	Allegheny	Pittsburgh	6	0.93
	Lancaster	Lancaster	3	2.69
	Lawrence	New Castle	3	6.60
	Philadelphia	Philadelphia	4	0.50
Texas	Bexar	San Antonio	4	1.45
	Dallas	Dallas	4	1.05
Washington	King	Seattle	6	1.60
Wisconsin	Dane	Madison	3	3.36

The deficit states fall into reasonably neat regional patterns. New York and northern New England comprise one of the great northern deficit regions. Despite the unparallelled success of the New York Yankees, the old Giants and Dodgers, and the new Mets, New York has become a very poor source of baseball talent. Low productivity extends westward through Michigan and Wisconsin, reaching a low ebb in Minnesota. The northern Plains are in the same category. Another very poor baseball region consists of Utah, New Mexico, and Arizona. Again in the case of Arizona, it is apparent that proximity to high-quality baseball (the outstanding university programs) does not (or has not yet) stimulate the local growth of athletes. One other scattered deficit area comprises Indiana, West Virginia, states which are surrounded by average to above-average production.

CITY AND COUNTY OUTPUT

Los Angeles is the leading baseball city in the United States (Table 8-2). One out of every fourteen major leaguers was born in the county of Los Angeles, giving it a 2.27 per capita rating. New York, Chicago, and St. Louis are next, in that order, but their combined total does not equal the Los Angeles output. Other important centers include Mobile, San Diego, San Francisco, Washington, D. C., Boston, Cleveland, Cincinnati, Pittsburgh, and Seattle, each accounting for at least six players.

Outstanding cities on a per capita basis are confined primarily to the southern United States. Mobile, Alabama, Little Rock, Arkansas, Sarasota, Florida, and Macon, Georgia are all deserving of special mention, as is tiny Martin County, North Carolina, which recorded a per capita rate of over 27 times the national norm (Table 8-2). Mobile can claim a premier group of black outfielders, which numbers Henry Aaron, Billy Williams, Cleon Jones, and Tommy Agee.

Aside from the southern communities, there are few that had per capita rates in excess of 2.50. Among the larger cities, St. Louis, Boston, and Washington, D. C. were in a class by themselves. The high St. Louis production extended across the Mississippi River to the industrial suburb of East St. Louis. High production was also characteristic of the entire Boston metropolitan area. Elsewhere, Omaha, Nebraska, Joliet, Illinois, Lancaster and New Castle, Pennsylvania, and Madison, Wisconsin are the only cities in this elite group.

CHANGES IN PRODUCTIVITY

Although there is a scarcity of geographic data on football and basketball players, there is a wealth of historical information on the origin of
baseball players. (See Chapter 3.) We have already examined the
spread of baseball from 1876 to 1958, but it seems appropriate to
look at the changes which have occurred since the expansion period.
To do this the 1950 major league rosters were examined. The 1950
sample consisted of 592 players from the spring training rosters of the
16 teams which existed prior to the expansion period. The 1950 pattern was basically similar to the 1970 situation with a few exceptions
(Table 8-3).

TABLE 8-3
CHANGES IN THE PRODUCTION OF PROFESSIONAL BASEBALL PLAYERS
1950, 1970

Rank		Number of players	Rank		Per capita rate
Top Ten total and per capita states in 1950					
1	California	58	1	Missouri	2.12
2	New York	46	2	Alabama	1.80
3	Pennsylvania	46	3	Oklahoma	1.65
4	Illinois	39	4	Rhode Island	1.62
5	Michigan	33	5	North Carolina	1.51
6	Missouri	33	6	Vermont	1.38
7	North Carolina	24	7	Idaho	1.32
8	Ohio	23	8	West Virginia	1.30
9	Alabama	21	9	Arkansas	1.27
10	Texas	20	10	Michigan	1.25
Top Ten total and per capita states in 1970					
1	California	124	1	California	1.97
2	Pennsylvania	41	2	Oklahoma	1.94
2	Illinois	41	3	Alabama	1.91
2	Ohio	41	4	Nevada	1.75
5	New York	39	5	Missouri	1.51
6	Texas	37	6	Idaho	1.50
7	North Carolina	27	7	North Carolina	1.47
8	Missouri	26	8	Arkansas	1.40
9	Alabama	25	9	Louisiana	1.30
10	Massachusetts	23	10	Nebraska	1.16
10	Michigan	23			

The West has recorded the biggest gains in terms of relative per capita production increases over the past twenty years. California is a much more important baseball state now, as is Texas and the Rocky Mountain region. In the South, Florida, Mississippi, and Louisiana have dramatically increased their contributions to the major leagues. On the other hand, Georgia, Tennessee, Kentucky, Virginia, and Missouri are relatively less important today. The importance of Pennsylvania, West Virginia, New York, and Michigan has declined significantly. Former dependence on the Northeast has shifted to the South and Far West, accompanying the spread of the game in those directions. The emergence of the black ballplayer during this period has also served to increase the productivity of states like Mississippi, Florida, and Alabama, and the District of Columbia. Baseball is finally becoming a "national" game.

TOWARD EXPLANATION

To conclude that there is a relationship between baseball player origin and climate is difficult to avoid. Today virtually all of the leading states possess a warm climate, allowing outdoor activity throughout most of the year. Conversely the long-winter states, with the exception of Massachusetts, are well below the national average for baseball player production. In the early days, in fact up through 1940, climate was far less important as evidenced by the high production in the Northeast. However, as the game spread and all people were given an opportunity to qualify for the big leagues, the comparative advantage of the warm weather states became apparent. Thus we can see that the role of the natural environment is constantly changing, and is dependent on a number of other factors (Fig. 8–3).

High school participation in baseball bears little relationship to the output of professional players. As discussed in Chapter 4, per capita participation in high school baseball does not exhibit the pronounced regional pattern characteristic of football and basketball (see Fig. 4-4). New Hampshire, Vermont, Ohio, and Minnesota are the only states with as much as twice the normal participation. The Midwest is a region of above-average participation, as is the Southwest and the Pacific Coast. The South and the Atlantic Coast states with their high output of major leaguers are uniformly low when it comes to high school participation.

It is obvious that the high-participation states are not the best producers of major league players. In fact, New Hampshire and Ver-

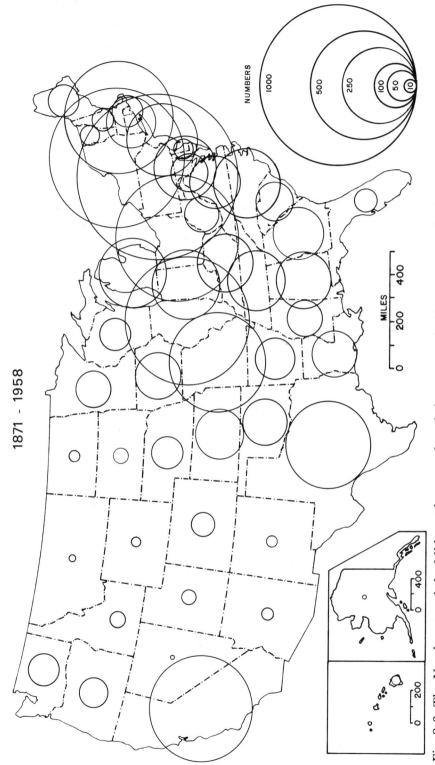

THE ORIGIN OF MAJOR LEAGUE BASEBALL PLAYERS

1871 - 1958

NUMBERS

1000
500
250
100
50
10

MILES
0   200   400

0   200

0   400

Fig. 8.3 The Northeast and the Midwest have produced the most major leaguers over the long run, but in recent years the climatic advantages of California and the South have come to the fore.

mont have sent forth none of the present crop. And there are only two Minnesotans currently playing in the major leagues. Oklahoma is the only state that ranks high in both per capita participation and the development of major leaguers. High school emphasis in the South apparently suffers from the conflict with spring football practice, a conflict which is not so common in other areas.

In most places, baseball is not as important a high school sport as football or basketball. The high school game is frequently subservient to other forms of competitive organization, such as American Legion, Babe Ruth, Pony, and similar types of summer leagues. The great concentration on Little League programs, typical of most American communities, has taken its toll on the players in the advanced group (13 to 18). In general, the facilities, publicity, and attendance deteriorate after Little League. Hence, older players are faced with a less stimulating baseball environment. For this and the other reasons referred to above, per capita participation in high school baseball is probably a poor indicator of the community support situation.

Tradition must also be an important variable where baseball excellence is concerned. There is no other reasonable explanation for such bastions of the game as St. Louis, Boston, and Washington, D. C. Each of these cities was a baseball pioneer, and the game's strength has been maintained despite the inherent disadvantages which face the big city athlete. (See Chapter 3.)

9 / The Recruiting Game: Football

The recruitment of collegiate athletes from high schools and junior colleges throughout the United States can be portrayed as a spatial model. It involves the spatial arrangement of athletic production and consumption, individual spatial decision-making on the part of the athletes and the recruiters, and group decision-making on the part of university officials, governing boards, and the general populace. The pattern of recruiting has been greatly influenced in recent years, particularly since 1950, by the strong desire of geographically remote universities to gain national exposure through the medium of athletics. As a result, numerous recruiting forces (in this case, geographical points) have been added and have served to make the "recruiting game" a much more spatially complex phenomena.

A spatial model of recruiting can be set up as follows. One major element of the model involves the geography of production. It has been demonstrated that athletic production varies considerably from place to place. Some areas are producing many more athletes than others. This is due to a discontinuous distribution of population, great spatial variation in the emphasis placed on different sports, variation in social-economic character, climatic variations, and so on. Thus recruiters are confronted with identifying the locations of collegiate prospects, selecting those people on which to concentrate, and luring them to the desired playing location, a place that in most instances is removed from the athlete's home location. The second important element of the model involves the spatial arrangement of playing opportunities, or the points of consumption. This might best be referred to as the *market*. The market has even less resemblance than the production function to the distribution of population (Tables 4-2 and 4-3).

To further complicate the model, there is a hierarchy of markets for the potential athletes. The so called "big time" schools constitute one segment of the market and should realistically be divided into at least two groups. These can be based on athletic budgets which are highly correlated with the successful pursuit of national honors. In addition to the big time market, there exists the scholarship-subsidized state college group, the small state colleges, and a wide range of private institutions. Most of these are operating on a very limited athletic budget. The effect of the distance between the production regions and the market varies considerably at different levels within the hierarchy. The really big name universities are much better at overcoming the friction of distance than are the small state colleges. Thus the highly financed schools have the potential to recruit from all the lucrative production regions, while the small state and private colleges are usually confined to their immediate locales.

Hence the recruiting pattern of a single university or regional grouping of universities should reflect their location relative to the location of available athletes. If they are situated within or near a region of high productivity, most of their recruiting should be local; if not, it should be spatially linked with the closest source region or regions.

A spatial model of athletic recruiting cannot stop with the analysis of production and consumption fields. For many athletes, it is no longer a direct move between their high school site and the site of the college which they select. A growing number are making an intermediate stop at a junior college. Many of these two-year schools now serve as "farm clubs" to the major universities. Junior college locations then must also be considered in any realistic model because they provide intervening opportunities within the consumption field.

Other variables which demand inclusion are the geographical experiences of recruiters and coaches, the distribution and interest of alumni, and the strength of the attachment that athletes from various sections of the country have for their local area. The geography of recruiting at any given college will reflect the geographical experience of its coaches and the strength of their contacts with other areas. For example the recruitment of Michigan or Illinois boys to a given university, as opposed to New Jersey or California athletes, may simply mean that the coaches have more experience and influence in the former states. Recruiters also possess a given set of perceptions in regard to where the best athletes come from. These perceptions are related to their own place experience and, to some extent, reflect their place pride. A recruiter who is strongly attached to his state or culture region will seldom leave that region for recruitment purposes. In the same vein, an athlete who is strongly attached to his area will be reluctant to select a school outside his perceived cultural region.

Alumni play a large (but difficult to measure) role in the recruitment game. They donate funds which enable the university to overcome the impediments created by distance. Their distribution is also a significant factor. A dispersed group is likely to be more effective than one which is located almost exclusively within the home region. The Notre Dame and the Armed Forces Academy alumni have access to the chief production fields. The Notre Dame radio network reaches all sections of the United States and has wielded a great impact through the years. It provides an excellent example of alumni influence.

The model must also take into account the athletes themselves. For after all, it is they who make the spatial decisions which transfer them from the production to the consumption fields. Each athlete is influenced by the extent and nature of local playing opportunities and his own degree of place pride or identification. His decision is affected by many things over which he has little or no control; the distribution of various alumni, recruiters, his own perceptions, and those of his family and friends. The net result is a spatially complex, yet reasonably predictable, athletic migration pattern.

FOOTBALL RECRUITING

Every college football expert knows that a successful program is dependent on the superior recruiting of both players and coaches. Good recruiting, in most instances, results in good teams, which are proliferated through time. The collegiate recruiting game is frenzied and in recent years, the bidding for the best athletes has become very intense. For after all, there is very much at stake. In this era of scholarship-subsidized athletics, the name of the game is winning. Sadly, many of the old grads' purse strings are more easily loosened by his school's gridiron accomplishments than by its academic achievements. In addition with spiraling athletic costs, it has become even more important to attract a full house to every contest. The only dependable road to that end is a championship-calibre team.

So many schools are now engaged in the big time football business that the supply of talent has become severely strained. Added to this is an almost complete reliance on a multi-platoon strategy, with specialists required at all positions. Hence, there are many more positions to fill than there are top prospects available. As a result of this increasing imbalance between supply and demand, all sorts of irregularities in the (ostensibly rigidly controlled by the NCAA) market have occurred.[1] Numerous violations of the athletic scholarship rule which limits support to room, board, and tuition have been recorded, but if we are to believe the commentary of coaches and athletes, it must be concluded that the majority of the excesses have gone unnoticed and unpunished.

The best schoolboy athletes are often contacted by fifty or more universities. Much has been said about the pursuit of the "blue chip" or "boss stud boys"; the campus visits, the fatherly coaches, attractive coeds, flashy convertibles, and assured degrees.[2] Several prominent college stars have jokingly referred to taking a pay cut upon signing professional contracts. Regardless of what the extent of the recruiting violations may be, such cheating undoubtedly takes place in all sections of the country and is probably a neutral factor where the interregional movements of athletes are concerned.

INTERREGIONAL MIGRATION

By subdividing the United States into nine football production and consumption sectors, a broad view of the interregional migration of college recruits can be obtained (Fig. 9-1). The most important export areas are Pennsylvania–Ohio, California, the Midwest, and the Northeast. The Pennsylvania–Ohio region is the chief donor to the South Atlantic universities and a major exporter to the Northeast, the Midwest, and the West. Pennsylvania, which loses more than three-fourths of its high school players to universities in other states, is a leading source of athletes for the Atlantic Coast and Southern Conferences, the Ivy League, Indiana, Florida and even Arizona (Fig. 9-2). In fact, there were Pennsylvanians playing in all but five of the states with major status recruiting budgets.

Ohio retains the bulk of its best high school football players (Fig. 9-3). The state provides more major college playing opportunities than Pennsylvania and relies heavily on its own schoolboy population. Indiana is the number one consumer of the Ohio surplus, but Illinois, Michigan, Florida, and New York have also been successful

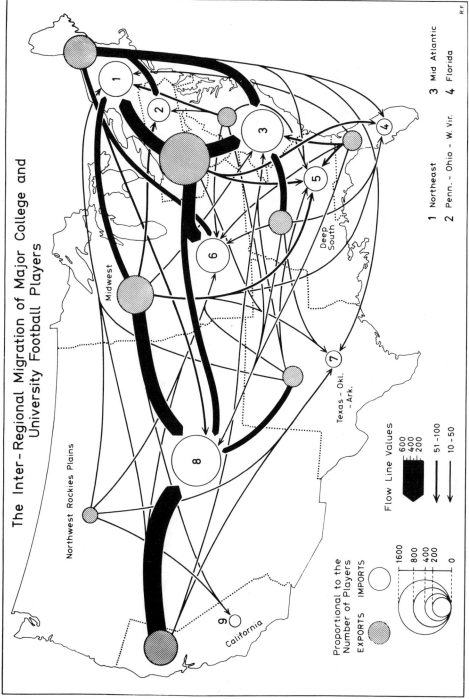

The Inter-Regional Migration of Major College and University Football Players

1 Northeast   3 Mid Atlantic
2 Penn. - Ohio - W. Vir.   4 Florida

Midwest

Northwest Rockies Plains

Deep South

Texas - Okl. - Ark.

California

Flow Line Values

600
400
200

51 - 100

10 - 50

Proportional to the Number of Players

EXPORTS   IMPORTS

1600
800
400
200
0

Figure 9.1

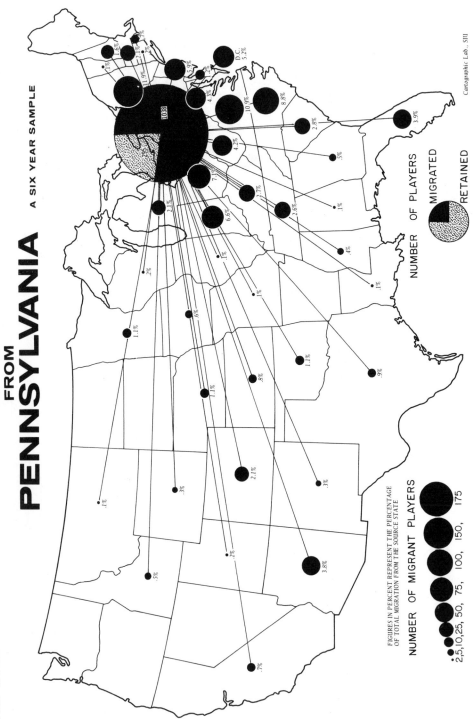

THE MIGRATION OF MAJOR COLLEGE & UNIVERSITY FOOTBALL PLAYERS

FROM

PENNSYLVANIA   A SIX YEAR SAMPLE

Figure 9.2

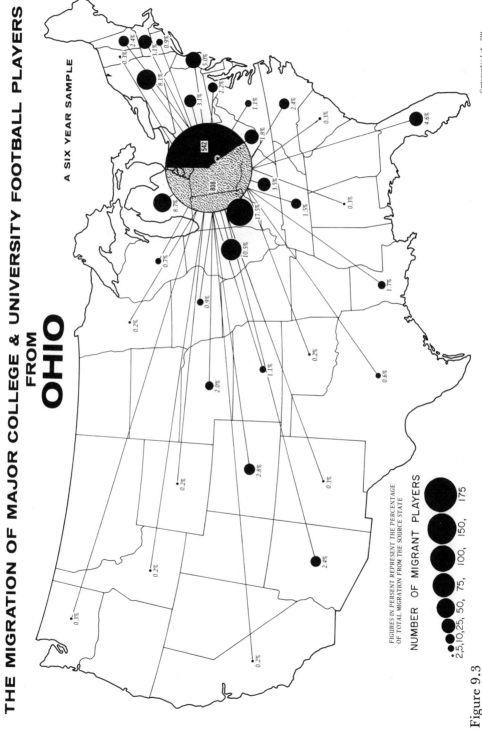

THE MIGRATION OF MAJOR COLLEGE & UNIVERSITY FOOTBALL PLAYERS

FROM

OHIO

A SIX YEAR SAMPLE

542

808

2.4%
0.3%
3.1%
0.9%
8.1%
5.0%
3.1%
2.2%
1.1%
2.4%
1.8%
0.3%
4.6%
8.7%
3.5%
1.5%
0.3%
17.5%
0.7%
10.5%
1.7%
0.9%
0.2%
0.2%
0.6%
2.0%
1.1%
0.3%
0.2%
2.8%
0.3%
0.2%
2.4%

FIGURES IN PERSENT REPRESENT THE PERCENTAGE
OF TOTAL MIGRATION FROM THE SOURCE STATE

NUMBER OF MIGRANT PLAYERS

2,5,10,25, 50, 75, 100, 150, 175

Cartographic Lab., SIU

Figure 9.3

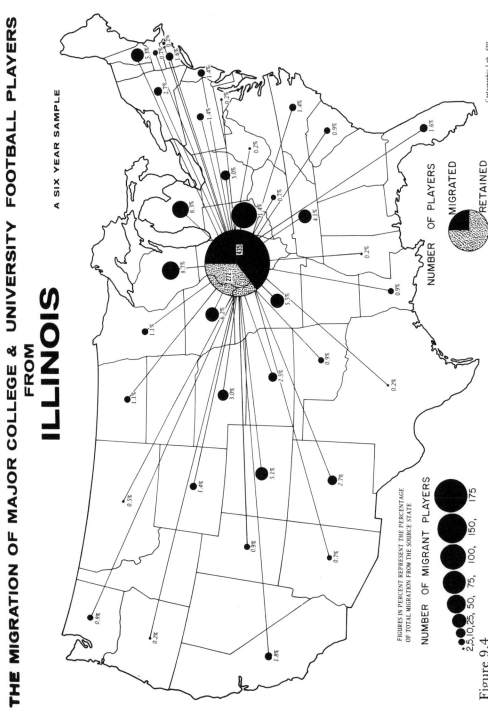

THE MIGRATION OF MAJOR COLLEGE & UNIVERSITY FOOTBALL PLAYERS

FROM

ILLINOIS

A SIX YEAR SAMPLE

NUMBER OF PLAYERS

MIGRATED

RETAINED

NUMBER OF MIGRANT PLAYERS

2,5,10,25, 50, 75, 100, 150, 175

FIGURES IN PERCENT REPRESENT THE PERCENTAGE
OF TOTAL MIGRATION FROM THE SOURCE STATE

Cartographic Lab., SIU

Figure 9.4

raiders (Fig. 9-3). Compared to Pennsylvania, though, the Ohio geographical impact has been slight.

Most of the high school players who leave California are recruited by Pacific Coast universities in Oregon and Washington or by members of the Western Athletic Conference. Utah alone absorbs 25 percent of the exports, and together with Washington and Oregon, consumes over half the California total. The impact of California decreases rapidly with distance. Very few recruits get beyond the Great Plains except in the case of Notre Dame and the Naval Academy, where the ever-present and persistent alumni have overcome the distance barrier.

The Midwest furnished the bulk of the Big Ten's needs. It has also made a significant contribution to the development of the Big Eight as a premier football conference. Boys from the Midwest have helped Missouri, Nebraska, and Kansas to national honors. They have also done much to bring football respectability to the Western Athletic Conference. In the Midwest, Illinois has provided most of the regional surplus (Fig. 9-4). Even the Ivy League, particularly Dartmouth and Yale, has been aggressive in seeking out what they have labeled scholar-athletes from the Midwest.

Many of the Illinois boys, particularly those from the Chicago area, do their playing in Indiana, Michigan, and Wisconsin (Fig. 9-4). The great majority leave the state, and it has been this inability to retain many of the "blue chippers" which has led to the recent demise of University of Illinois football. But Illinois' loss has been Nebraska's, Missouri's, and Indiana's gain. Even Tennessee has profited from recruitment in the "Illini" territory.

THE NORTHEAST

Those players recruited from the Northeast usually end up at schools in the Atlantic Coast and Southern Conferences. The members of the two conferences are highly dependent on New Jersey, New York, and of course, Pennsylvania talent. Over 75 percent of the New Jersey boys leave home to compete (Fig. 9-5). They are widely sought within the northeastern region. Their presence is also felt in the Midwest, particularly at Notre Dame. The 1971 Cotton Bowl triumph over Texas was fueled by Joe Theismann of South River and backed up by four other New Jersey teammates. Gridders from New York are not as heavily recruited as their New Jersey neighbors. Over fifty percent are consumed in the immediate vicinity (Fig. 9-6). Massachusetts is a major supplier to the Yankee Conference and the

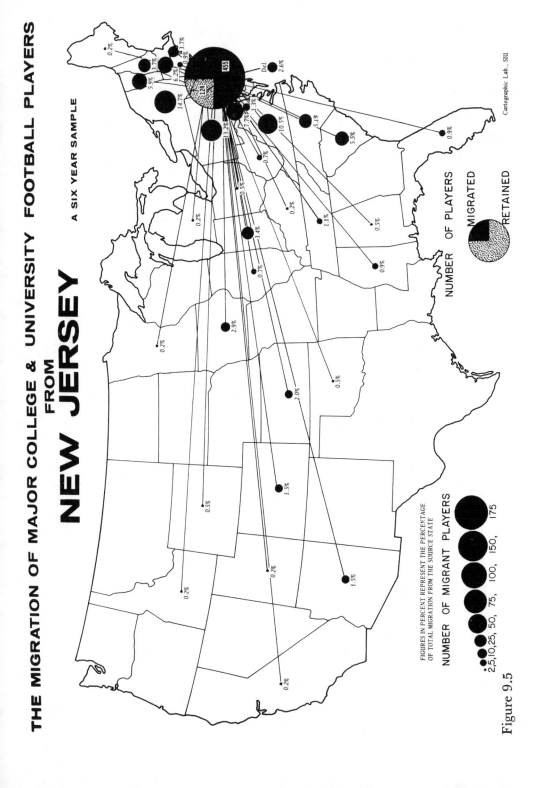

THE MIGRATION OF MAJOR COLLEGE & UNIVERSITY FOOTBALL PLAYERS

FROM

NEW JERSEY

A SIX YEAR SAMPLE

NUMBER OF PLAYERS

MIGRATED

RETAINED

FIGURES IN PERCENT REPRESENT THE PERCENTAGE
OF TOTAL MIGRATION FROM THE SOURCE STATE

NUMBER OF MIGRANT PLAYERS

2,5,10,25, 50, 75, 100, 150, 175

Cartographic Lab., SIU

Figure 9.5

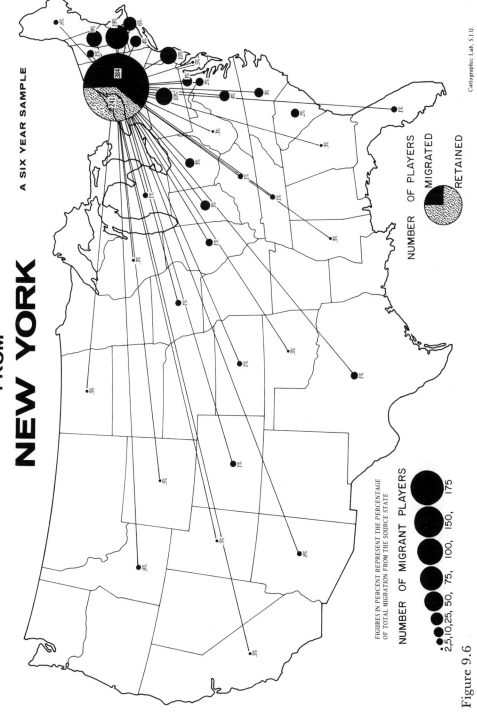

THE MIGRATION OF MAJOR COLLEGE & UNIVERSITY FOOTBALL PLAYERS FROM

NEW YORK

A SIX YEAR SAMPLE

NUMBER OF PLAYERS

MIGRATED

RETAINED

FIGURES IN PERCENT REPRESENT THE PERCENTAGE OF TOTAL MIGRATION FROM THE SOURCE STATE

NUMBER OF MIGRANT PLAYERS

2,5,10,25, 50, 75, 100, 150, 175

Cartographic Lab, S.I.U.

Figure 9.6

THE MIGRATION OF MAJOR COLLEGE & UNIVERSITY FOOTBALL PLAYERS
FROM
MASSACHUSETTS
A SIX YEAR SAMPLE

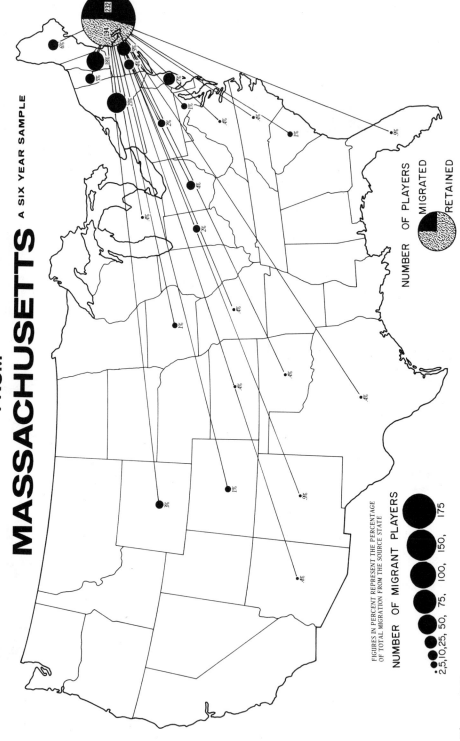

NUMBER OF PLAYERS

MIGRATED

RETAINED

FIGURES IN PERCENT REPRESENT THE PERCENTAGE OF TOTAL MIGRATION FROM THE SOURCE STATE

NUMBER OF MIGRANT PLAYERS

2,5,10,25, 50, 75, 100, 150, 175

Cartographic Lab. S.I.U.

Figure 9.7

Ivy League (Fig. 9-7). The Commonwealth has had little impact in
the Middle Atlantic region, but several Boston area products have
made the long trip to Wyoming and Colorado.

THE SOUTH

Only minor flows of players stem from the Deep South, Texas, and
Florida, and, considering the number of schools and people in the
Deep South, there has been little contact with other areas. Georgia,
Alabama, and Mississippi are exemplary of the limited out-migration
from the region (Figs. 9-8, 9-9, and 9-10). It is obvious that most
of the exports go no further than the culturally similar South-Atlantic
zone. Those "Yankees" who come in, with the prominent exception
of Joe Willie Namath, seldom penetrate further than Tennessee.

Until recently, a substantial proportion of the southern exports
were blacks who moved along a modern day "underground" railroad,
particularly to schools in the Midwest. Big Ten record books docu-
ment the accomplishments of many blacks who would have otherwise been denied the opportunity of playing first-class college football. Today though, the emergence of high-calibre football at predominantly black schools such as Grambling, Texas Southern, Alcorn A & M, Jackson State, and Florida A & M has stemmed the
tide of migration.

In Texas most of the hugh high school output is employed at
home (Fig. 9-11), and those who leave seldom stray far. Oklahoma
alone recruits over 35 percent of the "defectors," and much of the
Oklahoma University success story can be attributed to them. In
contrast to Pennsylvania, Texas retains more than 80 percent of its
athletes. Apparently state loyalty is a very strong force. However,
with the spread of the Texas high school football legend, more of
the best prospects are opting to leave and the trend is virtually certain
to continue.

Florida is unlke the other southern states (Fig. 9-12). Its schoolboy gridders are competing in most of the states east of the Mississippi River, and also out west, especially in Kansas, a fact that strongly
suggests that Florida is culturally different from the Deep South.

More than 50 percent of the interregional movement of players
is prompted by the deficit spending of universities in the vast Plains-
Rockies-Northwest region and in the smaller South Atlantic zone.
Both areas are characterized by schools which are trying to field
national class teams from a locally limited supply of top-flight
players. As a result, over 1300 players had to be recruited into the

THE MIGRATION OF MAJOR COLLEGE & UNIVERSITY FOOTBALL PLAYERS

FROM

GEORGIA

A SIX YEAR SAMPLE

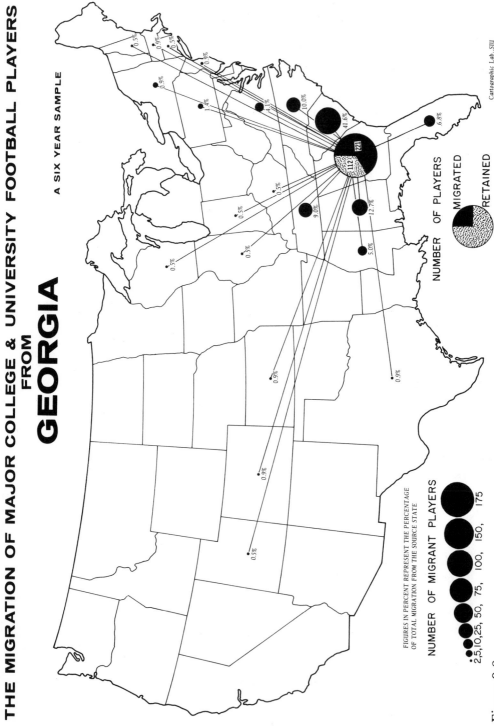

Cartographic Lab., SIU

NUMBER OF PLAYERS

MIGRATED

RETAINED

FIGURES IN PERCENT REPRESENT THE PERCENTAGE
OF TOTAL MIGRATION FROM THE SOURCE STATE

NUMBER OF MIGRANT PLAYERS

2,5,10,25, 50, 75, 100, 150, 175

Figure 9.8

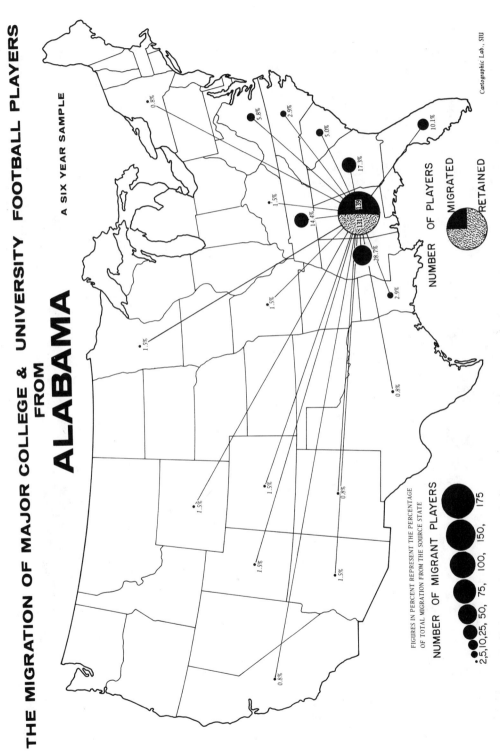

THE MIGRATION OF MAJOR COLLEGE & UNIVERSITY FOOTBALL PLAYERS FROM

ALABAMA

A SIX YEAR SAMPLE

NUMBER OF PLAYERS

MIGRATED
RETAINED

FIGURES IN PERCENT REPRESENT THE PERCENTAGE
OF TOTAL MIGRATION FROM THE SOURCE STATE

NUMBER OF MIGRANT PLAYERS

2,5,10,25, 50, 75, 100, 150, 175

Cartographic Lab., SIU

Figure 9.9

THE MIGRATION OF MAJOR COLLEGE & UNIVERSITY FOOTBALL PLAYERS
FROM
LOUISIANA
A SIX YEAR SAMPLE

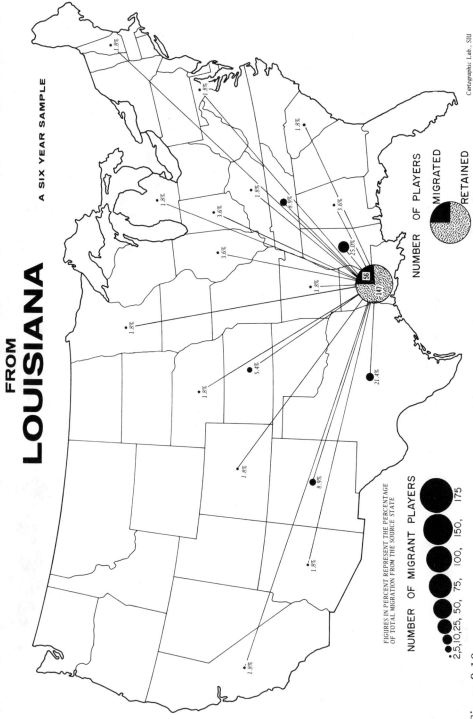

FIGURES IN PERCENT REPRESENT THE PERCENTAGE
OF TOTAL MIGRATION FROM THE SOURCE STATE

NUMBER OF MIGRANT PLAYERS

2,5,10,25, 50, 75, 100, 150, 175

NUMBER OF PLAYERS

MIGRATED

RETAINED

Cartographic Lab., SIU

Figure 9.10

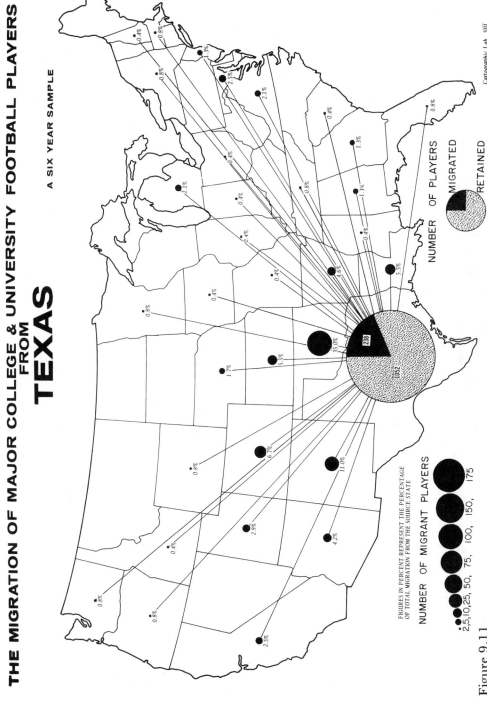

THE MIGRATION OF MAJOR COLLEGE & UNIVERSITY FOOTBALL PLAYERS

FROM

TEXAS

A SIX YEAR SAMPLE

NUMBER OF PLAYERS

MIGRATED
RETAINED

FIGURES IN PERCENT REPRESENT THE PERCENTAGE
OF TOTAL MIGRATION FROM THE SOURCE STATE

NUMBER OF MIGRANT PLAYERS

2,5,10,25, 50, 75, 100, 150, 175

Cartographic Lab., SIU

Figure 9.11

THE MIGRATION OF MAJOR COLLEGE & UNIVERSITY FOOTBALL PLAYERS

FROM
FLORIDA

A SIX YEAR SAMPLE

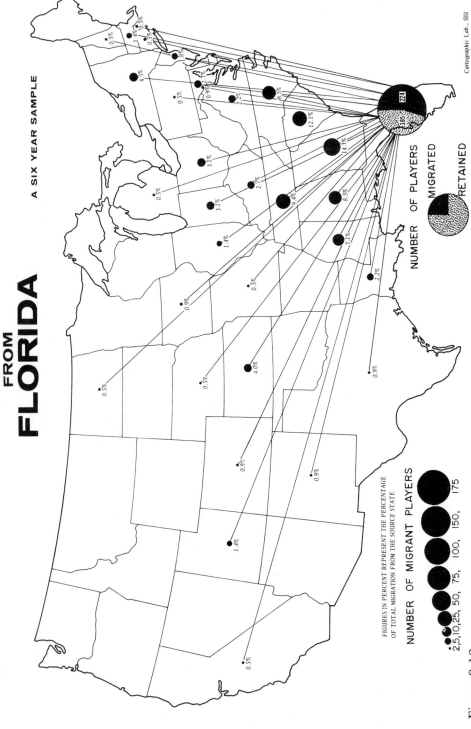

FIGURES IN PERCENT REPRESENT THE PERCENTAGE
OF TOTAL MIGRATION FROM THE SOURCE STATE

NUMBER OF MIGRANT PLAYERS

2.5, 10, 25, 50, 75, 100, 150, 175

NUMBER OF PLAYERS

MIGRATED

RETAINED

Cartographic Lab., SIU

Figure 9.12

Inter-Regional Movements of Football Players in the U.S.

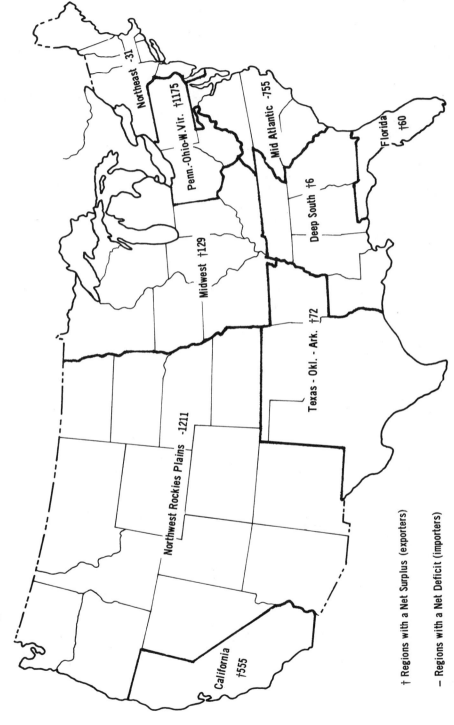

Northeast -31

Penn.-Ohio-W.Vir. †1175

Mid Atlantic -755

Florida †60

Deep South †6

Midwest †129

Texas - Okl. - Ark. †72

Northwest Rockies Plains -1211

California †555

† Regions with a Net Surplus (exporters)

− Regions with a Net Deficit (importers)

Figure 9.13

TABLE 9–1
INTERREGIONAL MIGRATION OF FOOTBALL PLAYERS

	Northwest, Rockies, Plains	California	Midwest	Texas, Oklahoma, Arkansas	Deep South	Florida	Mid-Atlantic	Pennsylvania, Ohio, West Virginia	Northeast	Total exports
	1	2	3	4	5	6	7	8	9	
Northwest, Rockies, Plains		41	19	32	1	1	1	2	32	129
California	539		33	24	2	7	16	2	11	634
Midwest	373	12		26	53	20	40	85	145	754
Texas, Oklahoma, Arkansas	124	7	16		42	4	13	2	18	226
Deep South	28	2	29	25		31	175	4	9	303
Florida	18	1	20	2	93		59	0	17	210
Mid-Atlantic	16	2	31	6	39	8		32	64	198
Pennsylvania, Ohio, West Virginia	162	9	375	26	56	67	401		364	1,460
Northeast	80	5	102	13	11	12	248	158		629
Total Imports	1,340	79	625	154	297	150	953	285	660	4,543

western area and nearly a thousand by the South Atlantic representatives (Fig. 9-13). Aside from the two large deficit areas, most of the interregional flow balances out, with midwestern and northeastern exports roughly equaling their imports (Table 9-1). Nevertheless, the sheer magnitude of player migrations is indicative of the heated competition for and the high cost of acquiring football talent in the present market.

THE CONFERENCES

The consumption of college football players can be further generalized at the conference scale. A few visual examples should suffice in illustrating some of recruiting previously referred to (see Figs. 9-14, 9-15, 9-16, and 9-17). Each of the sampled conferences have one recruiting area in common. The Big Ten, Big Eight, Atlantic Coast, and Western Athletic conferences all tap western Pennsylvania. The Big Ten confines its activities, more than any other conference, to member states. The Atlantic Coast staffs its teams almost exclusively with eastern players. Aside from western Pennsylvania, most of the recruits are from the immediate coastal zone. The Big Eight obtains many of its athletes from Chicago, Detroit, Cleveland, and Pittsburgh. It also relies heavily on California. The Oklahoma rosters have a Texas and California flavor, whereas the northern schools, particularly Nebraska and Iowa State, are manned by Illinois, Michigan, and Pennsylvania recruits.

The nation is the recruiting territory of the Western Athletic coaches. All the major source regions, except the Southern Mississippi hotbed, are represented on league rosters, and over half the players are from nonconference states, with California, Michigan, Pennsylvania, and Illinois most apparent. The conference epitomizes many of the problems which face collegiate athletics. All of the member universities are supporting big-time programs without benefit of home-grown talent. They need much bigger recruiting budgets and have had to cultivate numerous junior college arrangements to compete with schools nearer to the athletes. But to their credit it must be said that they are providing an entertainment form which would not otherwise be available in their sparsely populated regions.

Conference recruiting territories have evolved over long time spans. They reflect the territorial ideas of member coaches and the quality of local and regional schoolboy competition. Each coach has his own contacts: former players and professional associates, alumni,

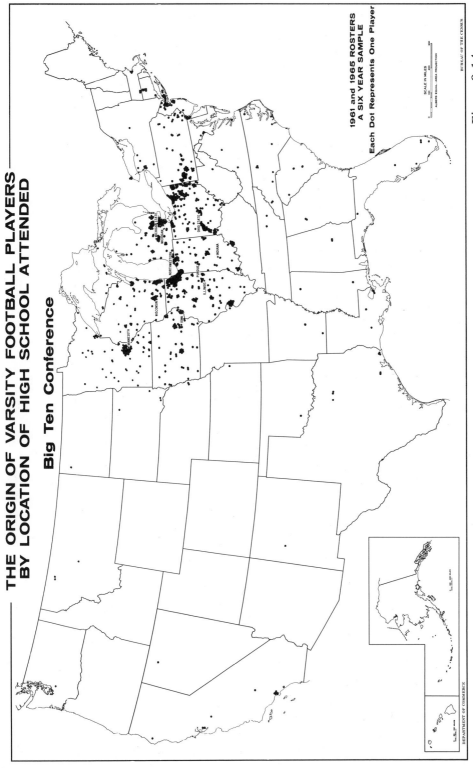

THE ORIGIN OF VARSITY FOOTBALL PLAYERS
BY LOCATION OF HIGH SCHOOL ATTENDED

Big Ten Conference

1961 and 1965 ROSTERS
A SIX YEAR SAMPLE
Each Dot Represents One Player

SCALE IN MILES

ALBERS EQUAL-AREA PROJECTION

BUREAU OF THE CENSUS

DEPARTMENT OF COMMERCE

Figure 9.14

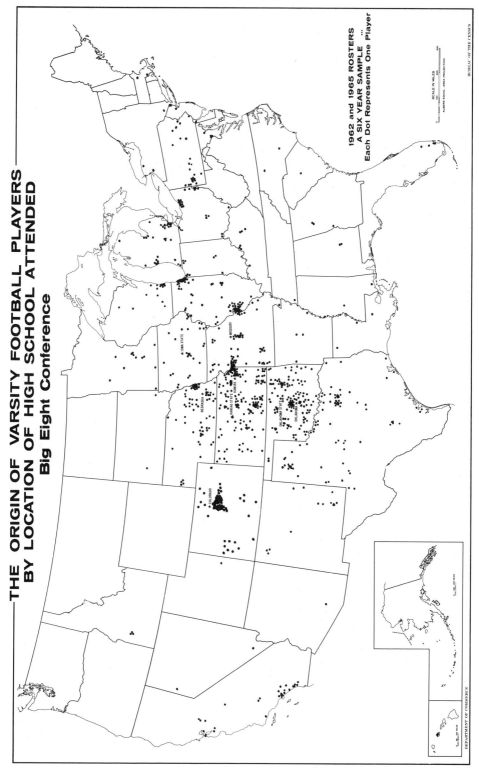

THE ORIGIN OF VARSITY FOOTBALL PLAYERS
BY LOCATION OF HIGH SCHOOL ATTENDED

Big Eight Conference

1962 and 1965 ROSTERS
A SIX YEAR SAMPLE . . .
Each Dot Represents One Player

SCALE IN MILES

ALBERS EQUAL AREA PROJECTION

BUREAU OF THE CENSUS

DEPARTMENT OF COMMERCE

Figure 9.15

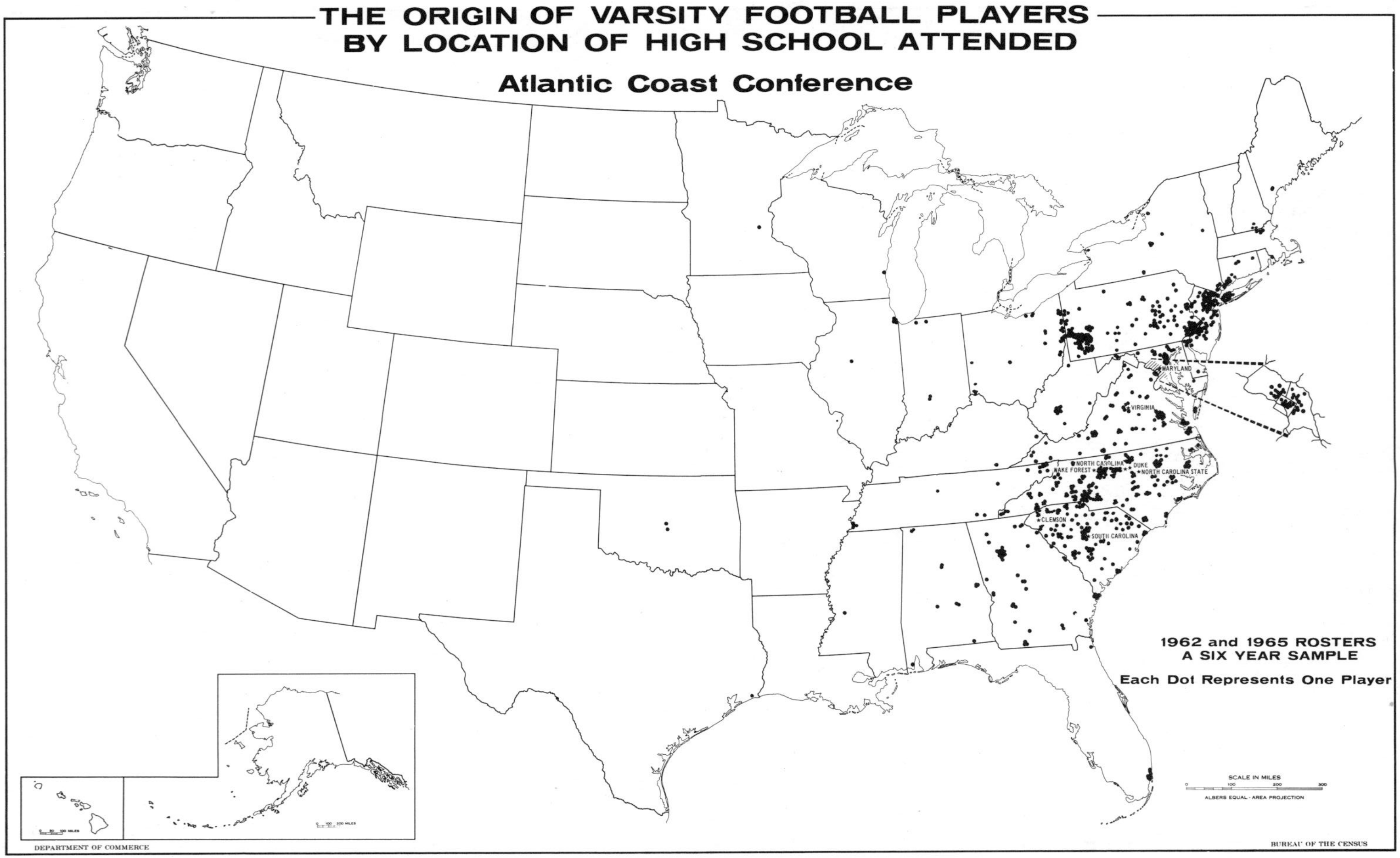
THE ORIGIN OF VARSITY FOOTBALL PLAYERS
BY LOCATION OF HIGH SCHOOL ATTENDED
Atlantic Coast Conference
MARYLAND
VIRGINIA
NORTH CAROLINA
DUKE
WAKE FOREST
NORTH CAROLINA STATE
CLEMSON
SOUTH CAROLINA
1962 and 1965 ROSTERS
A SIX YEAR SAMPLE
Each Dot Represents One Player
SCALE IN MILES
0 100 200 300
ALBERS EQUAL - AREA PROJECTION
DEPARTMENT OF COMMERCE
BUREAU OF THE CENSUS

Figure 9.16

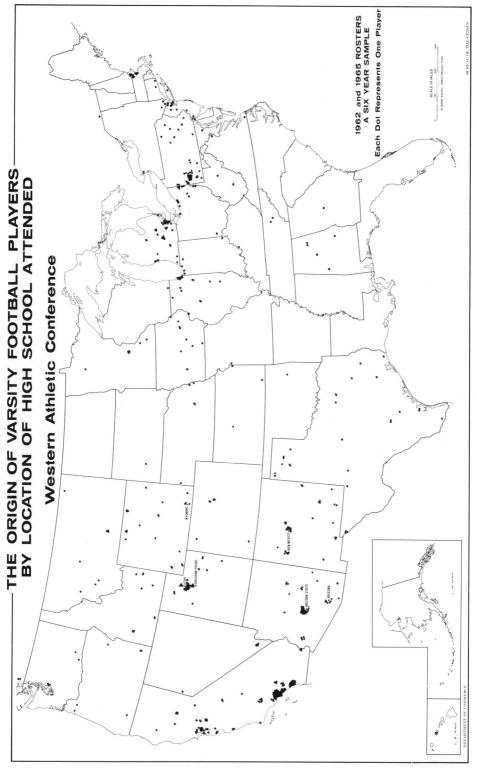

THE ORIGIN OF VARSITY FOOTBALL PLAYERS
BY LOCATION OF HIGH SCHOOL ATTENDED

Western Athletic Conference

1962 and 1965 ROSTERS
A SIX YEAR SAMPLE
Each Dot Represents One Player

Figure 9.17

Sport for sport's sake. Small college football in Minnesota. (Photo courtesy of Paul Bolstad.)

black market touters, Big Mammas, and so on. The immediate region is combed first, and depending on population density and the quality of play, it may fill much of the demand. Agreements with small colleges in regard to local prospects are not uncommon.

Recruiting strategies of any university are subject to drastic changes. A new coach, territorial raids by other coaches, and improvement in high school programs are all important. As a result, the geography of recruiting is extremely dynamic, as coaches are hired and fired, as new universities opt for big time football, as conference and scholastic requirements for athletes are altered, as "red shirting" rules are changed, and as an individual university's football fortunes rise and fall.

THE LITTLE PEOPLE

In the midst of the talent scramble by the major schools, there are over 500 "small" schools trying to pick up what is left. As we all know, some of the best players are overlooked or ignored by the "majors," and they often end up competing at a small college. However, the bulk of the small college recruits are a little bit smaller or slower than those at the big colleges. Even so, the competition for these players is extremely heated, as an examination of Oklahoma Collegiate Conference recruiting will illustrate.

With limited recruiting budgets, it follows that the smaller institutions will be confined in the territorial extent of their activities. This is illustrated in the case of the eight football playing members of the Oklahoma Collegiate Conference. Over 53 percent of the gridders participating between 1963 and 1969 came from within 100 miles of their respective colleges. At some of the schools, over one-half of the athletes were from within an hour's drive. However, there was considerable variation between the conference members. For example, Panhandle A&M, located in the almost peopleless high plains, could garner less than a quarter of its players from within a 100-mile radius (Table 9–2). Out-of-staters, including ten from Pennsylvania and eight from New York, represented 58 percent of the recruits. Conversely, Central State, located inside the Oklahoma City Metropolitan Area, got 75 percent of its footballers from the immediate vicinity and only 23 percent from out-of-state. Most of those came from Texas.

TABLE 9–2
THE ORIGIN OF OKLAHOMA COLLEGIATE CONFERENCE PLAYERS

School	Percentage of players within 100-mile radius	Percentage of players from out-of-state
Southwestern	42	38
East Central	50	32
Northwestern	55	43
Panhandle A & M	23	58
Central	75	23
Northeastern	50	36
Langston	61	11
Southeastern	68	23

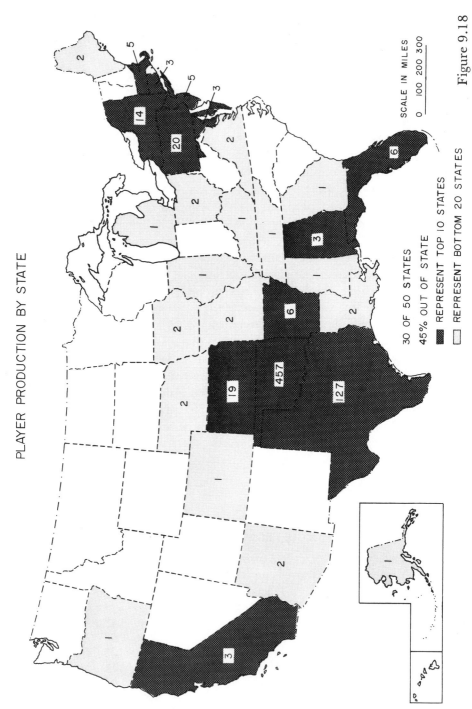

OKLAHOMA COLLEGIATE CONFERENCE

PLAYER PRODUCTION BY STATE

30 OF 50 STATES
45% OUT OF STATE

■ REPRESENT TOP 10 STATES
□ REPRESENT BOTTOM 20 STATES

SCALE IN MILES
0   100 200 300

Figure 9.18

MINNESOTA AND WISCONSIN INTERCOLLEGIATE CONFERENCE

(PLAYER PRODUCTION BY STATES)

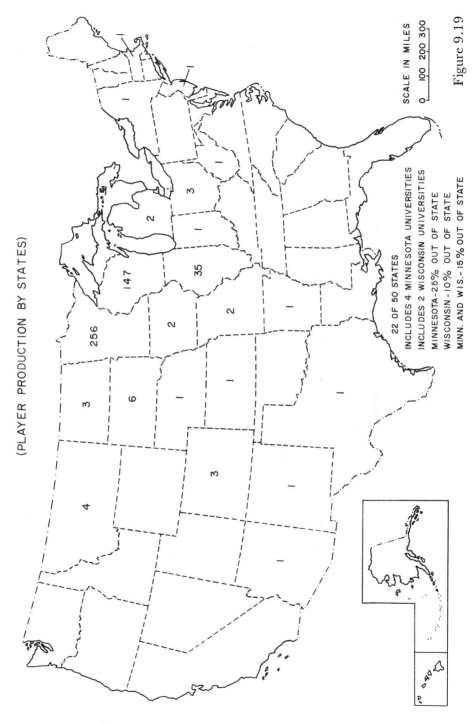

22 OF 50 STATES
INCLUDES 4 MINNESOTA UNIVERSITIES
INCLUDES 2 WISCONSIN UNIVERSITIES
MINNESOTA-25% OUT OF STATE
WISCONSIN-10% OUT OF STATE
MINN. AND WIS.-15% OUT OF STATE

SCALE IN MILES
0   100 200 300

Figure 9.19

TABLE 9-3
THE ORIGIN OF NORTHERN COLLEGIATE CONFERENCE PLAYERS

School	Percentage of players within 100-mile radius	Percentage of players from out-of-state
McAlester, Minnesota	39	42
Hamline, Minnesota	93	5
Concordia, Minnesota	50	40
St. Johns, Minnesota	82	22
Whitewater, Wisconsin	91	14
LaCrosse, Wisconsin	21	4

Oklahoma has supplied the bulk of the talent for its small colleges (Fig. 9-18), but as with the major universities (Oklahoma, Oklahoma State, Tulsa), the small colleges have relied considerably on Texas, which provided as many players as the rest of the states combined. Of the others, Pennsylvania, Kansas, and New York were the most important suppliers.

An examination of small college recruiting in Minnesota and Wisconsin revealed a similar dependence on local players (Fig. 9-19). Hamline College of St. Paul, Minnesota drew 93 percent of its players from a 100-mile radius (Table 9-3). The University of Wisconsin-Whitewater, obtained 91 percent from a similar area surrounding it. Coaches in the small conferences in Minnesota and Wisconsin make little attempt to seek out-of-state players, relying almost exclusively on alumni recommendations for this service.

THE MOVE TO THE BIG TIME

Success on the gridiron has led many universities to national prominence, and in some instances, it has been a harbinger of academic excellence. Exemplary of this rise are Michigan State, Texas, Notre Dame, and Stanford.

The past decade has witnessed the emergence of several newcomers to the ranks of major college football. It has also been a period in which numerous marginal football operations have disappeared in favor of minor sports and intramural competition.

The road to athletic prominence is not an easy one. A stadium must be built, alumni support must be assembled, coaches and athletes must be recruited, and large sums of capital must be allocated to the cause. One institution which has come a long way during the sixties is North Dakota State University. Located in

Fargo, the University of 6500 students was lacking a strong football tradition. Its successes were few, even in the North Central Conference, which has not been known for gridiron excellence. A close examination of the "Thundering Herd" demonstrates the drastic changes which have taken place in recruiting, coaching, alumni support, publicity, schedules, facilities, and capital outlays. Comparisons of the 1962 and 1966 rosters tell much of the story.

The 1962 Bison were only 34 strong and were led by just two coaches. Fifteen of the men who compiled a miserable 0–10 record were from North Dakota, nearly half of these from Fargo. Sixteen of the players hailed from Minnesota, primarily from the small towns in the western sector of the state. The other three were from Chicago and Winnipeg. The North Dakota State backfield averaged 173 pounds, and the line averaged just 195; blue chippers they were not. Publicity for the team was minimal, as illustrated by a small hand-typed press guide, limited newspaper and radio coverage, and a very small public relations budget.

By 1966, the "Thundering Herd" coaching staff had tripled, and the expanded scholarship-subsidized recruiting had doubled the squad to a total of 68 players. The growth of the coaching staff was accompanied by the construction of a new athletic office complex, new dressing rooms, and a general improvement of facilities. Recruiting brought in more North Dakota players than were represented on the 1962 squad. There were a total of 28, but only four were from Fargo. Minnesota furnished 21 of the players, with many from the larger towns and the Twin Cities metropolitan area. The expanded recruiting also brought players from Wisconsin (6), Illinois (2), New York (2), California (2), Wyoming (2), South Dakota (2), Florida (1), Iowa (1), and Michigan (1).

Not only were there many more players on the 1966 team, but they were also of considerably greater physical stature and ability. Team size had increased by approximately 30 pounds per man, and team speed was improved as well. The results on the scoreboard were even more spectacular. In 1965 the team was voted NCAA College Division National Champions and handily defeated Grambling in the Pecan Bowl. The past five years have witnessed continued success, with a gradual upgrading of the schedule accompanied by improvement in the North Central Conference. Although Bison football is not yet in a class with the major powers, it has made steady progress toward the "big time" and has developed most of the characteristics (fan mania, press, radio and television coverage, bowl

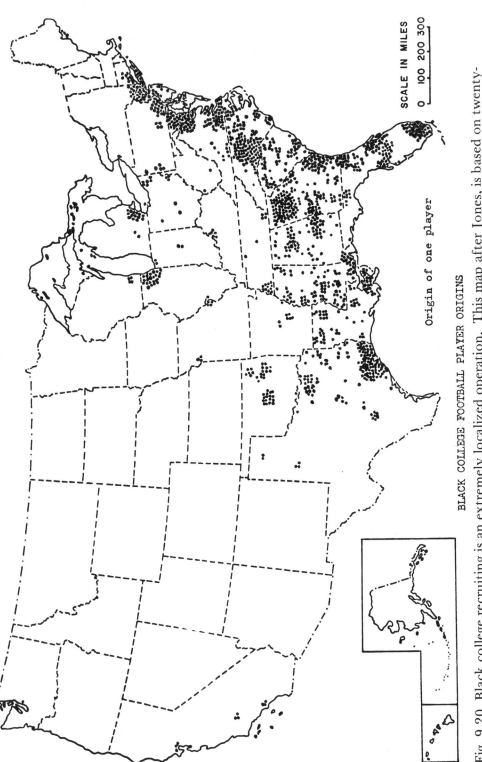

SCALE IN MILES

0 100 200 300

Origin of one player

BLACK COLLEGE FOOTBALL PLAYER ORIGINS

Fig. 9.20 Black college recruiting is an extremely localized operation. This map after Jones, is based on twenty-four of the sixty-two predominantly black colleges which sponsor intercollegiate football teams.

games) of the successful football giants. But the primary change has been the geographical basis of the recruiting effort, a change which demanded a substantial monetary investment in the football program.

The North Dakota State case is characteristic of the increased emphasis which has taken place at many institutions. Few have experienced such instant success, but many have allocated as many or more resources toward the development of football excellence. San Diego State, Northern Illinois, Arkansas State, Louisville, Grambling, North Dakota, Alcorn A & M, and West Texas State are but a few of those who have made tremendous strides during the sixties.

From a recruiting standpoint the nation's black colleges behave geographically similar to other small colleges (Fig. 4-20). Jones investigated the recruitment of gridders at 24 of the leading black institutions, concluding that the recruiting game was a minimum budget operation.[9] He found that most of the players were obtained within a 60-70 mile radius of their respective colleges. Only Chicago, Detroit, and New York City were significant exporters to the black college region. Even perennial stalwarts Grambling, Morgan State, and Alcorn A & M, recruited most of their players locally.

NOTES

1. David Dupree, "Playing the Game," *The Wall Street Journal,* October 8, 1970, p. 1. See also Richard Starnes, "An Unprecedented Economic and Ethical Crisis Grips Big Time Intercollegiate Sports," *The Chronicle of Higher Education,* Vol. III (September 24, 1973), p. 1 +, and the survey of the Carnegie Foundation for the Advancement of Teaching concerning intercollegiate athletics in the *New York Times,* October 24, 1929, pp. 22-23.

2. *Ibid.,* p. 1.

3. William J. Jones, "Black College Recruiting, A Geographical Analysis," unpublished Master's report, Oklahoma State University, 1973.

10 / The Recruiting Game: Basketball

The recruitment of high school basketball players by colleges and universities is in many ways similar to the situation that exists in football. As with football, migration from any area is a function of the number of local opportunities to play, the number of players available, and the strength of the demand for them from other regions. Each of these factors is closely interrelated. Local exposure to major college basketball has some influence on the extent and the quality of high school programs. This, in turn, affects local player output, eventually enhancing the reputation of the area in the eyes of basketball people (particularly recruiters) around the country.

THE ILLINKY SURPLUS

From an interregional viewpoint, two massive recruitment patterns can be identified (Fig. 10-1). Ths most imposing originates in the IllInKy region and includes a total of 39 states. The Midwest, Deep South, and Atlantic Coast zones are the prime benefactors. In addition, a great number of players are also lured to the Great Plains, the Rocky Mountain region, and Texas. This movement of players is a measure of the esteem in which IllInKy basketball is held by college coaches and recruiters around the country and reflects a production rate which substantially exceeds local consumption. Many of the best prospects have been recruited great distances from IllInKy at considerable expense to the universities involved and to the detriment of the area's own collegiate programs. The recent mediocrity

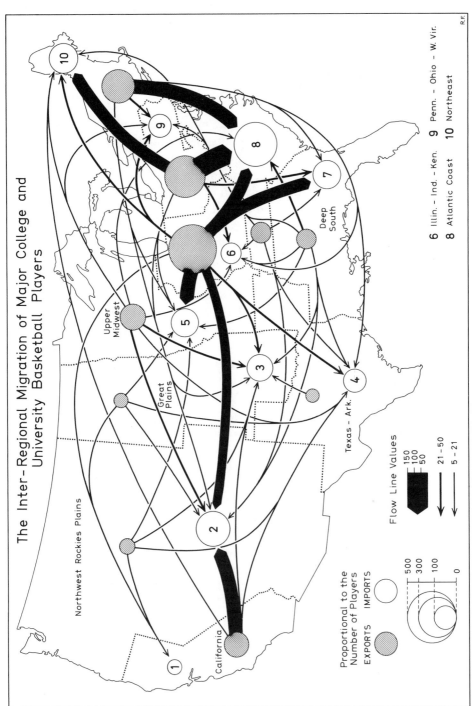

The Inter-Regional Migration of Major College and
University Basketball Players

Northwest Rockies Plains

Upper
Midwest

Great
Plains

California

Texas – Ark.

Deep
South

Proportional to the
Number of Players

EXPORTS   IMPORTS

500
300
100
0

Flow Line Values

150
100
50

21 – 50

5 – 21

6 Illin. – Ind. – Ken.   9 Penn. – Ohio – W. Vir.
8 Atlantic Coast   10 Northeast

R.F.

Figure 10.1

associated with formerly good basketball schools like Illinois, Loyola, Northwestern, Purdue, Depaul, and Kentucky, accompanied by the subsequent rise at obscure places (where basketball was concerned) like New Mexico, Mississippi State, Texas Western (UTEP), Houston, and Tennessee provides ample testimony. A lot of the best boys are leaving the area.

This situation has resulted in a more intense effort by the local coaches, which has already begun to pay dividends for Harv Schmidt at the University of Illinois and George King at Purdue. Perhaps the best example is Rick Mount, a national figure as a Lebanon, Indiana, schoolboy, who was beseiged with offers from all sections of the country. He finally selected Purdue University, which is only thirty miles from Lebanon. Schmidt is already noted for his talent searches throughout Illinois, and in three years had brought the state university back from the depths of the school's recent "slush fund" scandal.[1]

The extent to which the basketball heartland is combed by the talent hustlers is illustrated by the fact that nearly every serious basketball school has at least one IllInKy player on its squad. The overnight success stories of many collegiate basketball newcomers (examples include Houston, Southwestern Louisiana, Jacksonville, UTEP, and LSU) who have staffed their teams from this area, and from megalopolis, particularly New York City, Philadelphia, and Washington, D. C., provides ample testimony to the spatial impact of the region. Without Illinois and Indiana to draw on, it is doubtful that universities from Michigan, Wisconsin, Tennessee, Texas, and the states of the Deep South would be fielding respectable "big time" teams.

Players from IllInKy have made vast contributions to many college programs and have helped to elevate competition throughout the country. They have probably been the most significant geographical force in the diffusion of high-quality basketball throughout the United States. The University of Houston, a school which has recently evolved as a major power in college basketball, is an excellent example of the region's impact. By 1965, its first outstanding year, the Houston roster contained eight players from IllInKy and only two from Texas. The team that finished second to U.C.L.A. in 1967 had only one Texan. The emergence of the University of Texas at El Paso has followed much the same pattern. New Mexico and New Mexico State University, with half their players from Illinois and Indiana, are other cases in point.

Numerous high school coaches in the IllInKy region were queried relative to the collegiate recruiting effort there.[2] All of them believed that the world's best high school basketball was played in Illinois, Indiana, and Kentucky. A few volunteered that a quality game was also played in Ohio, the New York-New Jersey area, and "around" Philadelphia. This opinion was, of course, largely derived from written accounts in the popular press.

One coach from a small consolidated school in Southern Indiana, expressed it this way:

Yes I do feel that Indiana basketball ranks at the top, or near the top, in relation to other states. I am probably biased in this respect, but my thinking on the matter has become stronger in the past few years. I say this because, time after time, I receive mail from college coaches begging for Indiana basketball players. Just yesterday, a good-sized college in Minnesota called me and outright told me that they had to recruit some Indiana boys or their future in basketball would be dim. Of course, this is one case, but it has happened time after time.[3]

The head coach from Shelbyville, Indiana was more succinct stating, "Other states have good teams and players, but not as many as Indiana."[4] The feeling of basketball superiority is equally strong in Illinois, as these comments from Elgin indicate,

"The best basketball is played in northern Illinois and New York City. Elgin is a great basketball town, like others in this area including Rockford, Freeport, Lasalle–Peru, Joliet, and Aurora. I have sent 65 Elgin boys on to college ball since 1950."[5]

Even the Utah coaches believe that the interscholastic game reaches its zenith in IllInKy.[6]

Within the region, Illinois is the leading exporter (Table 10-1), and it ranks first nationally. Indiana is close behind, and both states have similar export patterns (Figs. 10-2 and 10-3). Illinois is a more significant supplier for Midwestern universities, particularly for those in Iowa, Wisconsin, and Missouri, while the Hoosier state is a more important supplier to Florida and Ohio. Together they have contributed to the programs of nearly every basketball school in the United States. The region's southern member, Kentucky, has made its impact primarily in the Deep South. Adolph Rupp, who compiled an extremely successful basketball record at the University of Kentucky, has been the most important geographical factor in the

TABLE 10-1
INTERREGIONAL MIGRATION OF COLLEGE BASKETBALL PLAYERS

From		1 California	2 Northwest and Rockies	3 Great Plains	4 Texas-Arkansas	5 Midwest	6 Illinois-Indiana-Kentucky	7 Deep South	8 Atlantic Coast	9 Pennsylvania-Ohio-West Virginia	10 Northeast	Total Exports
1.	California	–	91	10	5	1	1	1	3	1	6	119
2.	Northwest and Rockies	16	–	8	9	5	1	1	2	1	4	47
3.	Great Plains	6	12	–	8	7	1	1	1	0	2	38
4.	Texas-Arkansas	2	4	19	–	2	0	3	0	2	2	34
5.	Midwest	1	29	25	15	–	20	3	7	18	15	133
6.	Illinois-Indiana-Kentucky	6	60	37	30	100	–	85	87	25	24	454
7.	Deep South	0	6	7	8	6	7	–	23	5	7	71
8.	Atlantic Coast	3	9	4	6	4	10	18	–	10	16	80
9.	Pennsylvania-Ohio-West Virginia	4	14	13	4	17	23	22	147	–	84	328
10.	Northeast	1	10	11	15	10	17	19	102	33	–	217
	Total imports	39	235	134	100	152	80	153	372	95	160	1521

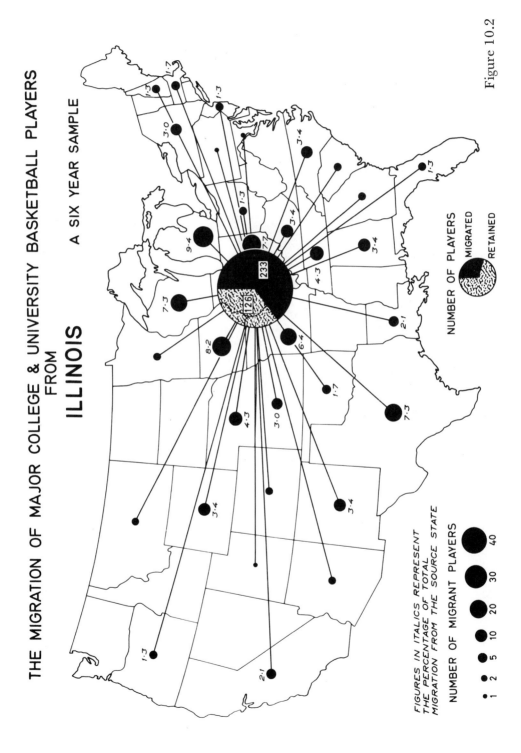

THE MIGRATION OF MAJOR COLLEGE & UNIVERSITY BASKETBALL PLAYERS
FROM
ILLINOIS

A SIX YEAR SAMPLE

FIGURES IN ITALICS REPRESENT
THE PERCENTAGE OF TOTAL
MIGRATION FROM THE SOURCE STATE

NUMBER OF MIGRANT PLAYERS

1 2 5 10 20 30 40

NUMBER OF PLAYERS

MIGRATED
RETAINED

Figure 10.2

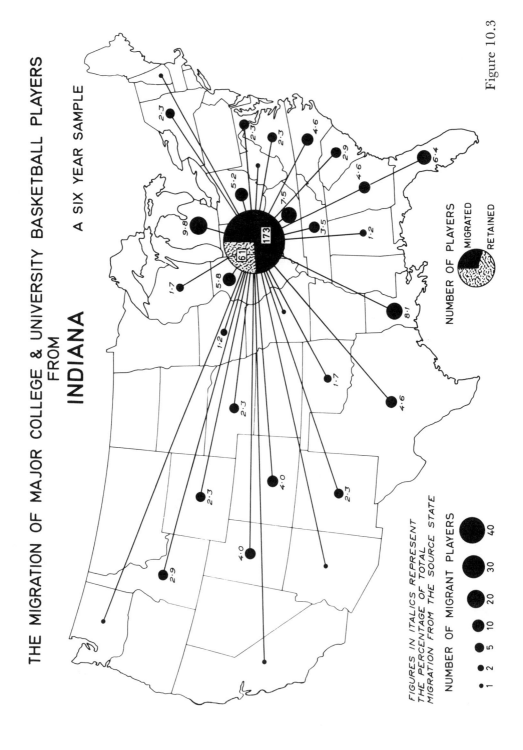

THE MIGRATION OF MAJOR COLLEGE & UNIVERSITY BASKETBALL PLAYERS
FROM
INDIANA
A SIX YEAR SAMPLE

NUMBER OF PLAYERS

MIGRATED
RETAINED

FIGURES IN ITALICS REPRESENT
THE PERCENTAGE OF TOTAL
MIGRATION FROM THE SOURCE STATE

NUMBER OF MIGRANT PLAYERS

1 2 5 10 20 30 40

Figure 10.3

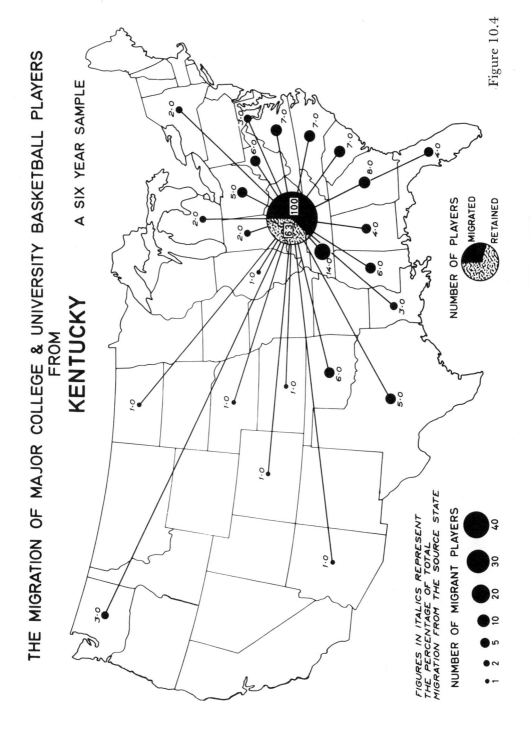

THE MIGRATION OF MAJOR COLLEGE & UNIVERSITY BASKETBALL PLAYERS

FROM

KENTUCKY   A SIX YEAR SAMPLE

NUMBER OF PLAYERS
MIGRATED
RETAINED

FIGURES IN ITALICS REPRESENT
THE PERCENTAGE OF TOTAL
MIGRATION FROM THE SOURCE STATE

NUMBER OF MIGRANT PLAYERS

1   2   5   10   20   30   40

Figure 10.4

South. His unparalleled success has pressed the Southern schools to improve their basketball programs, largely by recruiting high school players from his state and the Ohio Valley region (Fig. 10-4).

THE PENNSYLVANIA–OHIO SURPLUS

A second impressive flow of hoopsters branches out from Pennsylvania and Ohio (Figs. 10–5 and 10–6). This surplus of basketball skills has been attracted almost solely by the Atlantic Coast schools and a variety of northeastern universities. The Atlantic Coast region consumed 46 percent of the exports, and the Northeast 26 percent. The flow is very confined in comparison to that from IllInKy, with only eight states consuming ten or more players. Nevertheless, thirty-two states recruited from the region. The rosters at perennial stalwarts like Duke, North Carolina, Davidson, and South Carolina are generously sprinkled with Pennsylvania and Ohio products. For example, during the 1966-1967 season, the eight Atlantic Coast Conference teams included 20 Pennsylvanians, 13 New Jersey boys, 8 New Yorkers, and 6 from Illinois. Only 39 percent of the conference players were recruited from member states (Table 10-2). The 1971-1972 situation

TABLE 10-2
THE PRINCIPAL SURPLUS AND DEFICIT STATES

State	Consumption	Exports	Imports	Surplus	Deficit
Illinois	162	233	48	185	
Pennsylvania	167	184	41	143	
Indiana	101	173	40	133	
New Jersey	80	172	51	121	
Ohio	227	128	50	78	
Kentucky	110	100	47	53	
New York	304	177	127	50	
North Carolina	156	18	101		83
South Carolina	98	4	82		78
Texas	280	31	96		65
Utah	112	3	61		58
Virginia	121	21	75		54
Rhode Island	58	1	52		51
New Hampshire	58	2	45		43
Maryland	54	12	49		37

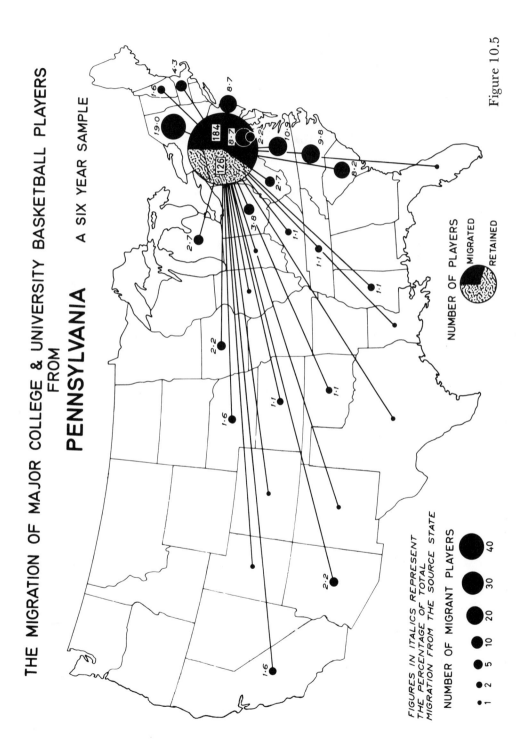

THE MIGRATION OF MAJOR COLLEGE & UNIVERSITY BASKETBALL PLAYERS
FROM
PENNSYLVANIA   A SIX YEAR SAMPLE

FIGURES IN ITALICS REPRESENT
THE PERCENTAGE OF TOTAL
MIGRATION FROM THE SOURCE STATE

NUMBER OF MIGRANT PLAYERS

NUMBER OF PLAYERS
MIGRATED
RETAINED

Figure 10.5

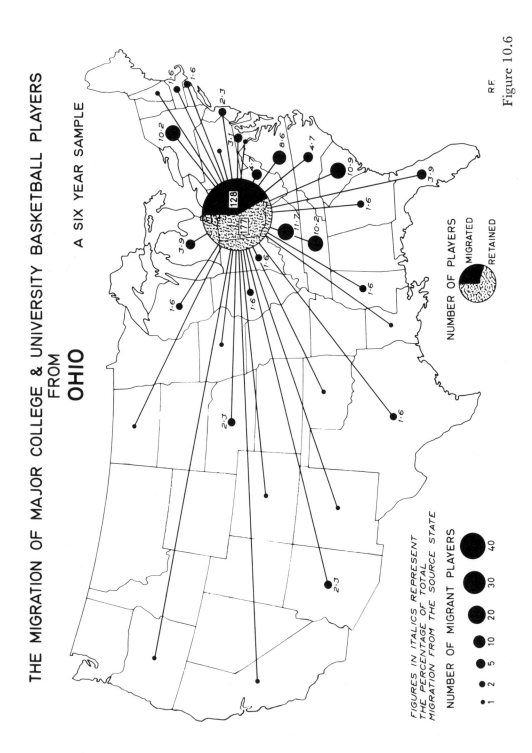

THE MIGRATION OF MAJOR COLLEGE & UNIVERSITY BASKETBALL PLAYERS

FROM

OHIO

A SIX YEAR SAMPLE

NUMBER OF PLAYERS

MIGRATED

RETAINED

FIGURES IN ITALICS REPRESENT
THE PERCENTAGE OF TOTAL
MIGRATION FROM THE SOURCE STATE

NUMBER OF MIGRANT PLAYERS

1 2 5 10 20 30 40

R.F.

Figure 10.6

was very similar, with 17 from Pennsylvania, 15 from New York, 8 New Jersey boys, and four each from Kentucky and Indiana.[7]

Most of the Pennsylvanians who migrate to the Northeast compete in New York and New Jersey (Fig. 10-5). The group is highly represented by boys from the Philadelphia area. This movement is partly offset by the flow of New Jerseyites into Pennsylvania, a phenomenon indicative of the local recruiting intensity within the megalopolitan zone stretching from New York City to Washington, D. C.

RECRUITING FROM THE NORTHEAST

The northeastern region is one of limited surplus, confined almost entirely to New York and New Jersey, states which rank third and fifth nationally on the basis of players exported. New Jersey sends out many more boys than it takes in, but New York's exports are nearly counterbalanced by imports greater in number than any other state (Figs. 10-7 and 10-8). Over forty percent of the exports from the two states stay in the Northeast, and of those who leave, nearly half journey no farther than the adjacent Atlantic Coast region. It is apparent that most eastern seaboard coaches regard the entire northeastern territory as their own. The migratory behavior of northeastern hoopsters is, in many ways, analogous to Texas footballers. The Northeast has its own style of play and a great pride in the previously described City Game. Hence, most of the eastern powers are manned by local products.

The demand for northeastern players is becoming more widespread, though, as the movement to the Midwest, Texas, and California indicates. Recently Marquette and U.C.L.A. have utilized New York and New Jersey talent to considerable advantage. The University of South Carolina, long the doormat of the Atlantic Coast Conference, has sprung forth as an independent basketball power through the almost exclusive use of New York products.

RECRUITING FROM CALIFORNIA

California is a principal donor to universities in the Northwest and in some sections of the Rocky Mountain zone (Fig. 10-9). Oregon, Utah, Washington, and Arizona are the major recipients. Californians have supplemented the heavy local production of college players in Utah and Oregon, helping to build several nationally ranked contenders in both states. Although players from California have been drawn

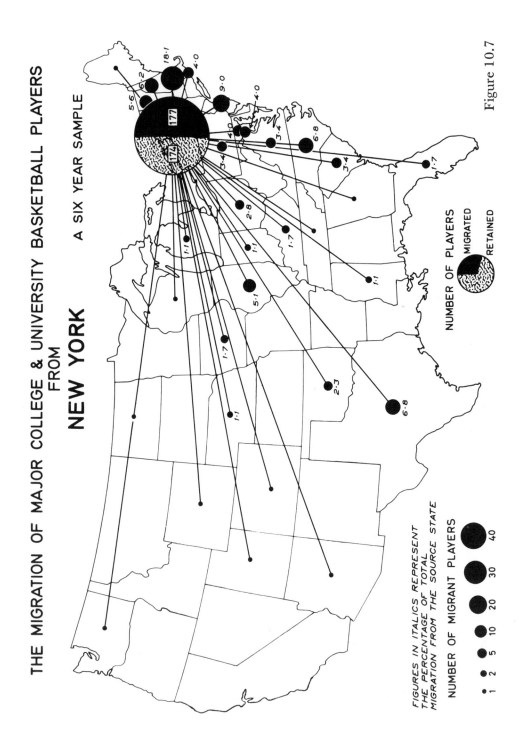

THE MIGRATION OF MAJOR COLLEGE & UNIVERSITY BASKETBALL PLAYERS
FROM
NEW YORK

A SIX YEAR SAMPLE

NUMBER OF PLAYERS
MIGRATED
RETAINED

FIGURES IN ITALICS REPRESENT
THE PERCENTAGE OF TOTAL
MIGRATION FROM THE SOURCE STATE

NUMBER OF MIGRANT PLAYERS
1 2 5 10 20 30 40

Figure 10.7

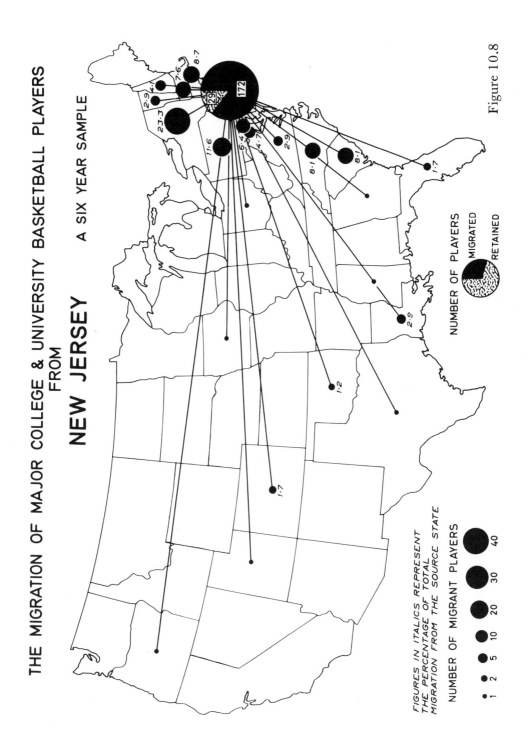

THE MIGRATION OF MAJOR COLLEGE & UNIVERSITY BASKETBALL PLAYERS

FROM

NEW JERSEY

A SIX YEAR SAMPLE

FIGURES IN ITALICS REPRESENT THE PERCENTAGE OF TOTAL MIGRATION FROM THE SOURCE STATE

NUMBER OF MIGRANT PLAYERS

1 2 5 10 20 30 40

NUMBER OF PLAYERS

MIGRATED

RETAINED

Figure 10.8

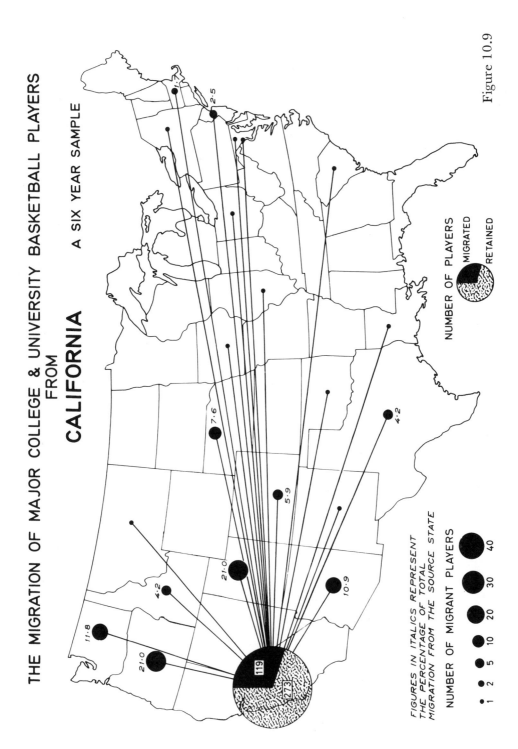

THE MIGRATION OF MAJOR COLLEGE & UNIVERSITY BASKETBALL PLAYERS
FROM
CALIFORNIA   A SIX YEAR SAMPLE

NUMBER OF PLAYERS
MIGRATED
RETAINED

FIGURES IN ITALICS REPRESENT
THE PERCENTAGE OF TOTAL
MIGRATION FROM THE SOURCE STATE

NUMBER OF MIGRANT PLAYERS
1   2   5   10   20   30   40

Figure 10.9

in significant numbers to locations as far east as Colorado and Nebraska, their attraction to recruiters dries up quickly in the Rocky Mountain region. The basketball and football migrations from the state are remarkably similar. In both sports, California serves the talent needs of the Pacific Coast and Western Athletic Conferences. Most schools in this area also tend to rely heavily on the IllInKy and Midwest areas. The contrast between Arizona, which recruits in California, and New Mexico, which is oriented toward Illinois, is most illustrative (Figs. 10–2 and 10–9).

The upper Midwest loses some of its output to recruiters from the Plains and Rockies. But only a few schools have found this region to be a key recruiting territory. The small loss is more than replaced by prospects from IllInKy, the source of two-thirds of the area's immigrants.

GENERAL PATTERNS

The outstanding high school basketball players are sought out regardless of where they live and are often besieged by more offers than they could possibly evaluate in any rational manner. The New York City metropolitan area and Philadelphia, along with Washington, D.C., Pittsburgh, Chicago, and Los Angeles are the hunting grounds of recruiters from all over the country. By visiting these six metropolises, the talent seekers could have gained access to over one-quarter of the major college players solicited during the last six years. Some of the best are products of the rigorous competition associated with high schools of multithousand enrollments.

Playing in the shadow of numerous city universities, coaches, scouts, and various under-the-table operators greatly enhances the probability of recruitment. In addition, the presence of alumni in major cities who possess widely scattered college loyalties has a similar effect. Notre Dame has been making its mark in the basketball arena through a massive recruiting effort in Washington, D.C., New York City, and Philadelphia. These players have brought success to teams as far apart as U.C.L.A. and Davidson and most recently to the University of South Carolina. Even though many of the superstars get away, the majority of the big city players perform locally, where opportunity abounds. As a result, teams like Villanova, Manhattan, Temple, Fordham, St. John's, Lasalle, St. Joseph's, Pennsylvania, Rutgers, Princeton, and Columbia seem to field strong entries with great regularity.

Fierce competition for the well-known high school stalwarts is to be expected. But there is also a substantial movement of the journeyman players across state and regional boundaries. Over 60 percent of the major college players participate outside their home states, and 35 percent cross over the broad regional divisions which were previously identified (Fig. 10-1). The general population mobility in the United States finds a great microexpression where basketball is concerned.

THE OVEREMPHASIZERS

On the basis of local population and the ability to groom potential college players, several states greatly overemphasize the college game. To some extent, this emphasis has occurred by the chance location of private schools within their political boundaries. The region generally encompassed by the universities of the Atlantic Coast and Southern Conferences is illustrative, with schools like Richmond, V.M.I., Davidson, Duke, Wake Forest, Furman, and Clemson all striving, and most succeeding, at major college basketball. However, even taking the role of the private institutions into account, the Atlantic Coast area is still overdoing it, relative to their current capacity to produce players.

The other kind of overemphasis is epitomized in the Rocky Mountain zone, approximating the areal extent of the Western Athletic Conference. As in the case of football, member schools and others in the vicinity are conducting athletic programs which can in no way be supported by the local population of high school talent. The region is providing more players than its meager population justifies, but there are too many programs for even phenomenal per capita outputs like Utah's to accommodate. Utah has produced college players at a per capita pace of nearly three times the national norm (Chapter 7). Yet over half of the Utah collegians had to be imported from other states. The Mormons have elected to include "big time" athletics in their three state universities and one major private institution, and this decision has necessitated a vast recruiting program. Similar decisions have been taken in sparsely populated Arizona, New Mexico, Wyoming, and Colorado. The other mountain states, Idaho and Montana, are beginning to follow their lead, having greatly increased their competitive ability during the last five years. This emphasis is possible because of high schoolboy output in other sectors of the country combined with less concern for subsidizing university athletic departments. This is in contrast to the relatively scant number of schools in Wisconsin, Minnesota, New Jersey, and even Illinois and Indiana, which are attempting to compete in the NCAA major college division (Table 4-3). It is interesting to speculate about the impact of a decision by the numerous midwestern and eastern state colleges and universities to go "big time." The surplus regions of IllInKy and Pennsylvania-Ohio would experience greatly increased levels of competition for their athletes, making it more difficult for the deficit region recruiters. Such a move could lead to a deterioration in Atlantic Coast and western area play, but it would likely prod the improvement of the high school game in both areas.

The development of good teams affords isolated universities national recognition which they might otherwise be denied. It seems to make little difference to local fans where the players come from, as enthusiasm in the Western Athletic and Atlantic Coast Conferences indicates. The University of Wyoming, which in past years has had as few as three natives on its football team and one in basketball, can claim some of the most hearty and involved supporters in the country.

DIFFERENCES BETWEEN THE MAJORS AND MINORS

As was demonstrated in the case of North Dakota State University football, the recruiting behavior of the major universities is very different from that of the small colleges. For basketball, data have been assembled on the 1971-1972 recruitment patterns of all of the four year colleges and universities in Indiana. The contrast between the NCAA and NAIA institutions is great (Figs. 10-10 and 10-11). Examining only those players obtained from within the state (over 70 percent of the total), we found that 58 percent of the NAIA players traveled less than 30 miles from their home to the college of their choice. Less than 30 percent of the NCAA competitors traveled such a short distance.

A careful look at each school's recruitment territory points up the relationship between the area they tap and the geographical variations in quality of high school basketball. For example NAIA members, Hanover, Tri-State, Oakland City, and Rose–Hulman are located in relatively poor player production regions. This results in recruitment of players from average distances of 68 miles, 96 miles, and 69 miles, respectively. In fact if those schools were eliminated from the NAIA group, the average distance drops to 30 miles per player. Note the clusters associated with most of the schools (Fig. 10-10).

The small college game is often played in a
"crackerbox gym" before sparse crowds, even
in the basketball heartland.

With more money and greater prestige, the larger universities
have, over the years, expanded their recruiting areas. Since only five
to ten players are brought in annually, distance has had little effect
on their behavior (Fig. 10–11). As a result they reach out farther
within the state and also penetrate farther out of state in an effort to
obtain the best prospects.

INSTATE RECRUITING OF COLLEGIATE BASKETBALL PLAYERS
BY NCAA INSTITUTIONS
1971 - 72

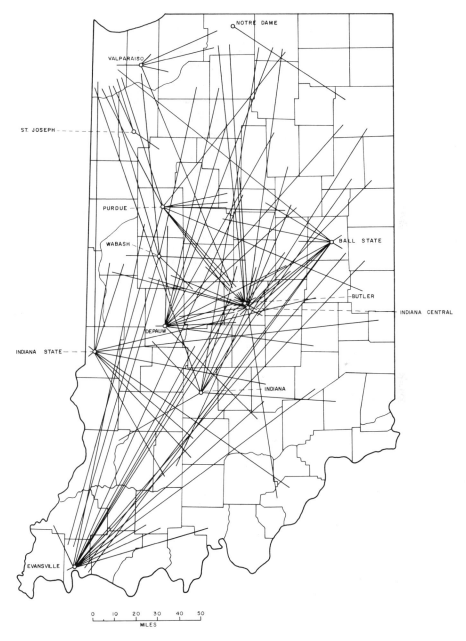

1 LINE INDICATES THE MIGRATORY ROUTE OF 1 PLAYER FROM HOME COUNTY

Fig. 10.10 After Roger Jenkinson, "A Geography of Indiana Basketball," unpublished doctoral dissertation, Oklahoma State University, 1974.[8]

INSTATE RECRUITING OF COLLEGIATE BASKETBALL PLAYERS
BY NAIA INSTITUTIONS
1971 - 72

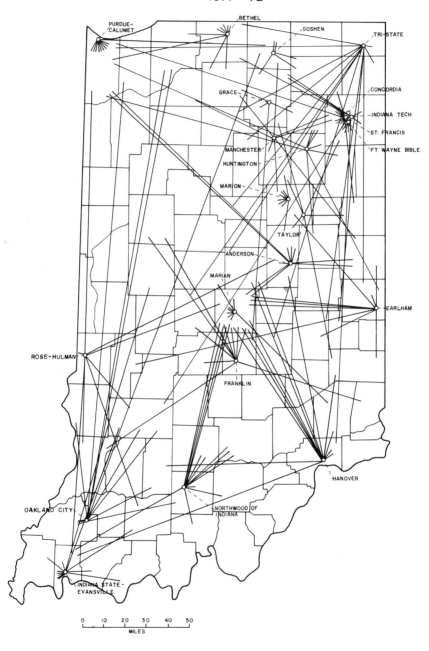

1 LINE INDICATES THE MIGRATORY ROUTE OF 1 PLAYER FROM HOME COUNTY

Fig. 10.11 After Roger Jenkinson, "A Geography of Indiana Basketball," unpublished doctoral dissertation, Oklahoma State University, 1974.[9]

NOTES

1. The slush fund administered by the booster club at the University of Illinois was brought to light in 1967. It involved illegal payment for travel and other items to athletes over a considerable period of time and resulted in a complete turnover in athletic administration.

2. Based on questionnaire sent to basketball coaches in selected states during 1970.

3. From a letter written by Al Harden, April, 1970.

4. Correspondence from Shelbyville, Indiana basketball coach, April, 1970.

5. Correspondence from Bill Chesborogh, Basketball Coach at Elgin, Illinois High School, April, 1970.

6. Correspondence from Spanish Fork, and Cedar City, Utah basketball coaches, April, 1970.

7. The 1971–72 data included the South Carolina University roster, even though it is no longer a member of the Atlantic Coast Conference.

8. Roger Jenkinson, "A Geography of Indiana Basketball," unpublished doctoral dissertation, Oklahoma State University, 1974.

9. *Ibid.*

11 / Women's Sport

Women's athletics have long been suppressed in the United States. Girls are just not encouraged to participate in organized sport to the extent that boys are, and those who do participate have only limited athletic career opportunities. Professional tennis, golf, and ice skating provide only a few slots for the very best of the women competitors. Some, like Mickey Wright, Billie Jean King, Kathy Whitworth, Margaret Court, Peggy Fleming, and Jane Blalock are fairly well known, but the majority are obscure compared to their male counterparts. Professional sport for women is so rare that the basketball and softball players, roller derbyites, and wrestlers are commonly viewed as freak attractions. They are entertainers first and athletes second. Our society has discriminated against the woman athlete much too long. Hopefully, if current trends continue, women will finally attain their rightful place in the realm of sport.[1]

GEOGRAPHIC VARIATIONS

The data on women's sport is extremely limited in contrast to that available for men. However, there is enough information to make some general place-to-place comparisons for the sports played and for the amount of participation. The International Federation of High School Athletic Associations has complied information at the state level on girl's interscholastic sport.[2]

Based on their data it appears that girls are at last being given the chance to become involved in interscholastic competition.

TABLE 11-1
GIRLS PARTICIPATION IN HIGH SCHOOL SPORT

States	Total participation in all girls' sports	State rank per capita	States	Total participation in all girls' sports	State rank per capita
Alabama	100	43	Montana	2050	18.5
Alaska	410	30	Nebraska	35,598	1
Arizona	2765	29	Nevada	1515	13.5
Arkansas	1500	36	New Hampshire	1993	16.5
California	no data	—	New Jersey	22,290	13.5
Colorado	1964	34	New Mexico	2300	25
Connecticut	7090	20.5	New York	no data	—
Delaware	1600	16.5	North Carolina	3800	37
Florida	1165	42	North Dakota	4450	4.5
Georgia	2448	39	Ohio	0203	35
Hawaii	2291	15	Oklahoma	5400	22
Idaho	189	41	Oregon	2100	33
Illinois	no data	—	Pennsylvania	no data	—
Indiana	23,100	8	Rhode Island	461	38
Iowa	no data	—	South Carolina	9750	12
Kansas	25,015	2	South Dakota	4200	6.5
Kentucky	5900	26	Tennessee	10,236	18.5
Louisiana	6955	27	Texas	42,795	11
Maine	475	40	Utah	no data	—
Maryland	5948	28	Vermont	2376	6.5
Massachusetts	21,288	9.5	Virginia	9352	23.5
Michigan	23,200	20.5	West Virginia	2107	32
Minnesota	no data	44	Washington	22,575	4.5
Mississippi	5090	23.5	Wisconsin	13,706	31
Missouri	18,098	9.5	Wyoming	2557	3

Marilyn Linsenmeyer is a woman athlete who doubles as a pom-pom girl. As a junior at Oklahoma State University she won the 200-meter hurdle event at the National AIAW meet held at Irvine, California during May, 1973. She also placed 4th in the high jump. Above, Marilyn is an easy winner in the Drake Relays 100-meter hurdles.

Though many states still discourage girls' athletics, the majority of them are now promoting basketball, track, field hockey, bowling, and softball. Using the International Federation data, we can analyze the geography of girls' participation in the same way that boys' participation was. A per capita index can be calculated for each state, based on the percentage of girls competing in each sport, relative to the national average.

There were probably on the order of 500,000 girls competing in high school interscholastic sport during the 1972–1973 academic year, a figure which represents less than 15 percent of the male participation. Texas was the leading state as measured by the number of girls involved. Nebraska, Kansas, Michigan, New Jersey, Massachusetts, and Washington were also high in the total participation category (Table 11–1).

From a per capita standpoint the highest participation centers in the Plains States, reaching its zenith in Nebraska and Kansas. Iowa with its reputation for outstanding girls' basketball should probably be grouped with the area, for it has over 15,000 girls playing basketball alone.[3] New England, New Jersey, and Delaware comprise another area of high female involvement. South Carolina and Tennessee stand out in a Southern region which is generally far below the national norm. Washington is also a high anomaly in the Northwest.

Basketball, followed by track and volleyball, are the leading girls' sports based on the number of participants. Tennis, softball, and gymnastics are also important. As would be expected there are pronounced regional differences in the sports which the girls are playing (Fig. 11–1).

Basketball is most popular in the Plains, New England, and in some parts of the South. It is almost totally absent in the western United States. Except for New England, girls track is popular in essentially the same States that basketball is. Kansas and Nebraska record the highest per capita participation. Volleyball is concentrated in a smaller number of states—the most important ones, Nebraska, Wyoming, Minnesota, Kansas, and Texas, all exceed the national average by four times. Virtually all the participation is located in the central third of the nation. The West and the South are void with the exception of Hawaii, Alaska, and South Carolina.

Tennis competition is sprinkled rather evenly about the country. Girls' tennis is available in all but a few states, and only three, Washington, Arizona, and Minnesota, substantially exceed the national average. Gymnastics is the major western activity. It is also a vital part of the programs in Minnesota, New England, Indiana, Virginia, South Carolina,

PARTICIPATION IN GIRLS' HIGH SCHOOL SPORTS

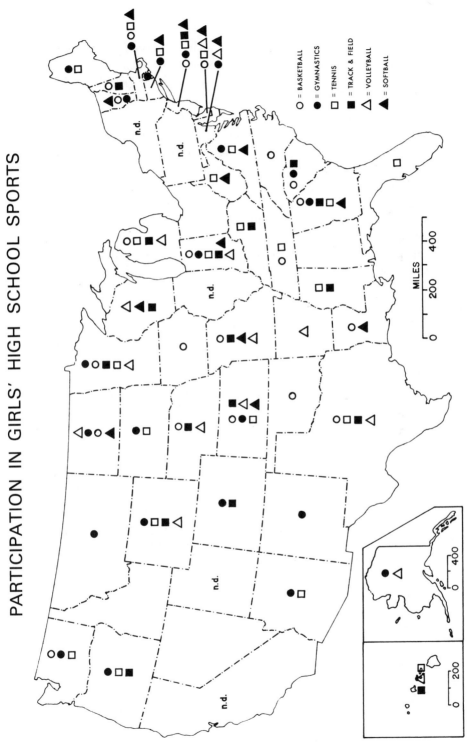

O = BASKETBALL
● = GYMNASTICS
□ = TENNIS
■ = TRACK & FIELD
△ = VOLLEYBALL
▲ = SOFTBALL

n.d.

MILES

0   200   400

SYMBOLS INDICATE THAT THE STATE'S PER CAPITA PARTICIPATION IS ABOVE THE NATIONAL AVERAGE

Figure 11.1

and Georgia. Softball is almost exclusively played in the Northeast, with a pocket of interest in Michigan, Indiana, and Missouri.

Is it apparent that high school athletics for girls vary greatly from place to place. It is clear that some states are according a high priority to the provision of competitive athletic experiences for girls, while others are completely ignoring their needs. Indiana, Kansas, and Minnesota appear to be supporting the most well-balanced programs. However, there is some evidence to suggest that even in these states, and in the others which rank above the national norm, the provision of athletics for girls is skewed toward the smaller communities. Bussett found a highly significant relationship between a state's rank in girls' per capita participation and its rank in the number of communities with between 2500–10,000 population.[4] Conversely, she found a negative relationship between participation and the percent of urban population. This suggests that the "in group" in the larger city high schools have been conditioned away from competitive sport. If the girls and their parents shun sport, it is very difficult to convince the school board to finance and promote viable programs. On the other hand, small-town girls are attracted to sport, which in their environment is a very acceptable and even laudable social outlet. In those states which take girls' sport seriously, it even represents a route to fame and attention.

INTERCOLLEGIATE SPORT

Women's intercollegiate athletics receive even less attention than high school sports. Scores of games (even those associated with regional, conference, and national championships), data on the players and coaches, and schedules of events are very hard to come by. Thus since we know so little at the national level, it is difficult to say anything definitive concerning place-to-place differences.

In an attempt to fill the information void, Mosely and Van Whitley undertook a preliminary study of women's intramural and intercollegiate sports.[5] Their study was based on responses from 86 universities located in 45 states.

Based on the number of universities that sponser teams, basketball proved to be the most popular intercollegiate and intramural sport (Table 11–2). Over 70 percent of the sampled institutions engaged in intercollegiate basketball competition. Tennis was a close second in popularity, followed by volleyball, field hockey,

TABLE 11-2
PARTICIPATION IN WOMEN'S INTERCOLLEGIATE SPORTS BY REGIONS

Sport	West, percent	South, percent	North Central, percent	Northeast, percent	National, percent
Basketball	80	57	92	67	73.5
Volleyball	87	61	84	43	69.5
Softball	87	11	60	29	43
Hockey	47	14	60	71	44
Kickball	7	0	0	0	1
Bowling	20	14	16	21	17
Tennis	73	71	72	64	71
Archery	7	7	4	21	10
Swimming	47	21	52	43	39
Fencing	7	11	21	14	13.5
Badminton	33	21	17	21	22
Golf	20	32	50	0	30
Table Tennis	7	7	4	0	5
Flag Football	7	4	0	0	2.4
Gymnastics	80	14	62.5	57	48
Track	67	18	42	7	32
Others	33	4	12	50	19.5

and softball. Gymnastics, swimming, and track were available to the women at over one-third of the responding universities.

Mosely and Van Whitley divided the nation according to the four major census regions and calculated the major sports for each region. Their findings indicated pronounced geographical variation in the games played (Fig. 11-2). Tennis is a major sport in all but the western region. The Northeast favors a field hockey–tennis combination, the Midwest basketball–tennis, and the South embraces volleyball and tennis. In the west volleyball, softball, and gymnastics are the leading activities.

There are strong indications that intercollegiate women's sport is entering into a tremendous growth phase. The Association of Intercollegiate Athletics for Women (AIAW) was established in 1972 for the purpose of coordinating activity at both the regional and national scale. It is an outgrowth of the Commission on Intercollegiate Athletics for Women (CIAW), which was set up just five years before. Under the CIAW the first national collegiate

REGIONALIZATION OF THE LEADING WOMEN'S INTERCOLLEGIATE SPORTS

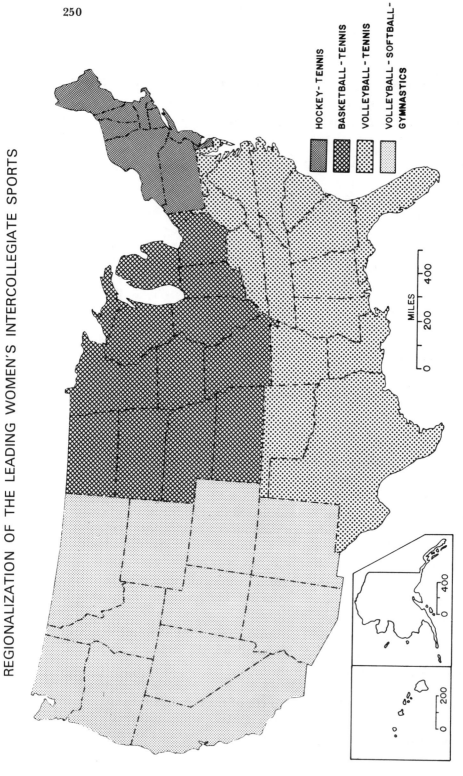

HOCKEY - TENNIS

BASKETBALL - TENNIS

VOLLEYBALL - TENNIS

VOLLEYBALL - SOFTBALL - GYMNASTICS

MILES

0   200   400

0   200

0   400

Figure 11.2

women's championship (gymnastics) was held in 1968. The equal
rights for women legislation should soon have a powerful influence
on those who control the intercollegiate athletic purse-strings. Already the University of New Mexico has reallocated $35,000 from
its men's athletic budget to help finance its women's sports program.
Many universities will have to follow suit, and in all probability with
substantially larger sums of money. This should allow for a great expansion in athletic opportunities for coeds and should provide a
training ground for the development of more lady professionals in
a wider variety of sports.

How will women's athletics be organized from a geographical
standpoint? Which universities will elect to participate? The
AIAW has divided the country into nine regions for the organization
of competition and the establishment of tournment sites. There
were 287 active member schools as of Spring, 1973. Over 30 percent of the membership was located in the Northeast. Another
region of strength focuses on Illinois, Ohio, and Missouri. California
and Utah are also well represented. The regions of lowest interest
appear to be the Deep South and the Southwest.

National and regional champions are now being crowned in
seven sports. The national tourney sites for 1973 included; Memphis
State, badminton, Queens, basketball, Iowa, gymnastics, Massachusetts,
golf, Idaho, swimming and diving, California State at Hayward, track
and field, and Utah, volleyball. The most successful universities
in recent years include Penn State, Illinois State, Illinois and
Southern Illinois, Brigham Young, Long Beach State, Queens,
Immaculata, and Mount Holyoke.

SPORTS CENTERS

There has been a strong tendency toward supremacy in a given sport
by either one university or by a small group of schools. For example,
the past three United States Olympic track teams have been dominated
by girls from Tennessee State University, although only one team
member was from the State of Tennessee. All but two of the Southern-
bred Olympians attended Tennessee State, as did a number of girls
from Indiana, Illinois, and Ohio. Aside from Tennessee State the
majority of the Olympians affiliated with track clubs independent of
the universities. A few—Los Angeles, Chicago, San Diego, and
Cleveland—dominated.

Gymnastics excellence is likewise a highly concentrated phenomena. Southern Illinois University has been the prime force. In
a sport where most of the competitors reach their peak before college
age, Southern Illinois has, in the last fifteen years, sent forth six
Olympians, four to the World Games, ten to the Pan American Games,
and over forty to major American competitions. As in the case of
track, the gymnasts have been attracted by the presence of a superb
coach, in this case, Herb Vogel.

California is superior in swimming and volleyball. Most of the
best swimmers are precollegians, who compete at the club level.
Exactly one-half of the Olympic swimmers from the 1960–1968
period were from California, while New Jersey and Pennsylvania
provided nearly 25 percent between them. Access to the water
and a winterless climate have been beneficial to the California programs, but one wonders why similar interest and expertise has not
evolved along the Gulf and South Atlantic coasts. Most of the northern swimmers are pool-trained in the wealthy suburban schools around
NewYork, Philadelphia, and Chicago.

Volleyball would appear to have similar outdoor roots. It is
known as a beach game in southern California and along the Gulf
coast of Texas. National women's competition has been dominated
by teams from the Los Angeles area, particularly Santa Monica and
Long Beach, and from Houston, Texas. Honolulu and Chicago have
also appeared in the National finals. Collegiate volleyball entered
into a growth phase in 1965, and the national tournament is now
attracting teams from New York, the Midwest, and the Southeast
in addition to those from California and Texas.

PROFESSIONAL PROSPECTS

Golf and tennis provide the greatest opportunity for women who aspire to a career in professional sports. The Ladies' Golf Tour has
followed in the footsteps of the PGA, its male equivalent. The 1973
tour had more events and significantly larger purses than ever before.
Thirty tournaments were scheduled with total prize money of nearly
$1,300,000. However fewer than 40 of the ladies earned over
$10,000. Thus despite this growth environment, golf provides an
opportunity for only a very talented few, and most of the aspirants
have virtually no chance for success.

Compared to golf, tennis is even harder to crack. After years of
small crowds and even smaller stakes, the sport has gained sponsor-

ship from a cigarette company. A tournament circuit has been established but only 16–32 women can compete in any event. Thus a grand and glorious living is available to the best players, but the probability of reaching the top is very slim.

What will the future bring for women professionals? Will the growth of sport at the collegiate level spawn professional leagues in basketball, softball, and perhaps even volleyball? Will the women join the men on the professional track circuit? What sections of the country will promote women's competition?

Given the fact that the small towns enthusiastically support girls' high school sport, it is tempting to speculate that they too might support professional basketball. The barn-storming lady pros are currently attracting substantial crowds in the small communities. It, therefore, seems possible that women's professional basketball could be successful, perhaps through the establishment of regional franchises, composed of submetropolitan-sized communities. The Iowa girls' basketball hysteria is spreading. Why should it stop at the high school commencement reception?

NOTES

1. For an interesting discussion of the female dilemma in sport, see M. Marie Hart, "On Being Female in Sport," in *Sport in the Sociocultural Process*, ed. by M. Marie Hart (Dubuque, Iowa: W. C. Brown, 1972), pp. 291–302. See also *Women and Sport: A National Research Conference*, ed. by Dorothy V. Harris, Penn State HPER Series (State College, Pennsylvania), November 2, 1973.

2. *Official Handbook 1972–73*, National Federation of State High School Athletic Associations, (Elgin, Illinois, 1974) p. 74–85.

3. "Les Girls in DesMoines," *Sports Illustrated*, February 17, 1969, pp. 72–74.

4. Carla Bussett, "The Geography of Participation in Women's High School Sport." Unpublished report, Oklahoma State University, May, 1973.

5. Karen Mosely and Ada Van Whitley, "Women's Intramural and Intercollegiate Sports in the United States." Unpublished report, Oklahoma State University, May, 1972.

12 / Other American Sports

Thus far we have devoted most of our attention to football, basketball, and baseball. For many Americans these "national" games are of little or no importance compared to the sport or sports with which they identify. It is impossible to comment here on the geographical aspects of all the "minor" games due to a paucity of information. However, we can say something about those played at the high school and college level and those for which information on player origins and facilities are readily available.

TRACK AND FIELD

As measured by the number of boys participating, track and field is in the same category with basketball. Approximately one out of every twelve high school boys is participating in track. Involvement in outdoor track reaches its peak in the Plains and North Central regions where six states exceed 2.5 times the national average (Fig. 12-1). It is lowest in the Northeast. Maine, Massachusetts, Rhode Island, and New York are especially low. Throughout the South, participation is also very limited as evidenced by Mississippi (.21), North Carolina (.35), and Louisiana (.39). In terms of performance the best track states are California and Texas. During the average year their athletes record the majority of the best times and performances in the running and field events.

The cross country situation is startlingly different from track. In some cases a state's low participation in track is offset by high par-

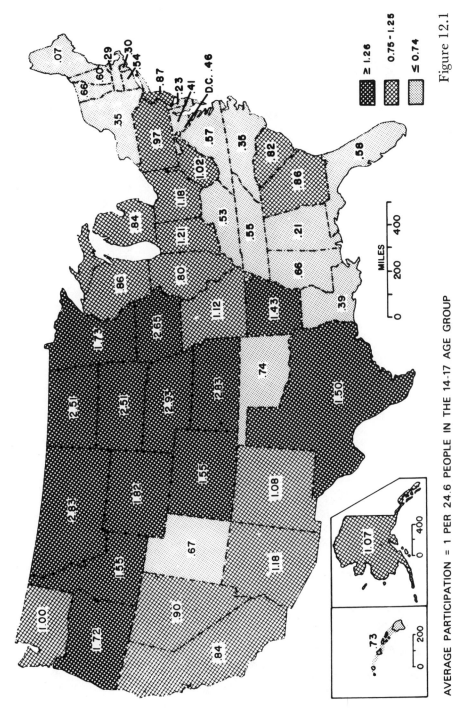

PER CAPITA PARTICIPATION IN HIGH SCHOOL OUTDOOR TRACK - 1971 - 72

Figure 12.1

AVERAGE PARTICIPATION = 1 PER 24.6 PEOPLE IN THE 14-17 AGE GROUP

≥ 1.26

0.75 - 1.25

≤ 0.74

MILES

0   200   400

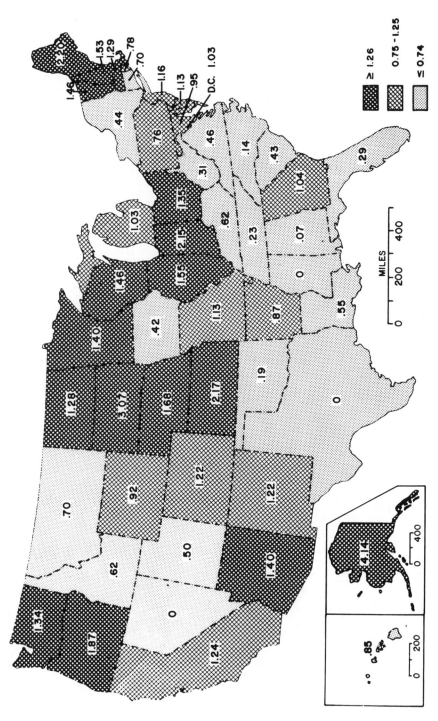

PER CAPITA PARTICIPATION IN HIGH SCHOOL CROSS COUNTRY   -   1971 - 72

AVERAGE PARTICIPATION = 1 PER 95.3 PEOPLE IN THE 14-17 AGE GROUP

Fig. 11.2 Based on Mosley and Van Whitley.

≥ 1.26

0.75 - 1.25

≤ 0.74

Amateur wrestling is one of the fastest growing sports in America.
It now outdraws basketball in many communities.

ticipation in cross country (compare Figs. 12-1 and 12-2). Per capita
involvement in cross country peaks in northern New England, the
Midwest, the northern Plains, and in the Pacific Northwest where it is
Alaska's major sport. As with track, participation in most of the
southern states is very low. Texas and Mississippi reported no participation whatsoever.

WRESTLING

Wrestling is the fifth leading high school sport on the basis of total
participation and has also experienced the fastest growth rate during
the last decade. However, there is still an extreme regional variation

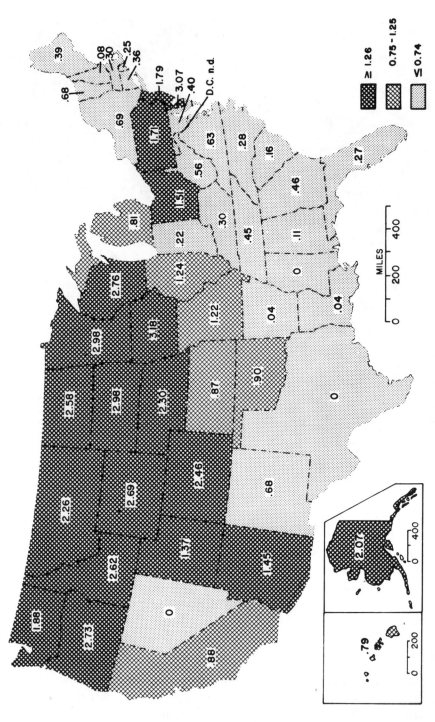

PER CAPITA PARTICIPATION IN HIGH SCHOOL WRESTLING - 1971 - 72

≥ 1.26

0.75 - 1.25

≤ 0.74

Figure 12.3

AVERAGE PARTICIPATION = 1 PER 59.8 PEOPLE IN THE 14-17 AGE GROUP

in the provision of wrestling programs (Fig. 12-3). Thirteen states, led by Iowa, which also places a high priority on collegiate wrestling, have participation of two or more times the national average. Two regions, New England and the South, are far below the national average. Mississippi and Texas reported no wrestling at all! New England has a composite index of only 0.30, while Alabama, Louisiana, Arkansas, South Carolina, and Indiana had indices of less than 0.25. In New England, hockey dominates at the expense of wrestling, while the poor showing of the South is consistent with their performance in most other high school sports. Oklahoma, the state with the most esteemed collegiate wrestling tradition, has surprisingly low high school participation. The similar situation in adjacent Texas and Arkansas is also difficult to explain.

GOLF

Of the 10 million active golfers in the United States, over 120,000 are male members of high school golf teams. Approximately one of every 64 high school boys participated in competitive interscholastic golf during the 1971–1972 school year. The leading golf states on a per capita basis include Iowa, Kansas, and Minnesota with indices of 2.00 or above (Fig. 12-4). Illinois, Texas, Nebraska, North Dakota, and Indiana exceed the national average by at least 50 percent. States with below-average participation are, for the most part, located in either the Northeast or the South. Low participation in New York, New Jersey, and Rhode Island appears to be a function of the large urban high schools and the lack of ample space for golf facilities. A combination of relatively poor support for education and the difficulties experienced by blacks trying to get on courses results in poor support for golf in southern high schools. Climate does not seem to be as important a factor as would be expected. Many of the cold states are above the national norm (Fig. 12-4). In fact, participation in golf, as with other sports, seems to be most affected by population density and the pattern of settlement.

Geographical differences in the importance of golf can also be measured by examining a place's ability to nurture and develop high-quality players. Geographical data are available on the touring professionals. Compared to other sports the sample of golfers is small, but nevertheless gives some insights concerning the geography of emphasis.

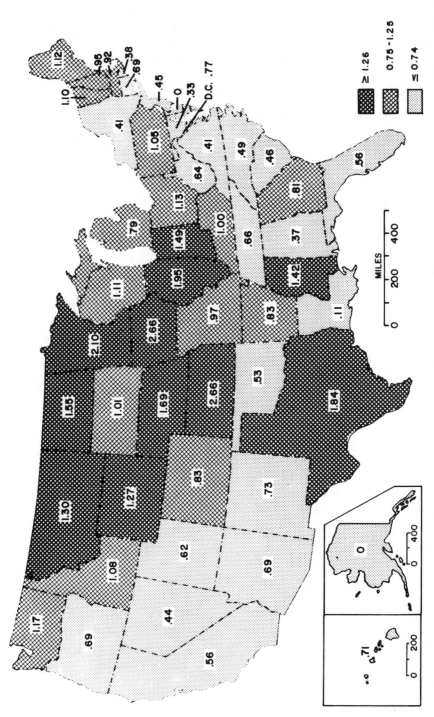

PER CAPITA PARTICIPATION IN HIGH SCHOOL GOLF - 1971 - 72

Figure 12.4

AVERAGE PARTICIPATION = 1 PER 132 PEOPLE IN THE 14-17 AGE GROUP

≥ 1.26

0.75 - 1.25

≤ 0.74

STATE PRODUCTION OF TOURING PROFESSIONALS

GOLF

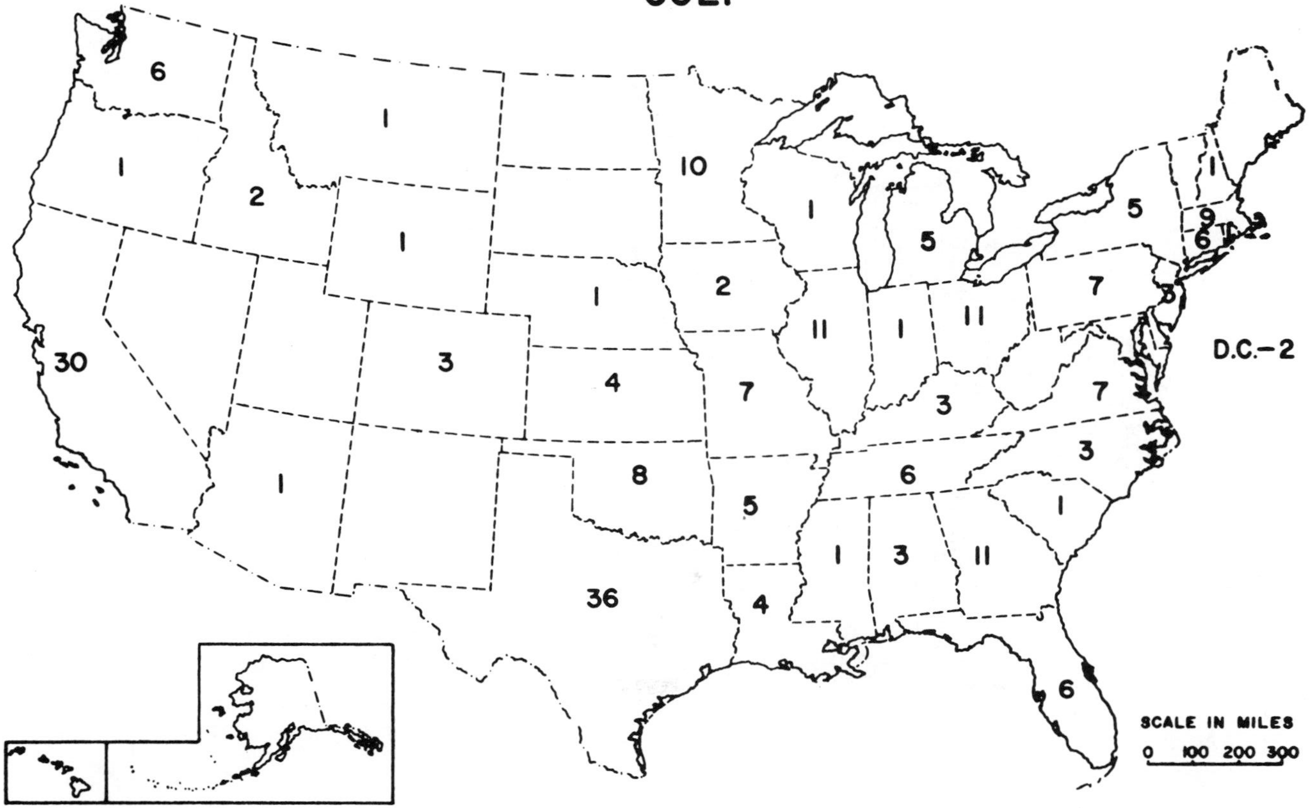

SCALE IN MILES

0   100   200   300

D.C.—2

SOURCE: 1971 P.G.A. TOUR BOOK

Figure 12.5a

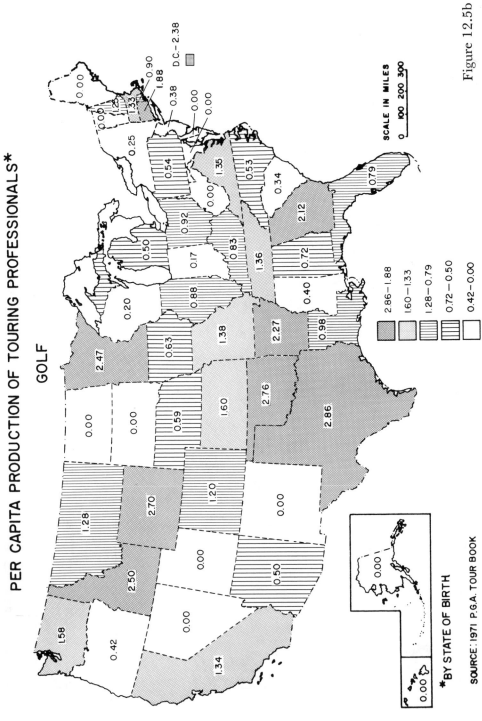

PER CAPITA PRODUCTION OF TOURING PROFESSIONALS*

GOLF

D.C. - 2.38

2.86 – 1.88
1.60 – 1.33
1.28 – 0.79
0.72 – 0.50
0.42 – 0.00

SCALE IN MILES
0   100 200 300

*BY STATE OF BIRTH

SOURCE: 1971 P.G.A. TOUR BOOK

Figure 12.5b

REGIONAL PER CAPITA PRODUCTION OF TOURING PROFESSIONALS
GOLF

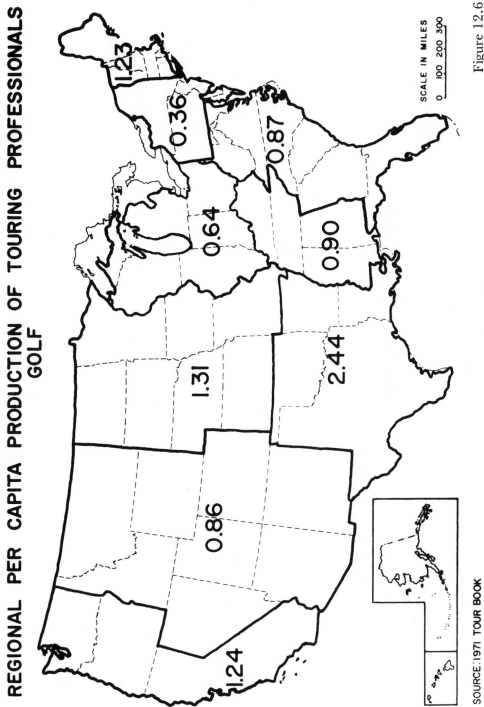

SCALE IN MILES

0   100 200 300

Figure 12.6

SOURCE: 1971 TOUR BOOK

There were 218 certified touring professionals in 1970. This group had access to competition in 41 major tournaments and over 20 lesser events. As is the case with other sports, the production of golfers shows considerable geographic variation (Fig. 12-5).[1] The "Sun Belt" states of Texas and California accounted for 30 percent of the touring pros. The per capita rate in Texas was 2.86, with California at 1.34. The effect of good weather on the development of golfers is also apparent in the southern Plains and in several of the southeastern states. Minnesota is by far the best state in the north, while Connecticut, Massachusetts, New Hampshire, and Montana are the only other states that rank above the national average. Of the large urban states, New York, Maryland, Michigan, and Indiana are each producing at rates of less than one-fourth the national norm.

The pattern of golfer origin is difficult to explain. A look at regional productivity gives a somewhat less confusing picture (Fig. 12-6). Climate would appear to be the most important variable, even though there are many exceptions including Florida, Alabama, and the Carolinas. Access to high school programs could be significant in the Texas and Minnesota cases and act as a deterrent in the South. However, with such a small sample we are probably safer in avoiding definitive statements about the types of environments which promote the development of outstanding golfers.

SOCCER

Soccer exhibits a strong regional concentration of participation. Only one high school boy in 100 plays soccer (Fig. 12-7). There are 26 states that reported no soccer competition whatsoever. The game is biggest in the Northeast, where the leading states and their respective indices are Vermont (9.71), New Hampshire (5.80), New Jersey (4.60), Maine (3.73), and Connecticut (3.51). Even New York and Maryland have more than twice the national average participation in soccer. Perhaps the proximity to western Europe and the relatively large proportion of recent immigrants has something to do with the northeastern affinity for soccer. Georgia, Hawaii, and Missouri, with its great tradition in the St. Louis area, are the only states outside the Northeast with above-average participation.

Although intercollegiate soccer competition receives scant attention from the press, there were 482 clubs playing the game during the 1971–1972 school year. The geographical distribution of partic-

PER CAPITA PARTICIPATION IN HIGH SCHOOL SOCCER   -   1971 - 72

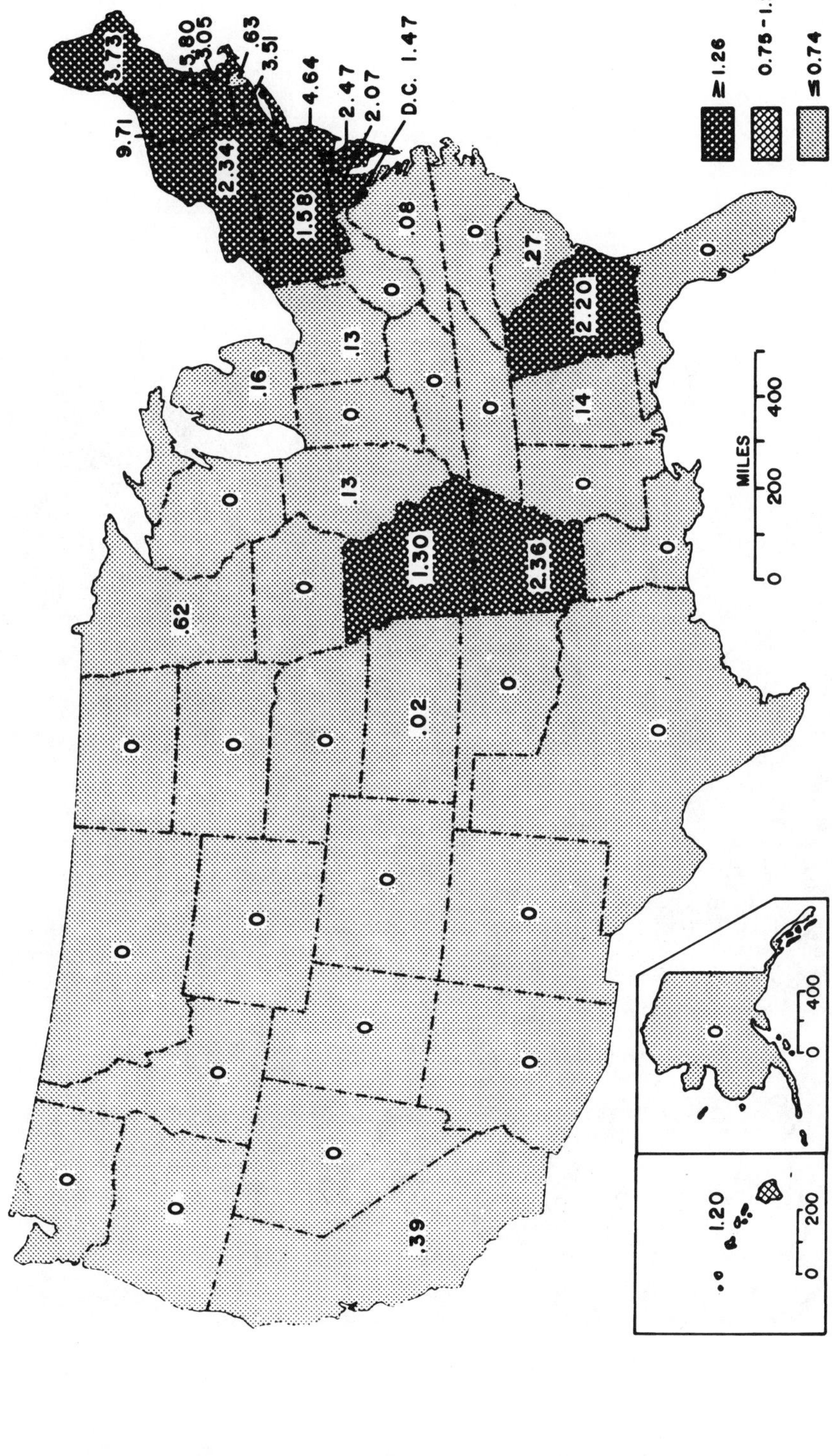

9.71

3.73

5.80
3.05
.63
3.51
4.64
2.47
2.07
D.C. 1.47

2.34

1.58

.08

0

.27

2.20

.16

.13

0

.14

0

.13

0

0

.62

1.30

2.36

0

0

0

.02

0

0

0

0

0

0

0

0

0

0

0

0

0

0

.39

≥1.26

0.75 - 1.25

≤0.74

MILES

0   200   400

Figure 12.7

1.20

0   200

0   400

0

AVERAGE PARTICIPATION = 1 PER 202 PEOPLE IN THE 14-17 AGE GROUP

Most amateur soccer is in the "sport for sport's sake" category.

ipation in these "minor" sports at the college level is quite similar to the interscholastic situation. Soccer is most important in the northeastern United States with New York and Pennsylvania alone accounting for nearly 25 percent of the teams. (See Fig. 12-12e.) Almost all of the schools in New England are competing. In addition there are 20 in New Jersey, 13 in Maryland, 11 in Virginia, and 17 in North Carolina. Ohio and Illinois are important soccer states. The sport is uncommon throughout most of the area west of the Mississippi River; California, with 37 intercollegiate teams, Minnesota, and Missouri are the only exceptions. The deep South has very little soccer competition outside of Florida. Despite the fact that many more American boys are playing soccer every year, the level of expertise is still far from that found in European and Latin American schoolboy circles. Except for St. Louis University, where most of the players come from the city's parochial league, the majority of the better collegiate teams are dominated by foreign players. In addition, the home-bred products have only a slim hope of making one of our professional clubs.

The attempt to introduce professional soccer to the United States on a massive scale was ill fated from the outset, primarily because there were too few native players and too few citizens who understood the intricacies of the world's most important sport. It would seem that the lesson to be learned from the experience is very plain. No sport (ice hockey may be an exception) can be introduced to a foreign area at the professional level before the general populace has adopted it, and it has become an integral part of the country's youth culture. Spaulding learned the same lesson many years ago when he attempted to foist baseball upon the English and west Europeans.

TENNIS

The pattern of tennis participation is very difficult to generalize. In a sport that approximately one of every 87 high school boys plays competitively, Washington, Idaho, and Arkansas are the only states with more than twice the national involvement (Fig. 12-8). Superb tennis weather has encouraged high participation in California, Arizona, and Texas. Many of the best players have come from these states. The best collegiate teams are usually from California and Texas. The good weather has had little effect in the South, perhaps because there have been few sponsors of quality teams. It is also likely that the windy environment of the Plains has reduced the emphasis there.

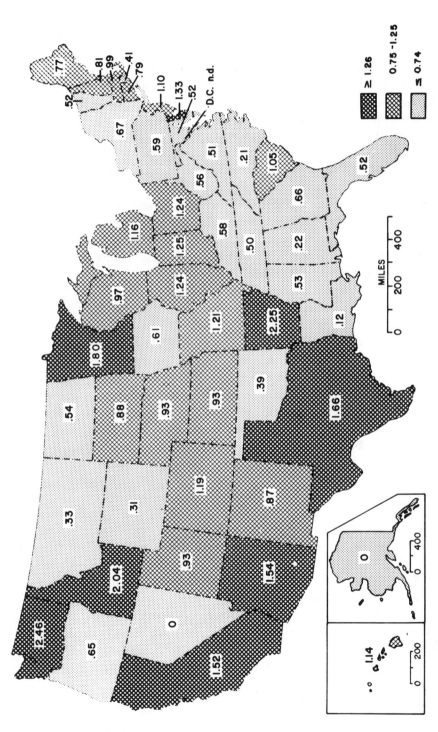

PER CAPITA PARTICIPATION IN HIGH SCHOOL TENNIS - 1971 - 72

Figure 12.8

≥ 1.26

0.75 -1.25

≤ 0.74

MILES

0   200   400

AVERAGE PARTICIPATION = 1 PER 173.5 PEOPLE IN THE 14-17 AGE GROUP

Tennis was until recently a sport associated with the wealthy and affluent segment of the American population. Tennis and golf clubs were developed to serve only a small percentage of the people. Inner-city courts were few and far between compared to the number available in suburbia and throughout the estate country. As a result, many of the best players were from wealthy families. The situation is gradually changing as evidenced first by Althea Gibson, and later by Arthur Ashe and a number of white players from modest backgrounds, but tennis is still a long way from being a sport of the masses.

SWIMMING

Swimming programs are sponsored in the high schools of all but seven states (Fig. 12-9). The highest participation states include Minnesota, California (which also has water polo competition), Hawaii, Iowa, Texas, and Georgia. Most of the Northeast, the South, and the Great Plains are far below average. For the nation, approximately one of 85 boys is a member of a high school swimming team. Thus even though we tend to associate California with swimming, as indeed we should considering its ability to produce Olympic champions, the fact is that there are four times as many boys playing football in California as there are in swimming programs.

Only a few universities really devote much attention to their swimming program. Indiana has won six consecutive NCAA titles (1968-1973) and has been challenged by virtually the same schools in each tournament (Table 12-1).[2] Since so few universities compete seriously, it has been relatively easy for newcomers like Tennessee and Washington to enter the title picture. Tennessee had its first swimming team in 1968 and finished second to Indiana in 1973! The recruiting behavior of the good swimming schools demonstrates that the talented people from all sections of the country are being funneled to just a select few institutions (Table 12-2).

TABLE 12-1
ORDER OF FINISH IN NCAA SWIMMING TOURNAMENTS, 1967-1971

	1967	1968	1969	1970	1971
First	Stanford	Indiana	Indiana	Indiana	Indiana
Second	USC	Stanford	USC	USC	USC
Third	Indiana	USC	Stanford	Stanford	UCLA
Fourth	Michigan	Yale	Michigan	UCLA	Stanford
Fifth	UCLA	Michigan	Yale	Cal. St.–LB	Cal. St.–LB

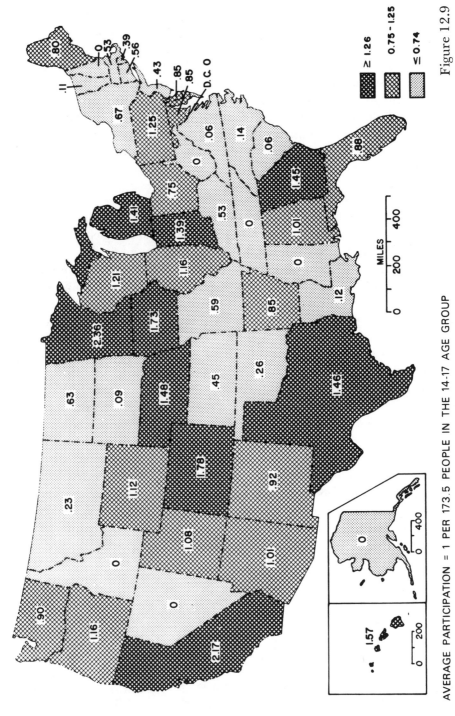

PER CAPITA PARTICIPATION IN HIGH SCHOOL SWIMMING   -   1971 - 72

AVERAGE PARTICIPATION = 1 PER 173.5 PEOPLE IN THE 14-17 AGE GROUP

Figure 12.9

≥ 1.26

0.75 - 1.25

≤ 0.74

TABLE 12–2
RECRUITMENT PATTERNS OF SWIMMERS BY MAJOR SWIMMING SCHOOLS, 1966–1971
Schools are listed in the order of percentage of out-of-state swimmers

Schools number of years	Percent in	Percent out	From other states		From foreign countries	
			Total	Average	Total	Average
Dartmouth (6)	3.4	96.6	24	13.2	0	0.0
Yale (6)	6.1	93.9	31	18.7	3	0.8
Indiana (6)	9.8	90.2	26	12.7	7	3.0
Tennessee (4)	15.2	84.8	16	9.7	0	0.0
Princeton (6)	17.9	82.1	23	13.3	0	0.0
Michigan (2)	28.4	71.6	15	11.5	3	2.0
Colorado State (5)	42.7	57.3	10	5.8	1	0.2
Michigan State (4)	43.4	56.6	13	8.5	1	0.5
Utah (1)	51.5	48.5	7	7.0	1	1.0
Washington (5)	67.2	32.8	10	3.8	1	0.4
Florida (6)	68.0	32.0	16	5.8	1	0.2
Kansas (5)	74.2	25.8	8	4.6	0	0.0
Southern California (6)	75.3	24.7	11	4.8	5	1.2
Oklahoma State (6)	83.2	16.8	9	2.0	2	0.3
Texas/Arlington (6)	89.5	10.5	6	1.5	2	0.7
UCLA (6)	90.0	10.0	2	0.5	4	1.8

Gymnastics has diffused to all parts of the United States. It has been given a considerable boost by the Olympic Games.

GYMNASTICS

High school gymnastics competition occurs in all but twelve states. Alaska with an index of 7.60 is the leader. The other Pacific Coast states are also substantially above the national norm. Other high-participation regions include the northern Plains and the far Southwest. Maine and Maryland stand out in the Northeast as does Georgia in the South—a region with almost no participation at all (Fig. 12-10).

Gymnastics has experienced tremendous growth in recent years. The sport has benefited from the publicity surrounding the Olympic Games as well as the increased stress on individual activities. Wom-

PER CAPITA PARTICIPATION IN HIGH SCHOOL GYMNASTICS - 1971 - 72

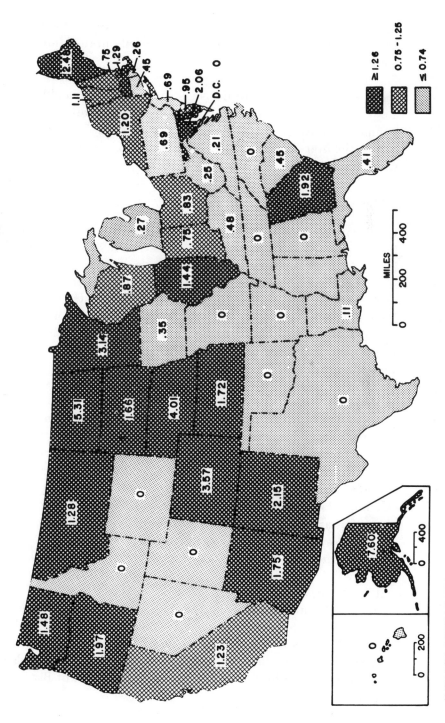

Figure 12.10

≥ 1.26

0.75 - 1.25

≤ 0.74

AVERAGE PARTICIPATION = 1 PER 391 PEOPLE IN THE 14-17 AGE GROUP

en's gymnastics is extremely popular too, although there are still nearly three times as many boys participating. Nonetheless there is a great potential for further expansion, especially in the Midwest and South.

Intercollegiate gymnastics programs are spread quite evenly across the country. California, New York, Wisconsin, and Illinois are the only states with 10 or more sponsoring institutions. Like swimming though, the number of quality programs is extremely limited. At the other extreme, Idaho and West Virginia are the only states without programs.

THE SNOW AND ICE SPORTS

Participation in sporting activities associated with snow and ice has been expanding at a very rapid pace since 1960. Skiing activity days have been increasing at a rate of over 15 percent annually, while snowmobiling or "ski-dooing," as it is popularly referred to, has become a winter way of life in many of our northern states, particularly Minnesota and Wisconsin. Hockey continues its diffusion to additional high schools and colleges each year to the accompaniment of a tremendous spurt in professional team expansion. Even curling continues to grow.

Participation in skiing at the high school level reaches its zenith in Vermont, Alaska, New Hampshire, Maine, and Colorado. These states as well as others in the Rocky Mountain region sponsor the country's best collegiate ski teams. However, the distribution of recreational skiers bears less resemblance to the distribution of annual snowfall. According to the Ski Trade Association, nearly 3 million "serious" skiers from all sections of the country spent over $1 billion in connection with the sport during 1972–1973, with over 100,000 ski enthusiasts being flown to Denver in that year alone.

Hockey is most popular as a high school sport in Minnesota, Massachusetts, and northern New England (Fig. 12–11). Delaware is the only mild-weather state of any importance. Of the 105 colleges fielding teams during 1972–1973, 20 are in Massachusetts, 17 in New York, and 12 in Minnesota (Fig. 12–11). The remainder of the schools are dispersed rather evenly through the cold belt. Hockey has become the dominant winter sport at a number of institutions including Denver, North Dakota, Michigan Tech, and Ferris Institute. It is also extremely important in the Ivy League and at a number of Big Ten universities (Fig. 12–12b).

Competitive skiing, like snow-mobiling, hockey, and curling, is
growing in popularity throughout the United States.

PER CAPITA PARTICIPATION IN HIGH SCHOOL HOCKEY, SKIING AND CURLING - 1971 - 72

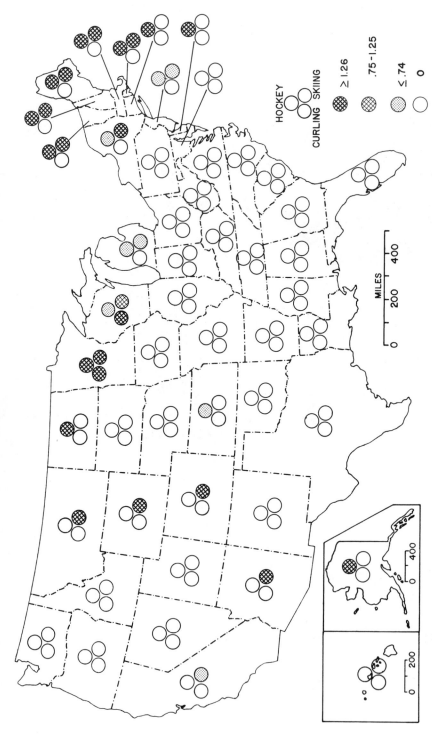

HOCKEY

CURLING SKIING

≥ 1.26

.75 - 1.25

≤ .74

MILES

0   200   400

AVERAGE PARTICIPATION = HOCKEY, 1 PER 699; CURLING, 1 PER 10,540; SKIING, 1 PER 1618.4 PEOPLE IN THE 14-17 AGE GROUP

Figure 12.11

Archery is one of the many sports which is enjoyed primarily as a recreational outlet, and is not characterized by the "winning is living" attitude.

THE REGIONAL SPORTS

Lacrosse and squash are the most spatially confined intercollegiate sports (Fig. 12-12). Almost half of the 118 lacrosse schools are found in three states: New York, Pennsylvania, and Massachusetts. The sport is also very popular in Maryland and New Jersey. Many of the players who stock the best eastern squads are from either Long Island, New York or Baltimore and adjacent suburbs. High school lacrosse has grown so rapidly on Long Island that there are now 5000 boys participating.

Although lacrosse is a northeastern sport, it has shown some signs of westward movement. There are now eight Ohio schools playing the game as well as representatives from Michigan, Wisconsin, Colorado, and California.

Crew, too, is essentially an eastern collegiate activity. Of the 73 sponsoring institutions, 16 are in New York and 13 are in Massachusetts. It has a particularly strong Ivy League tradition. In recent years this sport has migrated to the nation's coastal extremities par-

NUMBER OF COLLEGES AND UNIVERSITIES SPONSERING INTERCOLLEGIATE COMPETITION 1970 - 71
GYMNASTICS

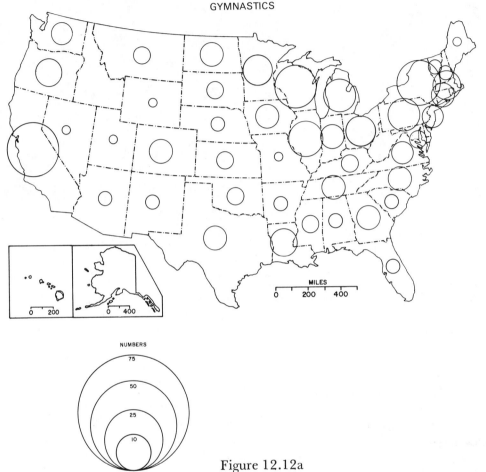

Figure 12.12a

ticularly to California and Florida. Washington and Oregon as well
as Wisconsin and Michigan are also putting strong national contenders
into the water.

Fencing, like lacrosse, squash, crew, and soccer, is basically a
northeastern sport. New York is the leading state with 22 schools.
New Jersey, Pennsylvania, and Ohio also sponsor a number of excellent programs. Fencing activity dwindles rapidly in the Midwest
and is virtually nonexistent in the Plains and Mountain region.
California again demonstrates that it has much in common with
the Northeast by sponsoring 17 fencing teams.

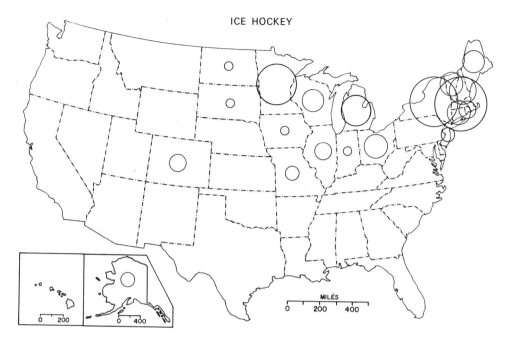

Figure 12.12b

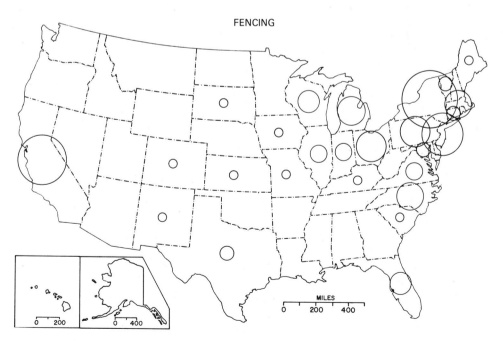

Figure 12.12c

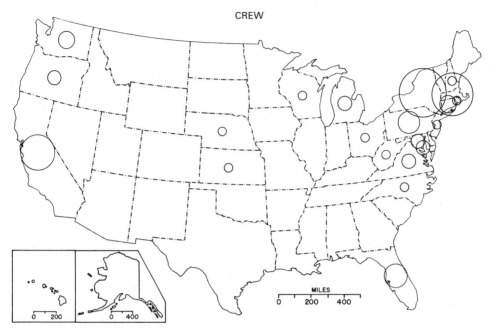

Figure 12.12d

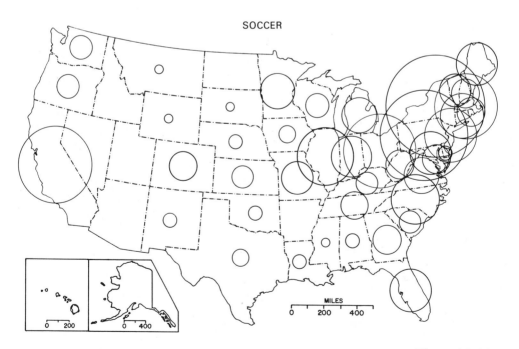

Figure 12.12e

Figure 12.12f

Figure 12.12g

There are numerous other sports being played in America. However, for most of them, quantitative information on place-to-place differences is either very scarce or has not yet been analyzed. For example, consider stock car racing. We are told that it is a southern phenonema, and Pillsbury has demonstrated that the majority of the first-class drivers do come from the South and that fan interest in the sport is probably highest there.[3] However, beyond that we have only sketchy data on the distribution and quality of facilities, attendance, prize money, and per capita participation in the sport.

There is some information on horse racing, bowling, billiards, and skating contained in the United States Census of Business. Sporting associations generally maintain files on the location of their membership, major events which they sponsor, and other data of geographical interest. Besides the written records there is a vast untapped source of personal expertise lurking around every place—high schools, universities, professional club offices, horse and dog shows, the track, athletic club, etc.—where sport is the business of the day.

NOTES

1. Mark M. Miller, "A Geographic Investigation of Professional Golf." Unpublished report, Oklahoma State University, May 1971.

2. For an account of the Indiana University involvement with swimming, see William F. Reed, "Its a Hoosier Title Wave," *Sports Illustrated*, Vol 34, March 22, 1971, p. 28.

3. Richard Pillsbury, "Carolina Thunder: A Geography of Southern Stock Car Racing," paper presented at the Annual Meeting of the Association of American Geographers, Atlanta, April 1973.

13 / Some Concluding Statements

This book has focused on several geographical aspects of sport in America. It represents a beginning, a first step toward the identification and examination of some of the basic issues—issues that must be better understood if there is to be a meaningful geography of sport. Although many of the findings are preliminary in nature, they do suggest the existence of a number of serious problems. If we accept the position that sport is a vital element of our society, these problems must be faced and eventually solved.

A major segment of the discussion has been concerned with the identification of sport regions and the spatial interaction which results from them. An attempt has also been made to account for the existence and development of these regions. Finally the origin and diffusion of the country's major games as well as their spatial organization has been addressed. The following discussion is an assessment of where we stand now and what might be done to improve this stance.

THE SPORT REGION

There are a number of areas in the United States that can be designated as sports regions, and most of them are dominated by one type of game. The epitome are the Texas football and the Illinois–Indiana–Kentucky basketball regions. However, there are a few areas like western Pennsylvania and northern Utah which are superior in more than one sport. There is also at least one noncontiguous region, the New York City, Philadelphia, Washington, D.C. basketball region.

In addition to the zones of emphasis and high athletic productivity, there are numerous places which assign sport a low priority. The state of Maryland is low in the production of quality players in each of the three "national" games. Much of the Appalachian and Ozark uplands are in the same category.

It is believed that the regionalization process used to identify the areas of dominance or neglect was the best available. However, it must be stated in all fairness that the method was biased in favor of high school athletic programs. We have assumed that the quality of an area's high school athletes in a given sport is closely related to the area's attitude and attachment to that sport. But outstanding high school football in a region should also be synonomous with high levels of interest in the collegiate and professional game. This correlation is well documented in the case of Texas, Pennsylvania, and Mississippi football, Ohio Valley basketball, and California baseball. There are exceptions however. New York City has low-caliber high school and collegiate football programs, while avidly supporting two professional teams. The Baltimore and Carolina situations are much the same with poor high school programs and well-developed professional or collegiate ones.

It is difficult to account precisely for the existence of the various types of sport regions. There is a multivariate explanation which seems to differ from place to place. The explanation for the Pennsylvania–Ohio football region includes a group of economic, ethnic, population, and political variables, in combination with a strong game-oriented tradition. Texas football thrives under a sharply contrasting socioeconomic situation and much more amenable climatic conditions. There are still other explanations for the Ohio Valley basketball scene.

It has become very apparent that sport does not usually thrive in places which are economically sick (there are a few basketball exceptions). Nor does it do very well in the densely populated central cities where high schools are large and recreational space is at a premium. To be sure, there are some very good city athletes, but they are being produced at the high price of ignoring many others who possess latent ability. Sport seems to be given highest priority in the small towns and cities, characterized by average income and a lack of intervening opportunities.

THE PRICE OF PRODUCING ATHLETES

It has been demonstrated that there is great geographical variation in the accessibility of American youth to participation in interscholastic sport. Some states have as many as twelve times the per capita high school participation of others. In general, the densely populated sections are providing far less opportunity to participate. And the relationship between low participation levels and juvenile crime and drug abuse is inescapable.

There is also lower per capita participation in many of the regions which lead in the per capita generation of high-quality athletes. For example, there is a much greater percentage of Nebraska and Wyoming high schoolers playing basketball in comparison to Indiana and Illinois boys, but there is a much higher per capita production of good players from the latter two states. This relationship between participation and the productivity of class athletes raises a serious question regarding the role and meaning of interscholastic, and to some extent, intercollegiate athletics.

One purpose of interscholastic athletics is to provide pure recreation for participants and spectators. At the other extreme, its purpose is to produce winning (at all cost) teams, specialist athletes, community prestige, and satisfied supporters. The first extreme is rare, but there are many programs whose goal is slanted more toward recreation than toward winning for the sake of the community. This type of program allows for a greater number of participants in a variety of sports but does not produce as many major college and professional athletes. The second extreme is generally found in regions dominated by one sport and tends to produce specialist athletes who have a higher probability of recruitment by a major college.

There are more universities investing more money in athletics than ever before. The specialist programs are, in large measure, a function of the growth in the number of "big time" football and basketball schools. Now is the time to examine closely the wisdom of this policy and to carefully analyze its effects on the high school level. It is the time to evaluate the NCAA and NAIA stance on athletic scholarships. The 1972 NCAA decision to limit football scholarships to 30 per year was a step toward placing athletics back in a more realistic perspective. It should actually give more athletes a chance to participate as opposed to warming the bench. However, the "major powers" are complaining and demanding their own division within the NCAA so that they can establish their own rules on aid to athletes. The next few years should witness the establishment of policies which will influence the direction of collegiate sport through the rest of the century. Great care and prolonged debate are indeed in order.

The spread of major college athletics to all sections of the country has necessitated a massive movement of players. As a result, recruiting becomes more competitive each year. This, coupled with the desire of more institutions to go "big time," is causing athletic budgets to spiral at unprecedented rates. As the collegiate powers become increasingly professionalized, this may now be the time to establish territorial limitations on recruiting. It might also be feasible to place all those potential players who have no college preference into a draft similar to the ones used in professional sports. They could then be parceled out to those colleges within their territory that were interested in their services. This suggestion may be unattractive to those who view "big time" collegiate sport as an amateur affair and accept the position that athletes select a college for education first and sports second. However, most of the recent evidence suggests that major collegiate competition should be placed on the professional end of the amateur–professional continuum.

We now have a situation in which the professional tail is wagging the amateur dog. The professional clubs are influencing the collegiate programs, and they in turn are effecting change at the high school level. Improvement of football at Nebraska or Arizona State causes greater effort to be put forth by the respective states' high schools. High school programs, which at one time were on the recreational end of the scale, move to the serious side. The goal moves from fun to winning and the grooming of specialist performers. This is fine if the ultimate goal is to produce highly qualified players. However, it is not a reasonable course if the goal is to give the maximum number of schoolboys the chance to participate in organized athletics.

With a growing national awareness of sport, this is the time to carefully evaluate local athletic objectives. Given the geographical variation in programs throughout the United States, there are many excellent laboratories in which to study sport and its ramifications. For a start we could compare Minnesota with Texas, and Maryland with Pennsylvania and examine the variation in the role of sport in those places and the different effects it has upon the individual athlete and the nonparticipants.

TOWARD SPATIAL REORGANIZATION

The spatial organization of American sport is far from optimal, in large measure because it is a part of the American educational system. The location of high schools is a function of settlement patterns. Small and scattered settlements traditionally produce a pattern of small dispersed high schools. The dense population of most large cities results in centrally located schools with relatively large enrollments, and the practice of each high school having only one varsity team per sport has discriminated against students enrolled in the larger schools. Opportunity to participate could be made more equitable by simply changing this ancient and revered practice.

The accessibility of high school students to participation in athletic competition is painfully analogous to voter representation prior to reapportionment. The rural voice was proportionately much stronger than the urban one. America has largely solved that problem but has not addressed and probably does not even know about this one. The city kids must be given more opportunity to experience competitive sport. It will require a complete reorganization and rethinking of the role which high school sport is to play, but it must be done. The benefits could very well be monumental.

The spatial organization of intercollegiate sport also favors the sparsely populated areas, as well as those with a large number of private colleges and universities. At the major college level, the imbalance is even more extreme. We have seen that the desire to have "big time" sport in out-of-the-way areas is tied to place pride and the need to call national attention to the locale. The price of building a major college contender is great, but the entertainment benefits may very well warrant it. Given the present attraction to intercollegiate athletics, it may be the most economical way to develop an entertainment complex and bring "glory" to a remote location. However, it would be much better if people would accept "big time" collegiate sport for what it is and alter the rules which govern its operation.

Professional sport could benefit from a considerable amount of geographical reorganization. As indicated earlier, the league and conference alignments do not make a great deal of geographical sense. Changes should be made in order to maximize competition between nearby places. The British and European achievements on this score could be very easily transferred to the American situation.

There is also an opportunity for additional expansion of major league franchises. The recent success of such maverick organizations as the American Football League, the World Hockey League, and the American Basketball Association suggests that there were a paucity of teams in existence. Also, there appear to be many more untapped markets throughout the southern, central, and north-western sections of the country. Miami, Birmingham, San Antonio, Tulsa–Oklahoma City, Louisville, Indianapolis, Honolulu, Phoenix–Tucson, Portland, and Seattle are a few of the prime possibilities. The regional franchise, as it exists in North Carolina (The Carolina Cougars), would seem a feasible alternative for groupings of medium-sized cities. A divisional system similar to that used in English football might also be tried. For example, major league baseball could be expanded to include sixty teams spread over three divisions. After each season, the best four teams in the third division would move up to the second division, whose best four would be promoted to the first. The bottom four in each division would be demoted to make room for the newcomers. Such a system has worked well in Britain and might be successful here.

THE CHALLENGE

The geography of sport is a broad and exciting subject. It offers great potential for the fuller understanding of society at the local, national, and world scales. It can also provide answers of prescriptive value. For example, some important questions are as follows: Where and how should amateur sport be expanded? How will given sports be received in different areas? Where are new professional franchises likely to succeed? How can the geographic organization of sport be altered at the high school, collegiate, and professional level to provide equal opportunity for participants and spectators alike?

We also need to know much more concerning the place of sport in total leisure behavior. Would the American population like to spend more of its leisure time on sport, if the opportunity were available? Given a constant amount of leisure time what kind of trade-offs would occur as a result of increases in sports participation? If city kids had the same accessibility to participation as small town kids, which of their present leisure activities would decline? Before decisions are made in regard to the increased provision of both schoolboy and professional opportunities we must answer this question.

We have examined only a few games and highlighted only a few places. In-depth studies on all sports, particularly with a world perspective, are vitally needed. A hard look at the Olympic Games is also in order, for the 1972 Olympics seemed to reflect the best and the worst of the people–place tie which makes a sport such a geographical phenomenon. Country first, athlete second seemed to be the rule of the day, thus making the Olympics an excellent laboratory for geographical investigation.

We need to know more about minority groups in sport. Why do some sections of the country emphasize women's athletics, while others ignore them completely? Where are blacks being given the greatest opportunity? What role do the black colleges play in collegiate sport?

There is much to be done if we are to realize the vast potential inherent in the geographic study of sport.

Bibliography

SPORT AND SOCIETY

Abstracts, Resumes, Third International Symposium on the Sociology of Sport, University of Waterloo, Waterloo, Ontario, August, 1971.

Beisser, Arnold R. *The Madness in Sports.* New York: Appleton Century Crofts, 1967.

Bogart, L. "Television's Effects on Spectator Sports," *The Age of Television.* New York: Frederick Unger, 1956.

Boyle, Robert H. *Sport: Mirror of American Life.* Boston: Little, Brown and Co., 1963.

Browne, Ray B., Marshall Fishwick, and Michael Marsden (eds.). *Heroes of Popular Culture.* Bowling Green, Ohio: Bowling Green University Popular Press, 1972.

Caillois, R. *Man, Play and Games.* Translated by M. Borash. New York: Free Press, 1961.

Cozens, Frederick W. *Sports in American Life.* Chicago: University of Chicago Press, 1953.

Cozens, F. W., and F. Stumpf. "Implications of Cultural Anthropology for Physical Education," *American Academy of Physical Education,* No. 1.

Edwards, H. *The Revolt of the Black Athlete.* New York: The Free Press, 1969.

Elias, Norbert, and Eric Dunning. "Dynamics of Group Sports with Special Reference to Football," *British Journal of Sociology*, XVII (1966) pp. 388–401.

Gamson, William A., and Norman A. Scotch. "Scapegoating in Baseball," *American Journal of Sociology*, LXX (1964) pp. 72–73.

Gilbert, Bill, and Nancy Williamson. "Sport is Unfair to Women," *Sports Illustrated*, May 28, 1973, p. 88.

Gini, C. "Rural Ritual Games in Libya," *Rural Sociology,* IV (1939) pp. 283–299.

Goellner, W. A. "The Court Ball Game of the Aboriginal Mayas," *Research Quarterly*; XXIV (1953) pp. 147–168.

Harris, Dorothy V. (ed.). *Women and Sport: A National Research Conference*, State College, Pennsylvania, Penn State HPER Series, November 2, 1973.

Hart, M. Marie. *Sport and the Socio-Cultural Process*, Dubuque, W. C. Brown, 1972.

Hastorf, A. H. and H. Cantril. "They Saw a Game: A Case Study," *Journal of Abnormal and Social Psychology*; XL (1954) pp. 129–134.

Hayner, N. S. "Mexicans at Play-a-Revolution." *Sociology and Social Research*; XXXVIII (1953) pp. 80–83.

Hoffer, Eric. *The Passionate State of Mind.* New York: Harper and Co., 1955.

Hoffman, W. J. "Remarks on Ojibwa Ball Play," *American Anthropologist*, III (1890) pp. 133–135.

Kaplan, Max. *Leisure in America: A Social Inquiry*. New York: John Wiley and Sons, 1960.

Kenyon, Gerald S. "A Sociology of Sport: On Becoming a Sub-Discipline" in Roscoe C. Brown, Jr. and Bryant J. Cratty (eds.). *New Perspectives of Man in Action.* Englewood Cliffs, N. J.: Prentice Hall, 1969.

Kenyon, Gerald S., and Gredd (eds.). *Psychology of Sport Proceedings of the 2nd International Congress of Sport Psychology*, Washington, 1968.

Leggett, William. "Let's Hear it for Boro," *Sports Illustrated*, July 21, 1969, pp. 30–35.

Loy, J. W., and J. F. Elvogue. "Racial Segregation in American Sport," *International Review of Sports Sociology*, Vol. 4 (1970), pp. 5–24.

Loy, J. W., and Gerald S. Kenyon. *Sport, Culture, and Society*. London: MacMillan, Co., 1969.

McIntosh, P. C. *Sport and Society*. London: Watts and Company, 1963.

McIllvanney, Hugh. "Fierce Holy War in a Violent City," *Sports Illustrated*, January 15, 1968, pp. 40–43.

Mulvoy, Mark. "If You Love Me Tell Me So," *Sports Illustrated*, February 26, 1968, pp. 28–30.

Nolan, Alex (ed.). *Sport and Society*. London: Bowes and Bowes, 1958.

Olsen, Jack. "Six Dreary Days—Then Saturday," *Sports Illustrated*, October 12, 1964, pp. 74–76.

Pideggi, Sarah. "Mallets Across the Blinkin' Sea," *Sports Illustrated*, July 31, 1967, pp.22–25.

Poling, James. "How the Reds Pay a Champion," *Sports Illustrated*, March 26, 1956, pp. 36–37.

Reischauer, Edwin O., David Moore, Alfred Wright, and Fred R. Smith. "Sport in the Orient," *Sports Illustrated*, December 23, 1963, pp. 38–93.

Ribalow, Harold U. *The Jew in American Sports*. New York: Block Publishers, 1966.

Roberts, J. M., *et al*. "Games in Culture," *American Anthropologist*. LXI (1959) pp. 597–605.

Sage, G. H. *Sport and American Society*. Reading, Mass.: Addison Wesley Publishers, 1970.

Schafer, Walter E. "Sport, Socialization and the School," paper presented at the Third International Symposium on the Sociology of Sport, University of Waterloo, Waterloo, Ontario, August, 1971.

Scotch, N. A. "Magic, Sorcery, and Football Among Urban Zulu: A Case Reinterpretation Under Acculturation," *The Journal of Conflict Resolution*, V (1961) pp. 70–74.

_____. *Sociology and Cultural Anthropology of Sport and Physical Education*. Springfield, Illinois: Charles C. Thomas Inc., 1964.

Starnes, Richard. "An Unprecedented Economic and Ethical Crisis Grips Big Time Intercollegiate Sports," *The Chronicle of Higher Education*, VIII, September 24, 1973, 1.

Stumpf, R., and F. W. Cozens. "Some Aspects of the Role of Games, Sports and Recreational Activities in the Culture of Modern Primitive Peoples: The New Zealand Maoris," *Research Quarterly*; XVII (1947) pp. 198–218.

Sutton-Smith, B., and B. G. Rosenberg. "Sixty Years of Historical Change in the Game Preferences of American Children," *Journal of American Folklore*. Vol. 74 (1961) pp. 17–46.

Thompson, Richard. *Race and Sport*. London: Oxford University Press, 1964.

Thorstein, Veblen. *The Theory of the Leisure Class*. New York: The Modern Library, 1934.

Vanderzwaag, Harold. *Toward a Philosophy of Sport*. Reading, Massachusetts: Addison-Wesley, 1972.

Wohl, A. "Conception and Range in Sports Sociology," *International Review of Sports Sociology*, Vol. 1 (1966) pp. 5–18.

Yetman, N. R., and D. S. Eitzen. "Black Athletes on Intercollegiate Athletic Teams: An Empirical Test of Discrimination," in N. R. Yetman (ed.). *Majority and Minority*. Boston: Allyn and Bacon, 1971.

SPORT AND PLACE

Angell, Roger. *The Summer Game*. New York: Viking Press, 1972.

"Australian Football: 100 Minutes of Hard Work." *Sports Illustrated*, October 26, 1959, pp. 32–36.

Axthelm, Pete. *The City Game*. New York: Harper and Row, 1970.

Bingham, Walter. "Football From the Cradle," *Sports Illustrated*, November 13, 1961, pp. 46–51.

Blanchflower, Danny. "Just One Truth for Me." *Sports Illustrated,* June 10, 1968, pp. 40–42.

Brown, Geirlyn S. "The Day the All-Blacks Attained the Zenith," *Sports Illustrated,* November 20, 1967, pp. 26–28.

Carroll, Joseph. "The Gentle Irish," *Sports Illustrated*, August 28, 1967, pp. 40–46.

Carry, Peter. "A Bonanza in Red Springs," *Sports Illustrated*, June 28, 1969, pp. 42–45.

Chapman, Dwight, and Jeff Prugh. *The Wizard of Westwood*. New York: Harper & Row, 1973.

Cooke, Jerry. "Sports in the U.S.S.R," *Sports Illustrated*, December 2, 1957, pp. 37–62.

Cope, Myron. "The Proudest Squares," *Sports Illustrated*, November 1968, pp. 98–100.

Curry, George. "Whoosh Goes the Wasco Whiz," *Sports Illustrated*, May 3, 1971, pp. 61, 71.

Deford, Frank. "A City of Complexes," *Sports Illustrated*, April 1, 1968, pp. 60–64.

_____. "Aces are High in Evansville," *Sports Illustrated*, February 15, 1965, pp. 24–27.

_____. "My Baby is Called the Kahlahanah Koogahs," *Sports Illustrated*, January 19, 1970, pp. 38–41.

_____. "Your Time, Not Your Dollar," *Sports Illustrated*, May 12, 1969, pp. 72–76.

Furlong, Bill. "New Day in Green Bay," *Sports Illustrated*, December 12, 1960, pp. 35–39.

Gammon, Clive. "Cymru Am Byth," *Sports Illustrated*, February 9, 1970, pp. 59–64.

_____. "Irish Sport is Happy Mayhem," *Sports Illustrated*, October 10, 1960, pp. 35–39.

Jenkins, Dan. "The Disciples of St. Darrell on a Wild Weekend," *Sports Illustrated*, November 11, 1963, pp. 72–80.

Johnson, William. "A Big Night in a Lil 'Ol' Town," *Sports Illustrated*, September 30, 1968, pp. 36–38.

_____. "The Only Game in Town," *Sports Illustrated*, February 16, 1970, pp. 54–56.

Johnston, Richard W. "A Playground Divided," *Sports Illustrated*, May 3, 1971, p. 78.

Kahn, Roger. *The Boys of Summer*. New York: Harper and Row, 1971.

Kane, Martin. "The True Football Gets Its Big Chance," *Sports Illustrated*, March 27, 1967, pp. 22–24.

Kirshenbaum, Jerry. "Let Me Make One Thing Clear," *Sports Illustrated,* June 7, 1971, p. 48.

Kram, Mark. "An Odd Time in Du Quoin, Illinois," *Sports Illustrated,* August 30, 1965, pp. 24–31.

_____. "Leo's Bums Rap For The Cubs," *Sports Illustrated*, June 30, 1969, pp. 14–19.

Maddocks, Melvin. "New Awakening in Orr Land," *Sports Illustrated*, October 11, 1971, p. 32.

McDonald, Douglas. "Geographic Variation in Athletic Production: Axiomatic or Accidental?" unpublished Master's thesis, Department of Geography, Southern Illinois University, Carbondale, 1969.

McIlvanney, Hugh. "But the South Shall Rise Again (and Again)," *Sports Illustrated*, May 17, 1971, pp. 22.

Miller, Mark M. "A Spatial Analysis of Golf Facility Development in the United States, 1931–1970," unpublished Master's thesis, Oklahoma State University, 1972.

Olsen, Jack. "Pallacanestro Is the Rage," *Sports Illustrated*, February 13, 1967, pp. 62–66.

_____. "The Uproar in Philadelphia," *Sports Illustrated*, January 18, 1965, pp. 18–23.

Parker, Don. "Football in the Backyard," *Sports Illustrated,* November 11, 1957, pp. 22–27.

Peterson, Harold. "Earning a Varsity Letter Out West," *Sports Illustrated,* July 1, 1968, pp. 34–39.

Pillsbury, Richard. "Carolina Thunder: A Geography of Southern Stock Car Racing," paper presented at the Annual Meeting of the Association of American Geographers, Atlanta, April, 1973.

Ronberg, Gary. "An Icy Love-In With the Red-Hot Blues," *Sports Illustrated,* April 7, 1969, pp. 52–54.

_____. "This Campus Struggle is Resolved With Sticks," *Sports Illustrated*, May 27, 1968, pp. 59.

Rooney, John F., Jr. "The Geography of Participation in Inter-scholastic Sport: Toward Equal Opportunity in the United States," paper presented at the Annual Meeting of the Association of American Geographers, Atlanta, April, 1973.

Smith, Liz. "Crab Cakes and Tall Timber," *Sports Illustrated*, April 24, 1967, pp. 52–59.

Stowers, Carlton. "A Pride of Lions in Cattle Country," *Sports Illustrated*, November 1, 1971, p. 38.

Tannenbaum, J. A. "If Football Comes to Yellow Springs," *The Wall Street Journal*, September 23, 1971.

Terrell, Roy. "The American Game," *Sports Illustrated*, December 9, 1957, pp. 26–29.

_____. "This is Cricket," *Sports Illustrated*, August 28, 1961, pp. 22–23.

_____. "This Sporting World," *Sports Illustrated*, November 12, 1956, pp. 54–57.

Thaman, Randy. "A Geography of Rugby," paper presented at the Annual Meeting of the Association of American Geographers, Atlanta, April, 1973.

Tunis, John R. *The American Way in Sports*. New York: Duell, Sloan and Pearce, 1958.

Underwood, John. "The Only Game in Panquitch, Utah," *Sports Illustrated,* March 24, 1963, pp. 56–60.

Warden, William L. "Australia: Sporting Continent," *Sports Illustrated,* November 5, 1956, pp. 34–36.

Waugh, Alec. "What Rugby Means to England," *Sports Illustrated,* February 4, 1957, pp. 58–63.

_____. "We Expect Them to Storm the Gates," *Sports Illustrated*, September 6, 1971, p. 20.

_____. "Which is the Best Sports Country in the World?" *Sports Illustrated*, April 23, 1962, p. 28.

White, Charles W. "The Hoosier Madness," *Sports Illustrated,* December 19, 1965, p. 23.

Wind, Herbert W. "Around the Mulberry Bush," *Sports Illustrated,* March 3, 1958, pp. 56–64.

_____. "The Bouncing Ball," *Sports Illustrated*, February 24, 1958, pp. 52–62.

Wolf, David. *Foul.* New York: Holt, Rinehart and Winston, 1972.

Yates, Brock. "Warts, Love and Dreams in Buffalo," *Sports Illustrated,* January 20, 1969, pp. 44-46.

RECRUITING

Deford, Frank. "The Negro Athlete is Invited Home," *Sports Illustrated,* June 14, 1965, pp. 26-27.

Hendron, Booton. "How Colleges Gather in a New Crop," *Sports Illustrated,* June 18, 1956, p. 30.

Jenkins, Dan. "Pursuit of a Big Blue Chipper," *Sports Illustrated,* September 9, 1968, pp. 104-124.

Pearson, Ronald C. "Football Recruiting in Texas: A Spatial Analysis," unpublished Master's thesis, Oklahoma State University, 1972.

Rooney, J. F., Jr. "A Geography of Basketball," paper presented at the Rocky Mountain Social Science Meeting, Fort Collins, Colorado, May, 1971.

_____. "A Geographical Analysis of Football Player Production in Oklahoma and Texas," *Proceedings, Oklahoma Academy of Science,* Vol. 50, 1970.

_____. "Up From the Mines and Out From the Prairies: Some Geographical Implications of Football in the United States, *Geographical Review*; LIX (October, 1969) pp. 471-492.

Sage, George H., and John W. Loy. "Career Mobility Patterns of College Coaches: Geographical Implications of College Coaches," paper presented at the Annual Meeting of the Association of American Geographers, Atlanta, April, 1973.

GENERAL

Andrenano, Ralph. *No Joy in Mudville: The Dilemma of Major League Baseball.* Cambridge, Mass.: Schenkman, 1965.

Aristotle *Politics* VII.

Augustine *Confessions* VII: 17.

Avedon, E., and B. S. Smith. *The Study of Games.* New York: John Wiley & Sons, 1971.

Bouton, Jim. *Ball Four.* Cleveland: World Publishing Co., 1970.

Boyle, Robert H. "The Bizarre History of American Sport," *Sports Illustrated,* January 8, 1962, pp. 54–55.

Burton, Tom L. (ed.). *Recreational Research and Planning.* London: George Allen and Unwin Ltd., 1970.

Classen, Harold. *Ronald Encyclopedia of Football,* New York: Ronald Press Co., 1959.

Cope, Myron. *The Game That Was.* New York: World Publishing Co., 1970.

Daley, Robert. *The Bizarre World of European Sports.* New York: William Morrow & Co., 1963.

Danzig, Allison. *Oh, How They Played the Game.* New York: MacMillan, 1971.

Davenport, David S. "Collusive Competition in Major League Baseball," *The American Economist.* XIII (Fall, 1969) pp. 6–30.

Dunning, E. G. "Football in Its Early Stages," *History Today,* Vol. 13, December, 1963, pp. 838–847.

Eyler, Marvin H. "Origins of Contemporary Sports," *Research Quarterly,* XXVI (1961) pp. 486–489.

Gamson, William A., and Norman A. Scotch. "Scapegoating in Baseball," *American Journal of Sociology,* LXX (1964) pp. 63–64.

Glanville, Bryan. *People in Sport.* London: Secker and Warburg, 1967.

Hansen, Emanuel. *Sports in Denmark.* Copenhagen: J. Jorgensen & Co., 1963.

Jenkins, Dan. *Semi-Tough.* New York, Atheneum, 1972.

Johnson, William. "You Know You're not Getting Maudie Frickert," *Sports Illustrated,* January 26, 1970, pp. 30-36.

Jokl, E. *Heart and Sport.* Springfield, Illinois: Charles C. Thomas Inc., 1964.

_____. *Medical Sociology and Cultural Anthropology of Sport and Physical Education.* Springfield, Illinois: Charles C. Thomas, 1964.

Jones, J.C.H. "The Economics of the National Hockey League," *Canadian Journal of Economics,* II (February, 1969) pp. 1–20.

Jukala, Martti. *Athletics in Finland.* Helsinki: Werner Soderstorm Osakeyhtio Parvoo, 1932.

Katchmer, George A., *Values in Sports*. Englewood Cliffs, New Jersey: Prentice-Hall, 1965.

King, Larry. "Origin and Diffusion of American Rodeo," *Newsletter, Association of Pacific Coast Geographers,* Monmouth, Oregon, Fall, 1971.

Koch, James V. "The Economics of Big Time Intercollegiate Athletics," *Social Science Quarterly,* LII (September, 1971) pp. 248–260.

Kramer, Jerry. *Instant Replay.* New York: World Publishing Co., 1968.

Levy, W. *Three Yards and a Cloud of Dust.* Cleveland: World Publishing Co., 1966.

Loy, J. W. "Social Psychological Characteristics of Innovators," *American Sociological Review,* XXXIV (1969) pp. 73–82.

Mahoney, S. "Pro Football's Profit Explosion," *Fortune.* 70 (1964) 153–155.

Maule, Tex. "A Flare in the Dark," *Sports Illustrated,* June 3, 1968, pp. 60–64.

_____. "Bongo for the Golden Cut," *Sports Illustrated,* July 25, 1966, pp. 32–35.

McCormick, John. "Score One for Today's Students," *Sports Illustrated,* May 20, 1968, pp. 46–48.

Miller, Richard I. *The Truth About Big-Time Football.* New York: Sloan and Associates, 1953.

Mokray, William G. (ed.). *Ronald Encyclopedia of Basketball.* New York: The Ronald Press Company, 1963.

Moore, John H. "Football's Ugly Decade, 1893–1913," *The Smithsonian Journal of History,* II (Fall, 1967)

Moore, Robert A. *Sports and Mental Health.* Springfield, Illinois: Charles C. Thomas, Inc., 1966.

Morton, Henry W. *Soviet Sport* (ed. by M. Florinsky). New York-London: Collier Books, 1963.

Neale, Walter C. "The Peculiar Economics of Professional Sports." *Quarterly Journal of Economics.* LXXVIII (February, 1964) pp. 1–14.

Olsen, Jack. "In An Alien World," *Sports Illustrated,* July 15, 1968, pp. 28–43.

Peterson, Harold. "Baseball's Johnny Appleseed," *Sports Illustrated,* April 14, 1969, pp. 57–64.

____. "Pro Football on a Shoestring," *Sports Illustrated*, December 16, 1968, pp. 36–38.

Plato. *Republic.*

Plimpton, George. *Paper Lion.* New York: Harper and Row, 1965.

Rehberg, Richard A., and Walter E. Schafer. "Participation in Inter-scholastic Athletics and College Expectations" *American Journal of Sociology,* LXXIII (1968) pp. 732–740.

Rosenblatt, Aaron. "Negroes in Baseball: The Failure of Success," *Trans-Action,* IV (1967) pp. 63–64.

Ross, Murray. "Football Red and Baseball Green," *Chicago Review,* September, 1971, pp. 30–40.

Rottenberg, Simon. "The Baseball Players Labor Market," *Journal of Political Economy*, XXIV (June, 1956) pp. 242–258.

Russell, Dick. "Bloody Nights on the Lone Prairie," *Sports Illustrated,* March 23, 1970, pp. 49–51.

Shrake, Edwin. "A Lonely Tribe of Long Distance Runners," *Sports Illustrated,* January 9, 1967, pp. 56–62.

____. "Sis-Boom-Bah Goes Hip," *Sports Illustrated,* October 1969, pp. 44–45.

Slusher, Howard S. *Man, Sport and Existence.* Philadelphia: Lea and Feabiger, 1967.

Smith, Robert. *Illustrated History of Professional Football.* New York: Madison Square Press, 1970.

____. *Texas Inter-Scholastic League Bulletin,* 1970.

Thompson, R. *Race and Sport.* London: Oxford University Press, 1964.

Toynbee, Arnold J. *A Study of History.* New York: Oxford University Press, 1947.

Turkin, Hy, and S. C. Thompson. *The Official Encyclopedia of Baseball.* New York: A. S. Barnes and Company, 1951.

Voight, David T. *American Baseball.* Norman, Oklahoma: University of Oklahoma Press, 1968.

_____. "American Baseball and the Mission of America," paper presented at the Third International Symposium on the Sociology of Sport, University of Waterloo, Waterloo, Ontario, August 26, 1971.

Weiss, Paul. *Sport, A Philosophic Inquiry.* Carbondale, Illinois: Southern Illinois University Press, 1969.

Index

Anson, Pop, 25
Artificial playing surfaces, 17
Association of Intercollegiate
    Athletics for Women, 249
Athletic conference, 89, 90–95
Athletic equipment, 18
Athletic facilities, 16
Athletic production as a function
    of interscholastic participa-
    tion, 141–142
Atlanta Stadium, 9
Axthelm, Pete, 167–169

Baseball
    Arizona collegiate, 182
    collegiate, 36
    diffusion, 23
    Los Angeles as a baseball center,
        182
    origin, 23
    per capita production, 176–184
    total production of players, 176–
        182
    towns, 180–181, 186
Basketball
    attendance, 49
    the city game, 77, 167–169, 231
    deficit areas, 171–174
    interregional migration of play-
        ers, 220–224, 228, 231
    North Carolina, 89

origin and diffusion, 49
overemphasis, 86, 236–237
per capita production, 154–174
regions, 154–167
rule changes, 49
total player production, 147–154
underemphasis, 86
Basketball recruiting
    Atlantic Coast Conference, 228,
        231
    California, 235
    Illinois, 225
    Indiana, 226
    Kentucky, 156, 227
    New Jersey, 233
    New York, 232
    Ohio, 230
    Pennsylvania, 229
    the small colleges, 237–240
Baylor, Elgin, 49
Betts, John, 21
Busch Stadium, 9

Camp, Walter, 62
Chamberlain, Wilt, 49
Cincinnati Red Stockings, 23
Cincinnati, Riverfront Stadium, 10
Community prestige and sport, 15,
    23, 74, 86, 138, 165
Crawley, Marion, 163–164
Cricket, 6

"Dapper Dan" Club, 126
Diffusion
    baseball from 1876–1958, 25–26
    big-time collegiate sport, 19
    emergence of California, 36
    football power, 41–47
    professional sport, 19

Early English football, 38

Fan regions, 7–8, 97
Football
    American institution, 112
    black football schools, 116
    coaching migrations, 40–41, 43
    conference football recruiting
        territories, 207
    diffusion, 36, 40
    origin, 36
        collegiate game, 39
    overemphasis, 84
    production
        low production areas, 142
        per capita, 116–134
        state comparisons, 132–134
        total players, 112–116
    regional variation in players, 122
    spatial organization, 5
    underemphasis, 84
Football conference recruiting
    Big Ten, 207–208
    Big Eight, 207, 209
    Atlantic Coast, 207, 210
    Western Athletic, 207, 211
Football fever, explanations, 134–
    142
Football player recruiting
    Alabama, 201
    Florida, 204
    Georgia, 200
    interregional migration of foot-
        ball players, 190–191, 195,
        205–206
    Louisiana, 202
    Massachusetts, 198
    New Jersey, 195–196
    New York, 197
    Ohio, 190, 192

Pennsylvania, 190–191
    the small colleges, 213–219
    summary of black college recruit-
        ing, 218–219
    Texas, 203
Franchise relocations, 6–8, 24

Gallager, Edward C., 58
Geographical use of team rosters,
    102–108
Geography and the character of
    place, 3
Golf
    housing developments, 61
    origin and diffusion in U.S., 58–
        61
    professional, 259, 261–264
    role of Arnold Palmer, 59, 61
    spatial organization, 99–101
Grambling University, 103, 199
Grange, Red, 48

Halas, George, 48
High school sports
    athletic conferences, 67
    tournaments, 67

Iba, Henry, 170
IllInKy, 156–167
The IllInKy surplus, 220–228
Illinois
    Kankakee, 157, 160
    Pinckneyville, 161
    Hebron, 161
Illinois and Indiana State High
        School Basketball Tourna-
        ments, 161–164
Indiana
    Muncie, Central H.S., 163
    Lafayette, Jefferson, 163
International Federation of High
        School Athletic Associations,
        242
Iowa
    Girl's basketball, 169

Jabar, Kareem (Lew Alcindor), 49
Jenkinson, Roger, 239–240

Jones, William, 218–219
Junior college athletics, 95–97
  California junior college football,
    95

Little League baseball, 64, 77
Los Angeles, Chavez Ravine, 11

Major college playing opportunities,
    79
McDonald, Douglas B., 146
Measurement of regional variation
    in the role of sport, 15
Miller, Mark M., 59

Naismith, James, 49
National Association of Baseball
    Players, 23
National Association of Intercolle-
    giate Athletics, 89, 158,
    285
National Collegiate Athletic Associ-
    ation, 79, 86, 89, 102, 158,
    285
National Federation of State High
    School Athletic Associations,
    70
National games, 12
Nebraska, Lincoln, 3
  University of Nebraska football,
    3, 86
New Jersey, Union County, 154
New York City, Yankee Stadium,
    11
New York Knickerbockers baseball
    club, 23
North Dakota State University,
    case study in recruiting, 216–
    217, 219

Odle, Don, 164
Ohio,
  Massillon, 124, 135
  Stark County, 124
  Steubenville, 122, 125, 135
Ohio Valley, 167
  basketball, 158, 284
  football, 125

Participation in high school sport
    as a function of
  enrollment, 72–78
  income, 72
  population density, 78
  settlement patterns, 72, 78
  social emphasis, 78
Participatory activities, 64
PenWevO, 122–126, 135–136
Per capita classification system,
    108–111
Periodic sports markets, 99
"Phog" Allen, 170
Pillsbury, Richard, 282
Price of producing athletes, 285
Professional football origin and dif-
    fusion, 47
Professional sport, spatial organiza-
    tion, 97–99

Recruiting as a function of
  alumni, 189
  college location, 187–188
  distance, 188
  geographical experience of
    coaches, 188
  perception, 189
  player production, 187
Recruiting irregularities, 190
Regional preferences for sports, 74
"Rounders," 23
Rugby, 4–6, 38
  origin, 39
  Rugby School, 39
Rupp, Adolph, 172, 223
Russell, Bill, 49

Shaughnessy, Clark, 48
Social role of sport, 74
Spatial organization
  intercollegiate sport
    basketball, 82–83, 86, 88–89
    football, 79–81, 84, 87
  interscholastic sport, 66–67
  professional sport, 97–99
Spatial reorganization of sport, 287
Spatial variation in games, 4–5, 14–
    15

Spatial variation in intercollegiate
    sport participation, 264, 267,
    280
  crew, 277, 280
  fencing, 278–279
  gymnastics, 274, 278
  hockey, 274, 279
  lacrosse, 277, 281
  squash, 281
Spatial variation in interscholastic
    participation
  all sports, 70
  baseball, 76–77
  basketball, 74–75
  football, 72–73
  golf, 259–260
  gymnastics, 272–274
  regional sports, 277–282
  snow and ice sports, 274–277
  soccer, 264–267
  swimming, 269–271
  tennis, 267–269
  track and field, 254–257
  wrestling, 257–259
Spectator-oriented activities, 64
  locational characteristics, 65
Sport
  as an amenity, 18
  as a basis for urban renewal, 11–12
  and climate, 137–138, 169, 184,
      264
  of kings, 22
  and landscape, 8–11
  and place-pride rivalries, 5
  and religion, 140, 171
  and social attitudes 138, 140
Sport participation survey, 68–69
Sports page, 22
Sports regions, 102, 283–284
  basketball
    Appalachia (The Hatfield-
      McCoy Territory), 158
    Central Indiana, 159
    North-Central Illinois, 159
    IllInKy, 156–167
    Northeastern U.S., 154
    Southern Illinois, 160
    Utah, 170–171

Western Kentucky-Southern
    Indiana, 159
  The Western-Ohio (Miami
    Valley) Region, 158
football
    Texas, 127–128, 136–139
    Southern Mississippi, 127, 140
    PenWevO, 122–126
    San Francisco Bay area, 131
    Utah, 131
  identification, 102–108
  multiplier effect, 140–141
  origin and growth, 164–167
Stadium-building era, 47
Stock car racing, 282
Suburban vs. central-city athletic
    production, 117, 122
Swimming, recruitment, 271

Technology and the growth of
    spectator sport, 21
Television's effect on minor league
    baseball, 36
Tennis, 101
Texas Interscholastic League, 5
Thomas, Duster, 161, 165

Uniform sports regions, 8

Voight, David T., 6

Weiss, Paul, 7
Women's athletics, 242–253
Women's interscholastic sport, 248–
    251
  Iowa basketball, 246
  professional prospects, 253
  rural dominance, 248
  spatial organization, 251
  spatial variation, 243, 246–251
  sports centers, 251–252
Wrestling
  collegiate, 58
  Oklahoma State University, 1–2,
    58
  origin and diffusion, 50–58
Wright, Harry, 24
Wrigley Field, 1–2